Military Rule
in Africa

edited by
Anton Bebler

Written under the auspices of
the Center of International Studies,
Princeton University

The Praeger Special Studies program—
utilizing the most modern and efficient book
production techniques and a selective
worldwide distribution network—makes
available to the academic, government, and
business communities significant, timely
research in U.S. and international economic. social, and political development.

Military Rule in Africa

Dahomey, Ghana, Sierra Leone, and Mali

PRAEGER SPECIAL STUDIES IN INTERNATIONAL POLITICS AND GOVERNMENT

Praeger Publishers   New York   Washington   London

Library of Congress Cataloging in Publication Data

Bebler, Anton.
    Military rule in Africa: Dahomey, Ghana,
Sierra Leone, and Mali.

    (Praeger special studies in international politics
and government)
    "Written under the auspices of the Center of
International Studies, Princeton University."
    Bibliography: p.
    1. Africa, West—Politics and government.
2. Africa, West—Armed Forces—Political activity.
I. Princeton University. Center of International
Studies. II. Title.
DT476. 5. B4   966   72-91713

PRAEGER PUBLISHERS
111 Fourth Avenue, New York, N.Y. 10003, U.S.A.
5, Cromwell Place, London S.W.7, England

Published in the United States of America in 1973
by Praeger Publishers, Inc.

Printed in the United States of America

I am grateful to several institutions that supported my work on this study. I started it in 1968 as a Research Fellow at the Institute of International Politics and Economy in Belgrade, Yugoslavia. My research in London and Paris in 1969-70 was aided by grants of the British Council and the French government. I profited from a field trip to West Africa in 1970, sponsored by the Union of Yugoslav Youth and financed in part by UNESCO. The writing and editing of the text was accomplished in 1970-71 with the help of the Center of International Studies, Princeton University.

In the course of my work I have used the libraries and consulted experts of the following institutions (in chronological order): Institute of International Politics, Belgrade; Institute of Commonwealth Studies, London; University of London; British Museum; West African Studies Center, University of Birmingham; Institute of Development Studies, University of Sussex; Oxford, Cambridge, Manchester, Edinborough, and Strathclyde universities; Fondation Nationale des Sciences Politiques, Institut d'Etudes Politiques, Documentation Française, and Sécretariat Général à la Présidence de la République pour les Affaires Africaines et Malgaches (all in Paris); Centre d'Etudes de l'Afrique Noire, University of Bordeaux; International Labour Organization and African Studies Institute, Geneva; Scandinavian Institute of African Studies, Upsala; Institute of Oriental Studies, Prague; National Archives, Porto-Novo; University of Ghana Legon; Fourah Bay University College, Freetown; Institut des Sciences Humaines, Bamako; Boston University; Princeton University; Library of Congress, Washington, D.C.; University of Pennslyvania; New York Public Library.

My debts to individual Africans, West and East Europeans, Levantines, and Americans are so numerous that I could not possibly list them. My sincere thanks to all those in Africa and elsewhere who offered me hospitality, shared knowledge, and gave me time and advice.

I wish to express my gratitude to the staff of the Center of International Studies, Princeton University, and particularly to Joanne Weissman for excellent secretarial assistance.

CONTENTS

LIST OF TABLES AND FIGURES

LIST OF ACRONYMS

Dahomey

CMR	Military Revolutionary Committee (Comité Militaire Révolutionnaire)
CMV	Military Committee of Vigilance (Comité Militaire de Vigilance)
CRN	Committee of National Renovation (Comité de Renovation Nationale)
PDD	Democratic Party of Dahomey (Parti Démocratique du Dahomey)

Ghana

CPP	Convention People's Party
EAC	Economic Advisory Committee
NAL	National Alliance of Liberals
NLC	National Liberation Council
NRC	National Redemption Council
PAC	Political Advisory Committee
POGR	President's Own Guard Regiment
PP	Progress Party
RWAFF	Royal West Africa Frontier Forces

Mali

CDR	Committee for the Defense of the Revolution (Comité pour la Défense de la Révolution)
US-RDA	Union Soudanaise-RDA

Sierra Leone

APC	All People's Congress
CRC	Civilian Rule Committee
EAC	Economic Advisory Committee
NIC	National Interim Council
NRAC	National Reformation Advisory Council
NRC	National Reformation Council
SLPMB	Sierra Leone Produce Marketing Board
SLPP	Sierra Leone People's Party

West African Currencies

CFA	Frank CFA
FM	Malian Frank
Le	Leone
NC	New Cedi

Military Rule
in Africa

1

INTRODUCTION

Not many years ago prestigious professors and "experts" predicted a bright and stable future for the new states in Africa. All kinds of arguments were advanced to prove this point--a low incidence of violence, a low addiction to ideology and rigid doctrine, a more creative attitude toward law, and the greater flexibility and adaptability of African politicians compared to politicians from other areas in the Third World. Even the assassination of President Sylvanus Olympio of Togo in 1963 did not stop suppositions and predictions of this kind.

Nowadays we are more used to hearing the news of another coup in this or that African country. The number of countries that have experienced or still are experiencing military intervention in politics changes so often that it does not make much sense to give yet another rundown here. Suffice to say that during the last 8 years over 15 countries on the African continent have had the privilege of tasting military coups--well over half the total membership in the Organization of African Unity. Few people now are likely to contest the relevance of the topic I seek to tackle: the African military in politics.

Apart from the political interest created by events, this subject touches on the difficulties of many Third World countries, including those that have not so far seen their military step in. The range of these difficulties is impressive and even overwhelm-

ing--from economic, educational, and cultural under-
development, internal conflicts of various kinds,
and the weakness and fragility of "modern" institutions to dependence on richer and stronger states
and foreign capital. This list can be easily extended.

It does not require a wild imagination to sus-
pect that military intervention in Africa is related
to or flows from these problems and difficulties.
Yet numerous attempts by scholars to link political
crises to any particular set of circumstances or
characteristics have been defied by complex reality.
There seem to be at least as many combinations of
various elements or symptoms of political crises as
there are countries. Because of very different conditions found throughout the Third World, and also
in Africa, I decided to avoid sweeping generalizations
and concentrate on a small group of African countries.

When a journalist asked Colonel Khaddafi, the
head of the Libyan military junta, to explain the
success of his coup, the young colonel raised his
eyes to the sky and reverently said, "Allah All-
mighty." Unlike Colonel Khaddafi, I take a more
prosaic view of military intervention and cannot claim
any privileged access to information from such a
high source. One of the laic questions that has been
asked on numerous occasions remains whether, and to
what extent, military coups in the Third World result
from domestic factors and circumstances. Have not
at least some of them been engineered or teleguided
by foreign powers? I have paid particular attention
to the charge of neocolonialist intervention made
after the coups in Ghana and Mali that ousted the
"radical" presidents Kwame Nkrumah and Modibo Keita.
I believe that from an examination of pre-coup Ghana
and Mali one can learn at least some underlying
causes that make governments and regimes in the Third
World unstable and vulnerable.

Apart from the general social and political environment in the countries affected by military takeover, there also might be something about the armies
and military of these countries that makes them willing and able to easily overthrow civilian authorities.
It seems to me, as a number of scholars have suggested,
that the colonial legacy had to have considerable

bearing on the place of the African military in society and hence on the motives of coup-makers. Military intervention may reflect, with some delay, the tempo and forms of decolonization in Africa.

It is not enough to deal only with the "why's" of military coups, since we know much less about what happens afterward and the consequences of military rule in Africa. This is the reason I decided to examine the functioning of military rule in four African countries between 1965 and 1970. Historically speaking, military rule on the African continent is not new since many pre-colonial African states experienced long periods of domination by warlords, religious-cum-military conquerors, militarized monarchies, and so forth. However, the most modern varieties of military rule were not given enough attention by scholars, although these periods are at least as important to an understanding of the nature of politics in the Third World. Yet among the many books that treat the military in developing countries (see Bibliography), very few deal with military rule in Africa.

This study seeks to answer such questions as the following: How does the military govern after a successful coup? How does the military organize itself and the ruling junta? What kinds of relations does the military have with former politicians, civilian bureaucrats, trade unions, such corporate bodies as the universities, and with the population and its various groups? The substance and the style of military rule can be expected to depend a great deal on the social environment, on the capabilities of the military and on its reaction to the ousted regime. Another question I posed was whether military juntas can and really do ban politics, as many of them claim. I was rather skeptical about another claim often made by military rulers--namely, that they are unselfish and politically neutral suprapartisan patriots who represent the nation as a whole and act above narrow group interests.

In order to answer these and a number of other questions, at least tentatively and without claiming universal validity for my conclusions, I examined four African countries that have experienced periods of military rule in the recent past: Dahomey, Ghana,

TABLE 1

Dahomey, Ghana, Sierra Leone, and Mali: Basic Indicators

Indicator	Dahomey	Ghana	Sierra Leone	Mali
Population (in thousands, 1968)	2,410	7,945	2,403	4,654
Area (in square kilometers)	112,622	238,537	71,740	1,240,000
Density (per square kilometer)	23	35	34	4
Annual rate of population growth	2.0	2.7	1.5	1.9
Population per physician	31,300	13,310	16,440	50,710
Primary school enrollment (first level)	139,737	1,288,383	136,824	186,022
Primary school enrollment per 1,000 of population	58	162	57	40
Urbanization (in percentages)	8.3	12.3	7.1	4.7
Total GNP (in millions of dollars, 1968)	183	1,851	351	293
GNP per capita				
1960[a]	72	164	103	66
1966[a]	68	166	128	58
Net gain or loss				
1960-66[a]	-4	+2	+25	-8
1967[a]	72	213	156	70
1968[a]	80	230	150	60
Total number in army, navy, air force, gendarmerie	3,000	16,000	1,360	5,300

Total number in civil police	1,000	12,000	2,050	2,400
Total number in military and police	4,000	28,000	3,410	7,700
Number of army and police personnel per 1,000 inhabitants	1.7	3.5	1.4	1.7
Date of independence	August 1, 1960	March 6, 1957	April 27, 1961	September 22, 1960
Years of independence at the time military rule began	5.3	9.9	5.8	8.2
Number of changes of parties in power during independence (pre-coup)	2	0	0	0
Date military rule began	December 22, 1965	February 24, 1966	March 21, 1967	November 19, 1968
Duration of military rule in years	2.6	3.6[b]	1.1	3.5
Date military rule ended	July 17, 1968	September 1969[b]	April 26, 1968	By June 1972

[a]The discrepancies among these indicators are obvious and due, in part, to differences in methodology of calculating the GNP in Africa.

[b]The inauguration of the first post-coup civilian government took place in September 1969, but the first post-coup civilian head of state was inaugurated on August 31, 1970.

Sources: A. Kamarck, "African Economic Problems and Prospects," AR, January 1969, p. 19; United Nations, United Nations Statistical Yearbook (New York, 1969), pp. 57, 673, 770; UN Economic Commission for Africa, Demographic Handbook (New York: ECA, 1968). Data is for the period around 1961; UN Economic Commission for Africa, "Economic Indicators for Africa," JA, No. 474 (February 3, 1970), p. 36; D. Wood, "The Armed Forces of African States," Adelphi Papers, No. 27 (London: Institute for Strategic Studies, 1966); Lieutenant-Colonel Muguet, Les Armées Nationales des Etats Voisins: Nigérie, Ghana, Guinée, Mali, No. 712/A (Paris: Centre Militaire d'Information et de Spécialisation pour l'Outre-Mer, 1964); Ernest Lefever, Spear and Scepter (Washington, D.C.: The Brookings Institute, 1970).

Sierra Leone, and Mali. All are located in West Africa, but they have no common borders. Some basic statistics of the four states are shown in Table 1.

Of the four countries Ghana is undoubtedly the most economically and socially developed. Sierra Leone is one-third as large as Ghana and less evenly developed. However, it contains the commercialized and sophisticated area of Freetown, with the longest continuous British influence in West Africa.

These two former British possessions seem to be economically, and to a lesser extent socially, more advanced and viable than the two former French colonies, Dahomey and Mali. Dahomey is close to Sierra Leone in terms of primary and secondary education. It is probably more socially complex, but it is poorer. Mali is decidedly the poorest and the least fortunate country in the group as far as the known natural endowment is concerned. Mali also was the most adversely affected by changes brought about by the Europeans. The only landlocked country in the group, Mali, lost the important position of intermediary between the Near East, North Africa, and Tropical Africa and became a neglected backwater possession. However, since independence it has made great strides in education and in Africanization of its public services. Nevertheless, the three coastal states are still more advanced.

The four countries gained or were granted independent statehood between 1957 and 1961. They are comparable as far as modern military establishments are concerned. They possess relatively small professional armies, fashioned mainly after the British and French. Ghana has had by far the biggest, most complex, and sophisticated armed forces. It is followed by Mali, leaving behind Dahomey and Sierra Leone.

I have adopted a simple scheme of presentation. Following this introduction the reader will find four chapters that present succinct accounts of the relevant developments in Dahomey, Ghana, Sierra Leone, and Mali. Armed with this background information the reader hopefully will be able to appreciate the next three chapters in which I compare and analyze the experience of military rule in the four countries.

I also have projected some of the conclusions on the rest of Africa.*

---

*For a more thorough treatment of the existing literature, methodological questions, concepts, variables, and research techniques, hypotheses, and the Huntington-Janowitz controversy, see the author's Ph.D. thesis, "Military Rule in Africa: Dahomey, Ghana, Sierra Leone, Mali" (Political Science Department, University of Pennsylvania, 1972).

CHAPTER

2

DAHOMEY:
DECEMBER 1965-
AUGUST 1968

Le vraisemblable est rarement vrai au
Dahomey. (The plausible is seldom true
in Dahomey.)

M. A. Glélé

THE ROAD TO MILITARY
INTERVENTION

The advent of military government in post-independence Dahomey on December 22, 1965, was not an
entirely new phenomenon in Dahomeyan politics. The
Dahomeyan army was dragged to power once in October
1963, but soon relinquished it in favor of a group
of civilians. The 1965 coup followed an acute political crisis and two smaller coups in which civilian
politicians were the main protagonists. Behind the
facade of the ruling and only legal political party--
the Democratic Party of Dahomey (Parti Démocratique
du Dahomey or PDD)--there had been ceaseless rivalries
and feuds among traditional political clans with
more or less determinate regional bases. Two of
these alliances of notables were headed by the president of the Republic, S. Migan-Apithy of Porto-Novo,
and the vice-president of the Republic and chief
executive, J. Ahomadegbé-Tometin of Abomey. The
Apithy-Ahomadegbé tandem was born in the struggle to
unseat the first president of the Republic, H. Maga,
a Northerner who finally was ousted in October 1963.

By the autumn of 1965 tensions between Apithy
and Ahomadegbé broke into an open clash, ostensibly
over the legal issues of appointing the Supreme
Court.[1] The conflict between the president and
chief executive blocked the workings of the entire
national government with no constitutional remedy in
sight. The only way out was through a political action of the unified party. There, as well as in the
National Assembly and the general public, Ahomadegbé
enjoyed at that moment an undeniable preponderance
and Apithy found himself in almost complete isolation.
He was expelled from the party but refused to obey
party discipline and resign as president.

On November 16, 1965, a "People's Assembly"--in-
cluding the National Assembly, ministers, and members
of the party executive, auxiliary organizations,
trade unions, Society of Elders (Anciens), and the
army--was convened by the speaker of the National Assembly. It announced the removal of the president
and temporarily vested his power in Chief Executive
Ahomadegbé. It was a civilian coup, but Apithy refused to vacate the presidential palace in Porto-
Novo. Civilian elites lacked the coercive capacity
to bring the coup to a conclusive end.

During 10 days, the government tried to oust
Apithy physically and Ahomadegbé ordered the army
into action through Lieutenant-Colonel P. Aho, the
deputy chief of staff, bypassing General Christophe
Soglo, his superior and a one-time head of state.
The head of a civilian political clan thus tried to
bring the army on his side, exploiting a division
among the top brass. This led on November 28, 1965,
to a clash between Ahomadegbé and General Soglo.
The general assembly of Dahomeyan officers was convened in the military base Guézo in the capital
Cotonou, and a designated group of senior officers,
through intimidation, obtained resignations of both
Apithy and Ahomadegbé. A new provisional government
was formed under Tahirou Congacou, speaker of the
National Assembly.

In the background of political instability there
was a continuous deterioration of the economic situation and balance of trade, as well as budgetary difficulties. The budget deficit in 1965 was approaching $12 million out of the swollen budget of about

$33 million, over a half of which was disbursed on the salaries of over 18,000 civil servants.[2] The degree of even passive acquiescence to the governing administration dwindled sharply when Ahomadegbé pushed through a rather severe program of austerity measures in July 1965.[3]

The interim administration of T. Congacou lasted only about three weeks, the PDD was dissolved,[4] the old political parties promptly reemerged, and the army became the de facto power. The Congacou government tried to push through the divided National Assembly a constitutional reform bill abolishing the post of vice-president. But the new opposition coalition of Apithy-Maga blocked the effort. Technical violation of the existing constitution was unavoidable and agitation in the capital cities Cotonou and Porto-Novo further reduced the authority of the Congacou administration. Urged in private by a number of prominent civilians, the army officer corps, in a general assembly, finally decided to step in on the evening of December 21, 1965. There were some indications of possible violence if the presidential election was allowed to be held.

In a bloodless takeover, T. Congacou signed a letter of resignation demanded by officers and the Dahomeyan army became the master of the country, this time with the intention of running it for a while.[5] The military intervention resulted from a stalemate of legal institutions brought about by the inability and/or unwillingness of the three leading political blocs to make them function. Evaluations of the danger of a civil war varied substantially, although the military used this theme as the main public explanation of its action. The top army officers were not completely indifferent or unwilling to hold power for the sake of power, but the popular support among the relatively small politicized urban population was sufficiently widespread to make this aspect inconspicuous.

THE DAHOMEYAN ARMY

At the time of the coup the total armed forces of Dahomey consisted of 1,700 army troops, 1,200 gendarmes, 100 men in the air force, and about 1,000 civilian policemen.[6] The army had basically two infantry battalions and a pioneer battalion. The organizational complexity and technical level have been very low, the army has never had combat experience, and in the absence of any conceivable external danger the officers had plenty of leisure time. A large part of the effective was concentrated in and close to the main cities in the southern coastal part of the country. The super-police function in the hinterland has been carried out by the more dispersed six companies of the Gendarmerie.

Military expenditure in Dahomey stood at roughly $4 million a year. It constituted 2.2 percent of GNP and about 12 percent of the budget, twice higher than expenditures on education and three times higher than those on public health.[7] The army officer corps consisted of 43 indigenous officers, and under the terms of technical assistance France maintained 12 officers and 22 NCOs. The armed forces were well paid: majors had a higher salary than most civilian cabinet members and young second lieutenants had higher salaries than experienced administrators in the ministries.[8] In addition, there has been a rather extensive system of other privileges and allowances.

By late 1965 the Dahomeyan military had had only a very short period of operation as a national defense force and no modern military traditions of its own. The last French troops left Dahomey in March 1965.[9]

The Dahomeyan military was drawn into politics in the summer of 1963 by the Maga regime. Following the assassination of President Sylvanus Olympio of neighboring Togo in January 1963, the civilian politicians tried to prevent a wholesale military intervention by partial and controlled politization of the army and by bringing the top officers closer to the political elite. This attempt already had failed in October 1963 when President Maga was ousted and the army became the arbiter of the political game.[10] The ensuing politization of officer corps went hand in hand with the reduction of the army's isolation and growing "nationalization" of the army into the body politic. The officers soon came to believe that

13

the army and they themselves were "the incarnation of the nation."

THE FIRST SOGLO GOVERNMENT

Taking power in the name of the army, General Soglo declared that it "will return to the barracks as soon as it completes the task of national reconciliation" and that it was not "a Praetorian Guard."[11] To conform to this image the military drew into the new government several young intellectuals and technocrats without known political affiliation, who accepted the jobs with an understanding that there would be an end to traditional clannish and interest group politicking, that top priority would be given to economic development, and that the army as a whole would stay away from political rivalries. A general platform of the military-civilian government and its composition was formally discussed on December 23, 1965, during a meeting of about 100 prominent civilians and 30 military officers. This assembly, convened in the presidential palace in Cotonou by the military, served as an ad hoc substitute for the parliamentary institutions, which had been suspended or banned by the new government, together with the constitution, political parties, political activities, and municipal, local, and departmental councils.[12]

The assembly adopted a general resolution and elected 25 of the final 36 members of a national consultative body to the government, called the Committee of National Renovation (Comité de Renovation Nationale, or CRN).[13] Only three members of this deliberative consultative body were military officers, and it was headed by a lawyer. Its function was to be a kind of transmission belt to the population, as well as a sounding board.

The first Soglo cabinet was said to be the most technically competent in Dahomeyan history. Three ministries were headed by military officers and ten by civilians. The most dynamic role was played by young intellectual-technocrats and moderately radical ministers--M. Mensah, C. Vieyra, N. Soglo, and S. Adotevi. Thus a military-civilian coalition was created (see Figure 1).

FIGURE 1

Schematic Representation of the Decision-Making Structure During the First Soglo Government in Dahomey, December 1965 - Fall 1966

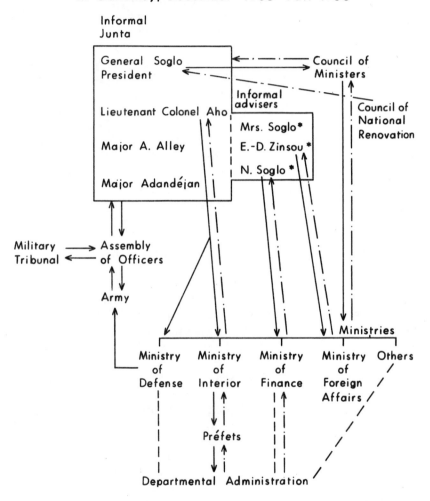

*Informal civilian associates to the junta

Key
——————→ Relations to subordination
— — — — Other types of power relations
—·—··→ Flow of information

As an example of decision-making that illustrates the relationship between various groups and institutions during the formative period of the first Soglo government, one can take the reexamination of diplomatic relations with the People's Republic of China. There were no pressing domestic reasons to revise relations with Peking, but it seems that the top brass was persuaded by foreign interests (the United States and also France) before the coup. Having made a decision, however, the military went to considerable lengths to convince its opponents on the issue within the military-civilian coalition. Most vocal and recalcitrant among them were young intellectual-technocrats and the trade union delegates in the Committee of National Renovation. Supported by elder statesmen, Roman Catholic clergy, and French interests, the military narrowly missed wrecking the barely established coalition. The issue was discussed first in the CRN and later taken to the Council of Ministers.[14] There the debate lasted for five days, and finally on January 1, 1966, the opponents gave up and the Peking embassy was given three days to leave the country.

In less vital areas of decision-making, General Soglo tended to act as arbiter and amiable paternalist in the Council of Ministers; only infrequently did he intervene and side with one group against another. Lieutenant-Colonel Aho had controlled the administration in the departments; but the préfets remained civilians, and there seems to have been no systematic intervention of the military in administration or in running ministries headed by civilians.

In the Council of Ministers the mode of arriving at final important decisions was procedurally vague. The three top military officers who participated in it, in addition to General Soglo and Lieutenant-Colonel Aho, had had no assignments beyond the areas of defense and security and technically were not bound by the principle of collective responsibility. There was no defined supreme body in the army, nor clear rules on how to handle confidential information or on who should participate in discussing the issues of governance, and how. In fact, crucial decisions were taken by an informal junta comprising three to five top officers, but the size and proce-

dures of this fluid body remained indeterminate.
Moreover each of its members could pass information
arbitrarily to lower echelons of the officer corps
in order to build up pressures and to influence the
final outcome. These were the potential seeds of
destruction. The top officers did not feel the need
to bring junior officers into decision-making, and
the institution of the general assembly of officers
remained inoperative most of the time.

During the first 10 months, the Council of Ministers operated rather smoothly and easygoing General
Soglo contributed to the lack of serious tensions.
In part this harmony was achieved at the expense of
the Committee of National Renovation, which gradually
became a debating society and a source of minor ir-
ritation to the power-holders.[15] The committee
viewed itself as the main link between the regime
and the population, a substitute for the parliament
and for a party. The top military brass and most of
civilian ministers grew weary of the CRN's pretensions
and looked at it as a purely consultative body. The
organization of the consultative bodies was envisaged
as comprehensively covering the whole territory with
departmental and local committees. In fact, the departmental committees never got off the ground.
Local and municipal committees were inaugurated officially only in November-December 1966, when the
national committee already had lost its influence and
momentum.[16] Furthermore there were no institutionalized and regularized ties between the consultative
bodies, horizontally or vertically. These were no
match for a centralized administration--the backbone
of the military rule supplemented by occasional direct contacts with the population.[17]

Weaknesses of the Soglo government and the areas
of disagreement between the military and the activist
civilian ministers came to the surface in August
1966 during a top-level seminar of "criticism and
self-criticism."[18] The military ignored the most
far-reaching recommendations of the seminar, but the
regime nevertheless was given an impetus and a program of action. "The Charter of the Nation" was announced on the radio by General Soglo on September 2,
1966.[19] It had a strong imprint of radical ideas,
but it seems unlikely that the general really intended

to implement the declaration. The ideas did not appeal to the still divided civilian elites or to the local French interests. To a degree, the charter sparked an unfavorable public reaction and the grumblings of trade unions heightened by the program of stiff austerity measures introduced in August. From a rather friendly acquiesence, trade unions shifted their attitude to one of subdued opposition. On October 1, 1966, they called a general strike of protest, but they backed off when confronted with guns and threats of massive layoffs. The Soglo government won the round, but from then on the trade union leadership was definitely in opposition.[20]

This crisis coincided with growing internal tensions in the government. Facing serious difficulties, the top brass acknowledged the bargaining power of the revived traditional political clans and economic interest groups and decided to maneuver between them. During a cabinet reshuffle and soon afterward, five younger activist ministers resigned and the crucial finance portfolio was given to B. Borna, the notorious former finance minister of President Maga. It was the end of a coalition between the military and the young technocrats. Instead, the military entered the political game as an interest group, possessing means of coercion. The government lost its dynamism and sense of direction, and the laxity, maladministration, and misappropriations of former times were on the way back. General Soglo's inability to provide leadership to the country became clearly visible.

THE SECOND SOGLO GOVERNMENT:
FROM CRISIS TO DOWNFALL

Dissatisfaction with the leaders spread to the army officer corps, which became more politicized but lacked institutionalized channels to express its opinions. In August 1966 Lieutenant-Colonel Aho managed to quell a wave of resentment.[21] Two institutions created in 1966--the Supreme Council and the Military Tribunal of Exception---indicated an increase in direct participation of military officers in running the country, but it was not enough for the younger, better-educated, and ambitious ones among them.[22]

Under pressure, General Soglo agreed in January 1967 to set up a military commission charged with reviewing the functioning of his government. It produced conclusions highly critical of the government, and soon two new bodies were created--the Superior Military Committee and the Military Committee of Vigilance (Comité Militaire de Vigilance, or CMV).[23] Both were designed to curb the power of General Soglo.

The CMV, headed by Major B. Sinzogan, became an intermediary between the Committee of National Renovation and the chief of state as well as a general watchdog body.[24] After about two months of coexistence the CMV finally displaced the civilian-dominated Committee of National Renovation in June 1967. However, the CMV had no executive powers and failed to assert itself in accordance with junior officers' expectations.

In a deteriorating economic situation General Soglo turned to France for help, and his pleas were heard. General de Gaulle's grand African design and the Nigerian civil war made him more magnanimous than the Dahomeyan clients had expected. In November 1967 General Soglo was received in Paris and was promised substantial aid. On his triumphant return to Cotonou on December 1 General Soglo declared: "We did not come back emptyhanded," thereby raising exaggerated expectations of white-collar state employees, who had long demanded an end to the mandatory 25 percent "solidarity tax" on their salaries.

On December 8 public schoolteachers went on a warning strike, and on the same day the government suspended all trade union activities in retaliation.[25] The strike spread to state post and telegraph employees and to the private sector. Arrests of 16 trade union leaders followed, after which the trade union federations announced an unlimited general strike.[26] At this moment General Soglo backed down and suspended the ordinance on December 8. The strike was called off on December 13.

However, the social crisis primarily over economic issues had strong repercussions in the military establishment. While the assembly of officers, convened on December 16, was in session again on December 17, Major M. Kouandété (chief of the cabinet of Lieutenant-Colonel A. Alley, the chief of staff),

Captain M. Kérékou, and several other junior officers staged a bloodless palace coup. Under their command the elite para-commando unit surrounded the villas of four top officers, put them under house "protective custody," and took control of the capital.[27]

The coup resulted from internal divisions within the armed forces and was directed by the middle and lower ranks against the top echelon of the military hierarchy. The plotters publicly explained their action by the failure of the Soglo government to effect economic recovery and national reconciliation; by General Soglo's failure to consult the officer corps and to bring them effectively into decision-making; by his intention to disregard the earlier promises of a return to civilian rule; and by waste, corruption, misappropriation, nepotism, and unseemly behavior of the top brass.[28] The authors of the coup were motivated to a significant extent by the desire to speed their own upward mobility for the sake of material rewards, prestige, and the possibility of playing a more important role in running the state. The ideological content of the cleavage was low.

December 17 was an intra-military coup with the declared purpose of terminating overt military intervention. However, the bone of contention in the military establishment was not the principle and legitimacy of military intervention but its form. The junior officers felt the military either should be complete masters or simply have a veto power without responsibility. Professional pride of the junior officers contributed to the December 1967 coup. The coup had no wide support either in the public or within the military establishment.[29]

THE GOVERNMENT OF THE
YOUNG CADRES

On December 17, 1967, the new junta broadcast over the radio "The Proclamation of December 17" by which it dissolved the Soglo government and the Military Committee of Vigilance and created a Military Revolutionary Committee and a provisional government charged with running current business. It further promised to set up a Constitutional Committee. A

20

new constitution was to be submitted to a referendum, and the people, according to a fixed timetable, were to elect new rulers freely and democratically. According to the published schedule the army was to withdraw to the barracks not later than June 16, 1968.[30]

Major M. Kouandété, the leader of the plot, became chairman of the Council of Ministers. Several days later his superior, Lieutenant-Colonel A. Alley, former chief of staff, whose attitude toward the coup had been ambivalent, was persuaded to assume the post of president of the Republic.[31] As another step to restore the corporate cohesion of the military, which had been badly affected by the coup, another senior officer, Major B. Sinzogan, was given the post of minister for external affairs. The dissatisfaction of the junior officers with the predominantly civilian government under General Soglo was reflected in the fact that only the very important ministry of finance, economic affairs, and plan was entrusted to the civilian P. Chabi Kao. A minister in the previous government, the chief lieutenant to and presumably an illegitimate son of ex-President Maga, he had been close to the Northern officers and knew well in advance of the impending coup. In the regionally balanced cabinet the other portfolios were distributed among three majors, three captains, and three lieutenants.[32]

The presumed ruling body, the Military Revolutionary Committee (Comité Militaire Révolutionnaire, or CMR), originally consisted of three captains, eight lieutenants, and three NCOs.[33] Captain Hachémé became its chairman. The role of the CMR was specified to consist of the supervision of the provisional government, the creation of a constitutional commission, and the investigation of the previous government. The membership of the CMR originally did not overlap with that of the Council of Ministers.

The entire system of military government under the young cadres (see Figure 2) was never stabilized or made orderly. The experience of running the state not only failed to heal the cleavages in the military establishment but exacerbated them. In a series of internal purges three senior officers of the new junta, all of southern origin, were dismissed: Cap-

21

FIGURE 2

Schematic Representation of the Decision-Making Structure Under the Young Cadres in Dahomey, December 1967-July 1968

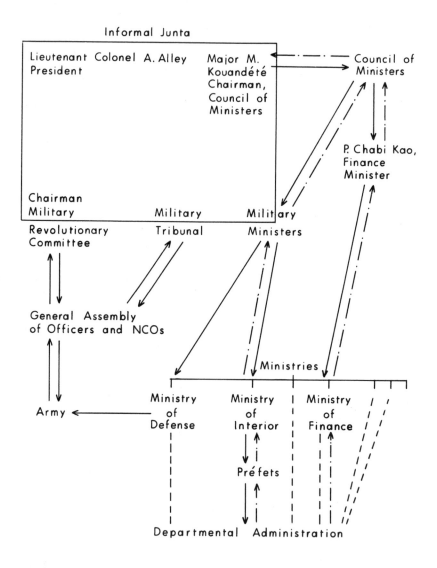

tain Hachémé, chairman of the CMR; Captain F. Johnson, director of national security; and Major L. Chasme, minister of justice. Major Chasme was the first victim of the Special Military Tribunal he himself had instituted shortly before.[34] He was found guilty of gross misappropriation and corruption. These changes shifted the balance in the military establishment in favor of officers of northern origin. In the absence of any external danger Dahomey could "afford" to have a rather ineffective and internally divided army. For a number of reasons the country avoided the fate of neighboring Nigeria.

In the informal power structure of government under the young cadres, a large group of about 90 politicized officers, NCOs, and even soldiers made up a kind of military parliament.[35] With no rules to guide their deliberations, the occasional gatherings of this informal body could not provide a common platform for the government. An interplay between the hierarchical distribution of roles and the informal power structure, based on prominence in plotting prior to the December 1967 coup and on direct control of the elements vital to state security, produced several fluid centers of power with very vague rules of the game.

An informal junta reappeared again, this time different and less stable than the previous one. The Alley-Kouandété tandem had been an uneasy alliance. Major Kouandété's power derived only in part from his official capacity as chairman of the Council of Ministers. More salient were his relations with junior officers and his control of the para-commando unit. Both President Lieutenant-Colonel Alley and Major Kouandété, as well as the most important ministers, were not members of the Military Revolutionary Committee, the intention being to associate a significant part of the officer corps to the government. It seems, however, that the proliferation of institutions of the new regime and the increased replacing of civilians in the top positions of authority in the capital did not appreciably bolster the impact of the military on decision-making and on the administration. In most ministries the officers were only figureheads, as they lacked specialized knowledge, expertise, and experience.

23

The impact of the young cadres outside the capital was negligible.

There had been several attempts to create consultative military-civilian machinery in the form of mixed military-civilian commissions to the Military Revolutionary Committee,[36] but these substitutes for the finally disbanded municipal and local committees of national renovation were short-lived and ineffective.

THE TERMINATION OF
MILITARY RULE

The military government stuck rather closely to the timetable of withdrawal announced in January 1968. Eighteen members of the Constitutional Committee were elected in the departments and twenty appointed by the government.[37] The Constitutional Committee was officially inaugurated on February 2, 1968, and a month later Chairman L. Ignacio Pinto, chief justice of the Supreme Court, handed the draft of the new constitution to President Alley.

The Constitutional Committee adopted provisions for a unified party suggested to it by the military[38] and proclaimed the army as guarantor "of the regime freely chosen by the people."[39] The top military officers campaigned for adoption of the draft, and on April 8 the electorate overwhelmingly endorsed it.

When it came to registering candidates for the presidency the military arbitrarily imposed its own limitations, barring the prominent political leaders. The Supreme Court declared this provision of the election law unconstitutional, but the government refused to comply, suspended the constitution, and temporarily dismissed the high court.[40] The traditional leaders condemned the military and waged a successful political campaign across the borders. On May 5, 1968, the Dahomeyan voter was given a choice of five unknown and unpopular candidates. The overall abstention rate was 74 percent, and the junta had to admit the defeat by annulling the election results.[41]

The economic, financial, and social situation, which had deteriorated since the fall of General Soglo,

24

became critical in late May-early June. Deprived of
the French budgetary subsidy, the young cadres were
still trying to meet the June 16 deadline to return
to a civilian regime. An abortive attempted internal military coup in early June and pressures from
Paris made them proceed faster.[42] On June 12 the
government convened a meeting of important personali-
ties of the former political formations and the
trade unions and of civic leaders to find a common
candidate for the presidency.[43] The meeting did not
produce a quick solution, and the impatient military
rulers unexpectedly announced their own candidate,
E.-D. Zinsou, a distinguished diplomat. This was a
victory for the Kouandété faction within the junta,
which contemplated a conditional withdrawal of the
army behind a facade of a figurehead civilian president.[44]

Zinsou was conferred the reins of power in the
name of the armed forces for "at least five years"
to "establish constitutional legality in order."[45]
It was in fact another palace coup, but Zinsou unexpectedly demanded and obtained a national referendum
to confirm his designation. This time the opposition
of the traditional leaders, barred again from return-
ing to Dahomey, was soundly defeated on July 28,
1968.[46] Deeply disturbed by the activities of the
traditional leaders and by political agitation, the
junta changed the day of inauguration from August 1
to July 17, 1968, and on August 1 dissolved the Military Revolutionary Committee. The army withdrew to
its barracks without glory to reappear again 16
months later after an uneasy period of de facto tutelage, which was ignored by President Zinsou.

During this period Lieutenant-Colonel Kouandété,
the chief of staff, avoided four attempted kidnappings
or assassinations, all originating within the army.
His former superior and rival, Colonel Alley, was arrested, tried, and condemned to 10 years in jail for
being associated with one of them. But of course
Alley served only several months.

In December 1969 Kouandété ordered President
Zinsou kidnapped in front of the presidential palace.
The tradition of bloodless Dahomeyan coups barely
survived, and the deposed president was transported
to Kouandété's native town in the North. The officer

corps was divided once again, and the architect of
the new coup was obliged not only to share power
with two other senior officers but also to cede the
chairmanship of the three-man Directorate to Colonel
Paul de Souza. Colonel Alley was set free, and the
military rulers reversed their decision to keep the
former presidents out of the country. The Directorate allowed Apithy, Maga, Ahomadegbé, and Zinsou to
present their candidatures in the new presidential
election.

The Dahomeyan voter was asked to the ballot box
in one region after another, with the exercise to
last through March 1970. But before the election
was over in all parts of the country, the junta an-
nulled it, justifying the decision by sectional violence. At that moment an electoral victory by H.
Maga was very probable and the annulment infuriated
the Magaists. They publicly threatened secession,
and the situation in the North became very tense.

At this juncture, the three "old leaders,"
Maga, Apithy, and Ahomadegbé, were brought together
by the French, who had had enough of Dahomeyan quar-
rels. The junta announced the creation of a three-
man civilian Presidential Commission--a collective
head of state. Each of the three leaders was to form
and to head the government in turn for two years.
The first round was given to Maga. Speaking at the
official handing-over ceremony, Lieutenant-Colonel
de Souza declared:

> The role that we have played in the coun-
> try's public life has often been criticised.
> We have been accused of going beyond our
> competence and favoring certain personal
> faults. . . . The political roles we have
> played . . . , for which we had not been
> originally trained, have certainly plagued
> the Army with differences. As we return to
> barracks, our greatest desire is to be able
> to settle the differences and resume our
> normal duties.[47]

And the military stayed in the barracks throughout the first two-year round of the presidential
troika. Even President Maga's frequent and eagerly

sought official and unofficial visits to distant lands did not seduce them to move in. But as the handing-over ceremonies approached, tensions and uncertainty rose. On February 23, 1972, Lieutenant-Colonel de Souza, army chief of staff, became the target of an unsuccessful assassination attempt. During the shooting the assailant, a sergeant-major, was killed. The center of the conspiracy turned out to be in the Cotonou garrison and in the Ouidah company, the notorious Praetorian Guard of Dahomey.

On the surface an internal military conflict, the plot seems to have had wider political objectives. Trying to eliminate Lieutenant-Colonel de Souza, the backbone of the perpetually squabbling Presidential Council, the plotters also were aiming at that body. As usual in Dahomey, the ringleaders' political background proved to be rather complicated. The order to move was given by Captain Lucien Glélé, a man with connections leading to ex-President Zinsou, but the executors were considered supporters of the then president, H. Maga. The latter circumstance immediately caused sinister apprehensions in the camp of J. Ahomadegbé, who was soon to succeed Maga.

But the real inspiration for this new Byzantine affair appears to have come from the perennial coup-maker, Lieutenant-Colonel M. Kouandété, who did not then have operative control of troops. A military tribunal sentenced him and three other coup-leaders to death. Earlier the authorities disbanded the Ouidah company.

The Presidential Council somehow survived the first orderly and legal change at the top in modern Dahomeyan history. In May 1972 a presidential ballet was performed and an ex-schoolteacher, H. Maga, handed his powers over to an ex-dentist, J. Ahomadegbé.

CHAPTER
3

GHANA:
FEBRUARY 1966-
SEPTEMBER 1969

THE BACKGROUND TO MILITARY
INTERVENTION

The advent of military rule in Ghana on February 24, 1966, was one of the most spectacular and widely publicized events in the modern history of Tropical Africa. It brought to an end 14 years of uninterrupted rule by Kwame Nkrumah and his Convention People's Party (CPP).

Independent since 1957, by 1966 Ghana had covered a long road from an Africanized Westminister model to a noncompetitive one-party political system with a docile and ineffective parliament.[1]

For years the only political party with significant support in all parts of the country was the CPP. Its leaders had succeeded in driving various opposition groups underground and their leaders to jail or abroad and in reducing the mechanism of elections to a mere symbol of popular support.[2] The CPP leadership also muzzled the conservative judiciary and reduced the autonomy of the civil service, the armed forces, and the university. Although it practically eliminated open political opposition, the CPP leadership itself had serious difficulties and was internally divided. It tried to maintain the heterogeneous anti-colonialist coalition that consisted of the new lower middle class, clerks, junior civil servants, occasionally employed primary school drop-outs, aggrieved and aggressive young semiliterate "commoners," small- and medium-scale indigenous entrepreneurs, and so forth.

The CPP leadership responded to the dwindling active support of the population, the proliferation of particularist movements and interest groups, and the resistance of the well-established indigenous urban elite[3] by increasing organizational efforts, by continuing to spread the CPP all over the country, and by extensively utilizing the manipulative and coercive powers of the state. In 1959 Nkrumah declared: "The CPP is Ghana" and "Ghana is the CPP."[4]

The reported CPP membership of 2.5 million formally encompassed the bulk of the adult population and most social, occupational, and professional voluntary organizations (trade unions, cooperatives, women's, youth, and children's organizations, and so forth) were integrated into the CPP system. The government also monopolized the press, radio, and television. As for the opposition, the CPP applied a full repertoire of suppression short of overt physical destruction: cooptation, intimidation, prohibition of organizations on regional, tribal, religious, and other grounds, deportation, modification of the constitution and of the electoral law, and so forth.

However, Ghana under Nkrumah did not become a totalitarian state in the European sense. "In practice the Armed Forces, the Civil Service, the Judiciary, the Universities, those engaged in Public Education, religious bodies, while subject to intermittent directives from the Party and President, continued to enjoy a considerable measure of autonomy and initiative."[5] This measure was dwindling, though.

It would be inaccurate and unfair to assign all responsibility for the "inflationary spiral of violence and coercion"[6] to the CPP leaders alone. The opposition provided the government with ample pretexts and justifications for doing away with various legal guarantees of liberal political democracy. President Nkrumah himself was the target of several unsuccessful assassination attempts in which a number of innocent bystanders and children were killed or wounded.

Despite its impressive size, the CPP system had a number of internal weaknesses. Numerous campaigns

to develop and strengthen the CPP organization had
not changed its original nature as primarily a vote-
getting and patronage-distributing machine. The increasing merger of the party and state hierarchy
failed to forge dependable links between party organizations horizontally and vertically and between
them and the auxiliary organizations.[7] Actual control by the national headquarters was weak, and efforts to evolve a viable ideology did not produce
self-discipline and devotion to the cause. One of
the reasons why the CPP came to reflect rather than
transcend Ghanaian society lay in the quality of
leadership. The overwhelming concentration of power
of the central political institutions in the hands of
K. Nkrumah, his growing isolation, the breakdown of
upward communication, divisions in the leadership,
and the defection of several capable organizers
weakened the staying power of the CPP regime from
within.[8]

One of the major underlying causes of this erosion was the shrinking material base of the regime
and the CPP leadership's inability to adjust to it.
Up until 1961 the previously accumulated public reserves in Britain, the high price of cocoa on the
world market, and good credit ratings permitted the
government simultaneously to effect great and visible
strides in economic and social development, to carry
out generous patronage activities, and to produce an
economic climate in which the new entrepreneurial
class and the party-state bureaucracy thrived. But
the unquestionable progress of the country was accompanied by a high proportion of waste due to the incompetence and carelessness of decision-makers, ex-
ceedingly unreasonable prestige spending, and outright corruption at all levels.

Deteriorating economic conditions and inflation
after 1960 brought the real wage index of unskilled
laborers in Accra to 89 points by December 1963, compared to 98 points at the time of independence.[9]
This deterioration alienated even industrial workers
from the CPP and helped precipitate an important
1961 strike in Tema-Takoradi. The eventual doom of
the CPP experiment in social engineering was caused,
in economic terms, by the opposing temporal trends
in commitments on the one hand and available resources

on the other. The CPP leadership badly miscalculated both the resource base and its own capacity to run the system and transform society. Ambitious over-confidence became self-deception on both the interna-tional and national scenes.

Having devoted so much of their energies to making Ghana look important in Africa and in the world, the CPP leadership in general and Nkrumah in particular took the desired for reality and seriously overestimated the manipulative capacity of a rela-tively small and strategically unimportant country to exploit rivalry among the big powers. The Ghana-ian need for external financing was rising when the United States and the USSR had reached a measure of mutual accommodation and had reappraised their African policies more realistically.[10] Nkrumah, despite his compromises and inconsistencies, tried to decrease Ghana's dependence on the West.[11] But the only coun-try that theoretically could help him to break away from the Western zone of influence--the USSR--had other priorities, already was overcommitted, had not overcome its reservations about him, and made only minor approaches in his direction.

THE GHANAIAN ARMED FORCES AND CIVIL-MILITARY RELATIONS UNDER NKRUMAH

The Ghanaian army originated in Britain's Royal West Africa Frontier Force (RWAFF) whose headquarters and two battalions were stationed in the Gold Coast.[12] At the time of independence the Ghanaian army had 7,000 men, commanded by 184 expatriates and 27 Ghanaian officers. The Africanization of the officer corps brought the percentage of indigenous officers to over 90 percent by 1962. The most drastic change occurred in September 1961 when Nkrumah dismissed the army's British commander, General H. T. Alexander, and about 200 British officers and NCOs.

The dismissals had nationalist as well as other external and domestic reasons. The presence of Brit-ish officers had been embarrassing to Nkrumah as he was endeavoring to play a prominent anti-colonialist and anti-imperialist role among nonaligned nations

31

and was maneuvering between the West and the East.
To underpin his activist and ambitious foreign policy
Nkrumah intended to expand the army, air force, and
navy, already among the biggest in Tropical Africa,
in order to be able to take "decisive military actions"
elsewhere on the continent.[13] An example of such
action was Ghana's participation in the UN peace-
keeping operation in the Congo. The Ghanaian con-
tingent, 2,624 men strong, spent almost two years
in the Congo, initially under the command of British
officers. Disagreements with General Alexander and
the British over the Congo operation and over Nkrumah's
intention to send 400 military cadets to Soviet
schools and academies and thus reduce Ghana's overwhelming reliance on British military schools also
contributed to the conflict. Another aspect of the
General Alexander affair was domestic and involved
the general's resistance to using British officers
and NCOs against the strikers in Secondi-Takoradi
at the time when Nkrumah attended the Belgrade conference of the nonaligned.[14]

The policy of accelerated Africanization and
Nkrumah's attitude toward the army remained ambiguous
and contradictory. In the first years after independence, some of the CPP leaders were conscious of a
possible "promotion blockage" and of the potential
desirability of maintaining professional standards.[15]
After the Major Awhaitey affair[16] and the military
coups in Pakistan and the Sudan, the CPP leadership
became apprehensive about its own military. With
the political barometer functioning poorly the CPP
leadership could not accurately monitor the spread
of silent political opposition, of which the army
and the police had become the most potent reserves.

A. A. Afrifa, one of the chief architects of
the 1966 coup, later related:

> What I wish to acknowledge publicly today
> is that I was encouraged and inspired in
> my resolution to help to overthrow the cor-
> rupt and oppressive regime of Kwame Nkrumah
> by the lectures and writings and the sus-
> tained campaign which Dr. Busia carried on
> within and outside this country in opposi-
> tion to the CPP, by his exposures of the

wrongs its leaders were perpetuating against
our country, and by identifying himself with
all those who stood against the malpractices
of the CPP. A fellow soldier, Major Alex
Duah, received a copy of one of the pamphlets he used to get into the country. This
one was entitled "No." . . . May I quote
him: NO to oppression and suppression, NO
to denial of Freedom of Speech, of Association and of Movement, NO to imprisonment
without trial, NO to spying, NO to a Police
State, NO to Deceit and Cheating whereby
many toil for few to "chop," NO to wasteful
projects, NO to scarcity of essential goods
and drugs, NO to crippling controls, NO to
Neo-colonialism. Under my master, the late
Lieutenant General Kotoka . . . , we said
NO in a more effective and decisive way than
Dr. Busia dared to ask.[17]

Aware of these dangers, Nkrumah had taken extensive precautions. After an abortive assassination
attempt in which an army warrant officer was involved,
Nkrumah decided that he could not trust British intelligence any more. He "asked the Soviets to fill
the vacuum"[18] and subsequently enlisted technical
assistance in security-related matters from the USSR
and East Germany.[19] With their help and equipment,
Nkrumah developed, under the growing President's
Office, his own intelligence and security system of
informers and bodyguards. After the next assassination attempt, this time involving a policeman, on
January 8, 1964, Nkrumah fired the top police officers including the commissioner and took away the
weapons of the recently armed National Police Service
and "utterly humiliated and rendered it impotent."[20]
Furthermore he placed the ICD (Criminal Investigation
Department) office under his direct control.[21]
    Through manipulation of promotion and by pitting
one senior officer against another, Nkrumah attempted
to divide the officer corps. His informers infil-
trated the army so conspicuously that their usefulness was seriously reduced. Nevertheless, the army
head of intelligence, Brigadier Hassan, Nkrumah's
appointee, had at his disposal a fairly good system

of early warning, but it eventually was "jammed" by too many alerts.

To divide the armed forces Nkrumah had built up a potent, well-armed, and well-paid rival to the regular army--the President's Own Guard Regiment (POGR), initially proposed by General Alexander as a relief duty for veterans. With superior fire-power and training provided by the Warsaw Pact instructors, strategically located around Flagstaff House (the presidential residence) and close to Accra, this elite guard became a deterrent to any coup attempt. Under loyal Colonel D. Zanlerigu, the POGR in 1965 counted 1,100 men and 50 officers, with a second battalion in training.[22] Confronted with objections by the top army officers to the removal of the POGR from the army command, on July 28, 1965, Nkrumah fired generals S. J. Otu and J. A. Ankrah from their respective positions as chief of defense staff and chief of army staff and retired them from the army.

Austerity measures, initiated by the government as economic difficulties grew, had been applied to the regular army but not to the security services and the POGR. Inflation substantially cut down the purchasing power of the soldier's pay, and the reduced appropriations for equipment, uniforms, travel, and so forth of army personnel negatively affected army morale. Its effectiveness diminished, the army had before its eyes the rival force, and some officers suspected that the army's existence itself was in danger (only after the coup did the army find plans to this effect in Flagstaff House). In June 1964 military training was introduced into the Workers' Brigades, numbering 7,000 men, but the project soon was abandoned; the brigades were never armed and did not become a serious para-military force. At the time of the Rhodesian crisis Nkrumah publicly advanced the idea of creating a "people's militia" and several thousand people were enrolled in the new Volunteer Brigade. The army became apprehensive that Nkrumah might send it to fight the Smith regime in Rhodesia and many officers strongly resented this on general political and professional grounds.

By 1965 discontent had spread over most of the army, affecting in various degrees the top brass, junior officers, NCOs, and enlisted men. In the upper echelons corporate grievances, insecurity, and normative cleavages played the most prominent role as the officers brought up in the British norms resented political interference, surveillance, promotion policies, and other violations of the armed forces' autonomy. Corporate insecurity was combined with the feeling of humiliation of those who had gone through a tour of duty in the Congo and with general political disagreement with the regime's policies.[23] Lower in the ranks the deteriorating conditions of service, the diminishing purchasing power of pay, and the demonstrative effect of the more privileged POGR were more important sources of grumbling and grievances. Despite the still persistent, although diminished, isolation of life in army barracks, the feeling of the military parallelled in varying degrees the general discontent of numerous groups in the population at large--the established urban elite, civil servants, some traders and entrepreneurs, traditional authorities and groups influenced by them, salaried employees with fixed incomes, cocoa farmers, and so forth. Some opposed CPP policies in part or almost totally, and practically all were hit by the falling cocoa prices, inflation, the economic slump, and severe shortages of essential goods on the poorly managed market.

On the other hand Nkrumah's policy of expanding and modernizing the armed forces resulted by 1965 in a large, by African standards, army of 14,000 men. In the absence of a credible external threat it consisted of 10 battalions--five infantry, two POGR, one paratrooper, and one reconnaissance. The air force and the navy had together 2,000 men.[24] From $8.3 million in 1959, the yearly defense allocations rose to $20.6 million in 1961 and declined steadily after that date to $15.5 million in 1966 (at 1960 prices and exchange rates).[25]

The disarmed Ghana Police Service with its intelligence function under the President's Office could not serve as a counterweight to an army establishment bent on carrying out a military coup. More centralized than in Britain the Ghana Police Service had risen from 6,200 at the time of independence to about 12,000 men, including approximately equal numbers of regular and escort police. In 1967 the police

had 71 expatriates and 45 Ghanaian officers; by 1966
the Africanization was complete.[26] In the 1964 reorganization of the police, J. W. K. Harlley, the
former head of the Special Branch, was appointed
commissioner.

THE COUP OF FEBRUARY 24, 1966

A number of people claim to have plotted to
overthrow Nkrumah prior to February 1966, including
Major-General J. A. Ankrah and Major A. A. Afrifa.
In this tense and precarious domestic situation
Nkrumah displayed a fatal lack of touch with the
reality in his country and an excessive preoccupation
with world affairs. Once again he left his finance
minister to deliver a tough and unpopular budget message[27] and embarked on a self-appointed mission to
bring peace to Vietnam. A large presidential party
departed for Hanoi on February 21, 1966. After a
welcome in Peking, Nkrumah learned that his regime
had just been overthrown on February 24, 1966.
    The coup was planned, initiated, and largely
carried out by Colonel Kotoka, aided by his subordinate Major A. A. Afrifa. The plan was drawn up by
the two on February 8. On February 15 Commissioner
Harlley was informed about the timing by Kotoka. The
cover for the movement of Colonel Kotoka's troops
was provided by war games, related to a possible
Rhodesian emergency.[28]
    The spearhead of the coup, 600 men from three
battalions of the Second Brigade stationed in Tamale
and Kumasi, started movements on 30-odd vehicles
from Tamale, 350 miles north of Accra, on February 23.
Colonel Kotoka informed the troops of the real aim
of the operation when they were 12 miles from Accra.
The reception to his revelation reportedly was en-
thusiastic. The movements did not cause alarm in
the capital because Major-General C. M. Barwah, acting defense chief of staff in the absence from the
country of Major-General Aferi, took it for another
false alert and because the police intelligence system was "plugged out" by Harlley. The first arrests
of senior military officers were made at 1:40 a.m.,[29]
and shooting at Flagstaff House started at 4:30 a.m.[30]

"Operation Cold Chop" was not a smooth and well-executed operation. It succeeded narrowly.

Colonel Ocran, commander of the First Infantry Brigade in Accra, vacillated and pretended loyalty to the government for several critical hours, and most of his brigade failed to join Colonel Kotoka's forces as had been agreed. The insurgents did not capture Flagstaff House--the main focus of the oper-ation--until 5:30 p.m., when they already controlled the country. The decisive move in the conflict was not military but political. The insurgents early seized the Ghana Broadcasting House, and at 6 a.m. Colonel Kotoka announced to the nation the end of Nkrumah's rule. This very soon immobilized the well-armed and -equipped Second POGR Battalion, whose early arrival would have doomed the insurrection. In a very short time the internal political decay of the regime was translated into a decisive military advantage for the insurgents and Nkrumah's impressive security machine proved to be isolated and ineffec-tive.

The presumably omnipresent and powerful party and its auxiliary organizations were nowhere in sight, and the attempts of several senior officials, including Defense Minister Kofi Baako, to do some-thing about the coup bordered on travesty.[31] Most of them were easily caught or surrendered voluntarily. A. A. Afrifa later stated, "We chose his [Nkrumah's] absence because we merely wanted to avoid bloodshed. We did not want to kill him either. . . . I wonder if they [the CPP ministers] did not escape too light-ly. They must thank Mr. Harlley that at least some of them were not killed."[32]

The coup exposed conflict within the armed forces. About 30 men were killed, mostly military personnel. The highest ranking victim was Major-General C. M. Barwah, who resisted capture. The top active offi-cers present in Accra were arrested,* and Major-

---

*Brigadier Hassan, director of military intelli-gence; Lieutenant-Colonel M. Kuti, national organizer, Workers' Brigades; Read-Admiral D. A. Hansen, com-mander of the navy; Vice-Marshal M. A. Otu, comman-der of the air force; Lieutenant-Colonel D. Zanlerigu,

General N. A. Aferi, chief of the defense staff, was dismissed.[33] Some of the top officers possibly would have joined the insurrection had they known about it in advance. But February 24 was a coup not only against the civilian government but at the same time against the top military hierarchy linked to the regime. Sincere commitment to a forceful change of regime on the part of the leading protagonists of the coup did not exclude other motivations based on the desire for upward mobility and professional security (Colonel Kotoka seems to have been particularly insecure in his position). They showed this eagerness for self-promotion soon after February 24. The police played no appreciable role in the coup itself; and the mass arrests of the CPP officials, carried out in the late morning and during the day, had no bearing on the military outcome of the insurrection. Commissioner Harlley offered the police headquarters to Colonel Kotoka, but Harlley's contribution was most important in setting the substance, tone, and style of the post-coup rule. The coup itself was an almost exclusively military affair[34] and was very warmly received by most of the population.

NATIONAL LIBERATION COUNCIL RULE

Manifest Goals and Policies

The shooting was still in progress around 10 a.m. on February 24 when the military-police junta that came to be called the National Liberation Council (NLC) was formed. The first meeting was held in police headquarters in the presence of only a few members of the new ruling body.[35] The first procla-

---

commander of the POGR; and an unspecified number of other officers as well as NCOs and soldiers of the POGR. According to General J. A. Ankrah, Lieutenant-Colonel D. Zanlerigu killed six disobedient soldiers. The victorious troops wanted to shoot seven defenders of Flagstaff House, including Zanlerigu, but General Ankrah intervened.

mation of February 26 named four army and three police
members, and the second and final list of the original NLC contained four army and four police members.[36]
A. A. Afrifa comments:

> We knew we would form some form of a revolu-
> tionary council. Originally we had planned
> to set up a small high-powered group of
> civilians. We were aware that as soldiers,
> we were not cut out to do politics. . . .
> But a civilian care-taker [government] had
> been tried in at least one African country
> and had failed. So we thought we could
> stand in briefly, and put things right as
> quickly as possible. The emphasis was on
> speed.[37]

Major-General Ankrah explained the insurrection
to the population in a radio broadcast on February
28. According to him, the army, with the cooperation
of the police, went into action because no one else
could "restore liberty, justice, happiness and prosperity." Ex-President Nkrumah allegedly forfeited
the Ghanaian people's trust when he established a
"one-man dictatorship." He also was accused of
bringing Ghana "to the brink of economic disaster by
mismanagement," thereby causing high inflation and
unemployment. Apart from legalist and general political grounds, Ankrah also mentioned a corporate reason for the revolt--the establishment of Nkrumah's
private army and security services "as a counterpoise
to the Ghana Armed Forces." The manifest goals of
the junta were "to put the country on an even keel,
politically, socially and economically," to "re-think
the economic set-up," to eradicate corruption, to
pacify and reconcile the country, and eventually to
restore constitutional government. The backbone of
the new regime issuing from the conservative revolution of February 24,[38] as clearly stated by Ankrah,
consisted of the armed forces, police, civil service
and other branches of the civilian bureaucracy, and
the traditional rulers.[39] The intention of the new
rulers, as widely understood in the country,[40] was
to restore as much as possible the social order and
economic system that existed in Ghana prior to the

CPP experiment in social engineering, i.e., the system in effect under the British.

This goal necessitated the attainment of two more immediate objectives: the political consolidation of the new order and economic recovery. The mode and style of pursuing these objectives were influenced by a number of often contradictory factors: sharp emotional reactions of the coup leaders to Nkrumah's rule and all associated with it; intolerance toward the CPP and apprehension of its latent strength even after its dissolution; and a fear of subversion and foreign invasion bordering on paranoia. Internal corporate circumstances, the army's posture of a unifying and reconciling force, and the persisting belief of some junta members that "soldiers should leave politics alone"[41] also had an impact on the NLC policies. Its initial popularity and the disarray and weakness of the opposition enabled the junta to implement painful and drastic austerity measures. Fortunately for the military rulers, Ghana enjoyed a moderately favorable external position and the cocoa market was improving.

During the NLC rule, national and local power and leadership were passed, under the aegis of senior army and police officers, "into the hands of the 'old establishment': the old elites of chiefs, professional men, wealthy traders, senior civil servants who tended to be older, better educated, wealthier, pro-British and who held higher traditional offices."[42] The junta solved the problem of internal legitimation of the new order by relying primarily on these social groups. A strong negative public reaction to some, but not all, features of the CPP rule assured the junta of important support, most clearly during the first year of its rule, among other segments of the population: cocoa farmers, petty traders, junior clerks, urban youth, and, notably, the new Trade Union Congress leadership representing workers and public servants.

Externally, the legitimacy of the new regime was challenged diplomatically for almost a year by several radical African regimes, particularly by Guinea. Other radical African regimes were less determined. The NLC restored diplomatic relations with Britain, which had been broken over the Rhodesian

40

issue. For the sake of legitimation the junta
stressed the elements of continuity in Ghana's external commitments and posture and declared itself
in favor of "true nonalignment" or neutralism.[43]
    Instead of maneuvering between the great powers,
as Nkrumah did, the junta tried to extract the utmost from the West alone by going as far to the right
as possible. The United States, West Germany, Britain, smaller Western countries, and the World Bank
and International Monetary Fund helped, but possibly
less than the junta had hoped. Economic and political realities outside and inside Ghana forced the
junta to revise the country's foreign policy only in
part and to effect a gradual evolution of its own
thinking from rabid anti-Communism to a more realistic reappraisal of conditions that had influenced
Nkrumah and continued to operate after his downfall.[44]
The NLC succeeded in significantly improving Ghana's
relations with its immediate neighbors and with "moderate" and pro-Western regimes elsewhere in Africa.
    A somewhat similar situation had developed with
respect to the proclaimed top-priority goal of economic recovery, stabilization, and changing internal
economic structures and the patterns of foreign trade
as well as economic and technical assistance. Here
too the junta could dismantle only a part of the extensive state intervention and welfare systems
erected under the CPP. It could not radically change
the more diversified pattern of external economic relations, in which the USSR and Eastern Europe had become important partners. Even when individual measures for reprivatization of the state sector and
selling unprofitable enterprises to foreign capital
made sense from the standpoint of short-run budgetary
solvency and accounting, the military-police government ran into vocal opposition in the country and
had to modify its stand.[45]
    The NLC, guided by domestic and foreign advisers,
had largely adopted the World Bank-International
Monetary Fund recommendations made to the Nkrumah
government in 1965 as a condition for financial assistance. The NLC abandoned the Seven-Year Plan and
tried to sell many of the 55 state-owned enterprises.
Of the 125 state-owned farms, only 39 were retained
by the State Farms Corporation and 20 by the Young

Farmers League.[46] In the reduced state budgets of
1966-67, 1967-68, and 1968-69, the NLC cut down on
the average per annum allocation for industry by
70.6 percent, on trade by 43.7 percent, transport
and communications by 37.1 percent, and agriculture
by 27.2 percent, but on the other hand kept increasing defense allocations by 22 percent per annum. Although the military severely criticized Nkrumah's
overly ambitious foreign policy, in fact the military
increased the budget allocations for foreign relations by 8.4 percent per annum.[47] The NLC liberal-
ized domestic and foreign trade and threw the doors
wide open to foreign capital.

Guided by a conventional and conservative economic philosophy, the NLC established three goals:
(1) the restoration of budgetary stability; (2) the
balancing of foreign trade; and (3) the consolidation of the foreign debt. Primarily by slashing development outlays and disinvestment in the public
sector, the NLC very substantially reduced the budgetary deficit. Through a decrease in imports by
one-third, a devaluation, and deflationary policies,
and thanks to better cocoa prices, in 1968, for the
first time since 1959, Ghana was close to a balance
in foreign trade and had a reduced balance of payments deficit of NC 48.3 million compared to NC 158.9
million in 1965.

However, the Ghanaian economy under the NLC did
not achieve the level of agricultural production of
the pre-coup period, despite a better-supplied internal market. From the phase of retrenchment and stabilization it was unable to reach the stage of accelerated growth. The annual rate of growth of the national economy registered 0.7 percent in 1965, 1.6
percent in 1966, 1.6 percent in 1967, 0.8 percent in
1968--all below the rate of population growth of
about 2.6 percent.[48] The GNP per capita at 1960
prices was falling throughout the NLC period--NC 142
in 1965, NC 138 in 1966, NC 137 in 1967, NC 134 in
1968, and NC 135 in 1969[49]--while contrary to its pro-
fessed goals the NLC increased public consumption.[50]
The NLC devoted very considerable efforts to stabilizing the external indebtedness of the country, of
which 80 percent was owed to the West. Although it
on several occasions threatened to, the junta never

42

repudiated even the more dubious among the total of
NC 889 million in debts contracted under Nkrumah.
Extensive lobbying and pleading with the friendly
West resulted only in a better debt structure, but
the total burden rose by 1969 to NC 1,003 million.[51]
The social cost of the NLC economic policies
was considerable. The number of employees laid off
in 1966-67 was close to 80,000 (61,838 in the public
sector), and the number of registered unemployed
climbed to 391,148 in 1967 and 423,115 in 1968.[52]
In 1969 the NLC tried to alleviate the problem of
unemployment by initiating the mass expulsion from
the country of non-Ghanaian Africans (this policy
was continued by the succeeding civilian government).
The policy of an eager and docile junior partnership
with Western capital was combined with nationalism-
chauvinism and xenophobia toward other Africans and
more mildly toward Levantines residing in Ghana.
The rising world prices of cocoa permitted the NLC
to raise the purchasing price paid to farmers several
times and thus assure their passive acquiescence to
the military regime, although the reduction in development spending negatively affected the countryside
too.

The Decision-Making Process

Both internally and in relation to the army,
civil service, and the governmental and consultative
bodies, the NLC underwent appreciable changes during
the three and one-half years of its rule.* Except
for the first day or two when the country was run by
the police, the NLC rule most properly should be
called a military-police-civilian coalition.[53] Lieutenant-General J. A. Ankrah proved a reasonably good
choice of an easygoing leader with a keen feeling of
the "sense of the assembly." There are only two
known NLC documents bearing the signatures of all its

---

*Lieutenant-General E. K. Kotoka was killed on
April 17, 1967, and the Council coopted Colonel E. A.
Yeboah. In 1969 Lieutenant-General J. A. Ankrah and
J. E. O. Nunoo resigned under pressure.

members, the initial Proclamation and the Disqualification Decree. All other measures were signed by the
chairman or deputy chairman of the NLC.

The relative strength of the top NLC members
changed considerably. From the beginning until his
death on April 17, 1967,[54] Lieutenant-General Kotoka,
the general officer commanding the GAF (Ghana Armed
Forces), was believed to be the strong-man of the
junta with a _veto_ power over its decisions. A cour-
ageous, strong-willed but rather harsh and unsociable
man, he did not make a good leader of a collective
body. During that period General Ankrah was close
to the position of a "swing-man." J. W. K. Harlley
mastered the position of a very influential second
or third in command and a real power-broker throughout the entire 1966-69 period. After Kotoka's death
the NLC had had difficulties reestablishing the internal balance. General Ankrah's position improved,
although several times he was openly challenged by
Brigadier Afrifa, who moved into the third position.
On April 2, 1969, Lieutenant-General Ankrah resigned
after the attorney-general's office, with the cooperation of Harlley's police, had found that a Nigerian
of dubious probity and integrity had collected over
$36,000 from various foreign firms. The money was
collected on behalf of General Ankrah "for the purpose of conducting research into General Ankrah's
prospects for the presidency at the forthcoming
elections." Ankrah was imprudent enough to collect
a part of these funds personally from businessmen.
After his disgrace, the National Liberation Council
"unanimously" elected Brigadier A. A. Afrifa to succeed him as the chairman of the council. It seems
that the senior deputy chairman, Harlley, deemed his
own being a policeman and a Ewe too big handicaps
for a chairman. After Lieutenant-General Ankrah's
disgrace and resignation on April 1, 1969,[55] Major-
General Afrifa assumed the chairmanship.

The NLC chairman also headed the Defense Council
(DC) consisting of the general commanding officer
and/or chief of defense staff,[56] commanders of the
army, navy and air force, inspector-general of police
or his deputy, director of Special Branch of the
police, principal secretaries in the ministries of
defense, interior, and communications, and if neces-

sary other officials by appointments. In addition, the Defense Council had a small staff headed by a senior army officer.[57]

Also under the NLC chairman was the National Liberation Council housed in the Osu Castle and staffed mostly by civil servants. The Office of Secretariat played an important role. Under the NLC chairman's supervision this office drafted proposed measures for preliminary discussions in the NLC, and once a decision was reached the office sent the measure to the attorney general's office, after which decrees, executive orders, and other legal acts were signed and promulgated by the NLC chairman.

All in all, the junta drew about 20 senior officers into the business of running the country. In most cases, and always when police officers were involved, these were double-job arrangements, as it was with the NLC members themselves. The army regional chairmen (governors) usually were local battalion commanders. In other cases army officers were seconded to top civilian jobs while retaining normal army pay, allowances, and seniority. The prevailing double-job arrangement permitted the military hierarchy to control both the army and the civilian administration, but the system spread manpower very thin so that in fact regional (civilian) administrative officers were running the countryside by proxy.

The pattern of relations between the NLC and civil service--the backbone of the military-police-civilian rule--also changed over time, the major landmark being July 1, 1967. One of the early measures of the NLC was to reestablish the Civil Service Commission, abolished by Nkrumah in 1965 in order to influence directly, through the Establishment Secretariat, appointments, recruitment, and promotions in civil service. The NLC restored the autonomy of the civil service as it had operated under the British. Having dismissed all Nkrumah's ministers, the junta left as heads of respective ministries and other agencies permanent secretaries who ran the country subject to NLC directives. This automony was reduced somewhat in the summer of 1966 when the junta decided to institute closer supervision of administration in the face of growing social problems, unemployment, inflation, and the end of public enchantment with the

change. The NLC divided unevenly among itself responsibilities of control over ministries and other
agencies.* The load on each individual NLC member,
while still attending to regular duties, made control very superficial.

Another important institution under the NLC
proved to be the Economic Advisory Committee (EAC),
which was a highly influential advisory-executive
body for almost a year and one-half (March 1966-
August 1967).** The EAC debated matters referred to
it by the junta, on its initiative, and questions
brought to its attention by ministries and departments trying to lobby at the top. A small body, the
EAC commanded extraordinary influence due to the top
priority given by the junta to economic recovery,
budgetary stabilization, restoring economic relations
with the West, and attracting foreign private capital.
After NLC action on its written recommendations the
EAC could act expeditiously through permanent secre-
taries--members of the body.

Apart from the Economic Advisory Committee, the
junta established a number of less important advisory,
advisory-executive, advisory-investigative, and

---

*General Ankrah was made responsible for the NLC
secretariat, ministry of external affairs, and several other bodies; J. W. K. Harlley supervised the
ministries of interior and of information, the attorney-general's office, and the Secretariat for
State Enterprises (where strikes were most frequent);
General Kotoka was entrusted with the ministries of
defense, labor, and health and social welfare.

**Chaired by E. N. Omaboe, a senior civil servant
and the chief government statistician under Nkrumah,
the EAC consisted of six senior civil servants (representing the most important economic ministries and
the Bank of Ghana) and R. S. Amegashie, dean of the
University of Ghana's School of Public Administration
and a successful businessman. The EAC met several
times a week, first in E. N. Omaboe's office in the
Bureau of Statistics; from September 1966 until September 1967 it was housed in Osu Castle, next to the
NLC office. The critics of the EAC charged that none
of its members held degrees in economics.

advisory-adjudicative bodies. In November 1966 the NLC appointed a Constitutional Commission, headed by new Chief Justice E. Akufo-Addo, and an Electoral Commission.

A Political Advisory Committee (PAC) came into existence on June 23, 1966, several months later than its presumed match, the Economic Advisory Committee. By this step the junta brought the most prominent politicians of the former opposition (they held at least a third of the initial 23 seats[58]), university academics, prominent paramount chiefs, and leaders of the Trade Union Congress, Chamber of Commerce, and religious and denominational groups into a measure of association with the government. This consultative assembly was given the Parliament House and its chairman, Justice Akufo-Addo later replaced by K. A. Busia, had weekly audiences with Major-General J. A. Ankrah.[59]

The PAC tried hard to compete with senior civil servants for influence exerted on the junta and with the EAC, since the latter also was making decisions of far-reaching political importance.* It never achieved an appreciable influence, although the importance of its individual members grew in time. Despite a community of values and some personal ties between the junta and the leaders of former opposition, the latter tended, rather impatiently, to view the military as mere caretakers for them and were highly critical of many civil servants who in the recent past had served Nkrumah and who were, in their view, responsible in part for Ghana's misfortune and corruption. The opposition leaders were privately in favor of cleaning up the civil service (this was done by the Busia government in 1969-70) and for a more resolute suppression of the residues of the CPP. Military rule for them was a welcome instrument as long as there was a need for reorganization.

---

*For instance the famous Abbot agreement was never referred to the Political Advisory Committee, and the matter was deemed to be technical and financial. The fact that E. N. Omaboe on several occasions consented to appear before the Political Advisory Committee is revealing as far as the relationship between the two bodies is concerned.

The junta on the other hand, with its residual distaste for politicians, did not take many of the PAC proposals seriously, treating them as self-serving propaganda and attempts to jockey for power. Besides, the Political Advisory Committee, biased heavily anti-CPP in its composition, represented only one part of public opinion.

And finally, the conservative judiciary, courts, and numerous commissions of inquiry into various aspects of the CPP rule played important roles in the stabilization and functioning of the NLC rule. The commissions, conferred with extensive powers, typically were chaired by an active or retired magistrate and included lawyers, accountants, and academics with non-CPP or preferably anti-CPP backgrounds.

The National Liberation Council rule during its first year could be schematically presented as shown in Figure 3.

This structure of governmental institutions underwent a substantial change after an almost successful counter-coup on April 17, 1967. Not quite satisfied with the performance of the civil service and sensitive to criticism in the army and among the former opposition and the intellectuals, the junta decided to reduce political power of senior civil servants and to exert a more direct control of the state. At the same time the move foreshadowed a gradual return to civilian government. On July 1, 1967, the NLC announced the appointment of 17 special commissions to head respective ministries. Three members of the junta assumed direct responsibility for key ministries.* Fourteen civilians became special commissioners.** There were mostly politicized civil

---

*General Ankrah took over the ministry of defense in addition to his duties in the NLC office and with the advisory bodies. All of the latter were abolished except the Economic, Administration, and Expediting committees. J. W. K. Harlley was to head the ministries of external affairs and the interior and the Chieftancy Secretariat, while Brigadier A. A. Afrifa was appointed special commissioner for finance.

**These special commissioners included E. N. Omaboe (economic affairs and Central Bureau of Statistics),

FIGURE 3

Schematic Representation of the Decision-Making Structure Under the National Liberation Council in Ghana, Spring 1966-Summer 1967

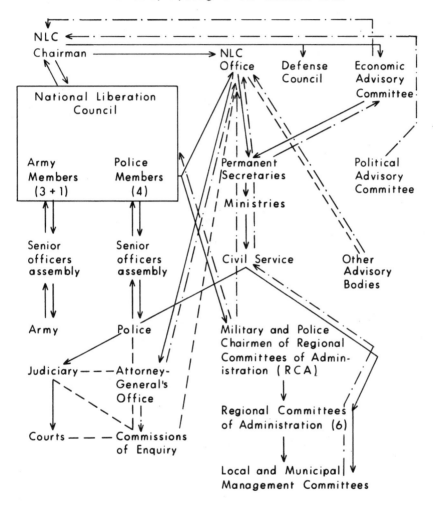

Key

⟶ Relations to subordination
--- Other types of power relations
—·—⟶ Flow of information

servants and prominent figures of the former opposition (V. Owusu) who had become close to the junta.[60] The new title of special commissioner was meant to indicate powers smaller than those of a minister and greater than those of a principal secretary.[61]

In the somewhat modified setup, the NLC became an inner cabinet, retaining the ultimate power to approve and to enact measures discussed in the Executive Council. The junta continued to hold its meetings separately and was not bound by a majority opinion in the Executive Council. Instead of the previous system under which all members of the junta had broad responsibilities over particular branches of administration, now only three were to guide four key ministries, this time more thoroughly and directly.

This was the highest point of the junta's undelegated interference in running the administration, and during the next two years the trend was toward greater and greater relinquishing of the chores of government and, most significantly, affording the former opposition the on-the-job training, visible symbols of power, and patronage credibility crucial in Ghanaian politics.[62] This movement accelerated after General Ankrah's removal in April 1969 and subsequent shifts in the NLC. The junta entrusted civilians with running the ministries of external affairs and of finance, retaining however the ministries of defense and of interior.

Concerned with the charges of alleged tribalist overtones of the coup on April 17, 1967--the three officers killed all happened to be Ewes--the junta decided to reverse the previous practice of appointing the chairmen of regional committees of administration (military-police governors) from among natives of the given region. From the summer of 1967 on, only the Northern and Upper Regions were exempt from the rule of having a non-native governor.

Since most of the Economic Advisory Committee members were made special commmssioners, the EAC, renamed the Economic Committee of the NLC, was steadily

---

V. Owusu (justice), R. S. Amegahie (industries and state enterprises), and J. V. L. Phillips (lands and mineral resource).

overshadowed by the Executive Council and in time lost its privileged position.*

The Political Advisory Committee was replaced by the slightly refurbished and more dignified National Advisory Committee, with roughly the same membership and influence. It consisted of 31 members, 14 of whom were civilian commissioners and only 4, former opposition leaders. Its influence did not increase.[63] As a part of the promised preparations for return to civilian rule, and also a reflection of its concern with the residues of the CPP influence, the junta established a semi-official Center for Civic Education, financed to a substantial degree by US and West German sources.[64] With official blessings the center was to spread the gospel of liberal parliamentary democracy; it was headed by K. A. Busia. (Busia resigned as chairman of the Political Advisory Committee and on April 30, 1969, when the ban on political activities was lifted, also as director of the center.)

The network of informal influentials around the junta also changed somewhat after the summer of 1970. The movement toward legalized civilian partisan politics had greatly contributed to the erosion of the internal cohesion of the junta. Latent, regionally colored coalitions of political and economic interest groups had found their way to individual members of the NLC by the close of 1968 or early 1969. General Ankrah's political ambitions had been suspected for some time,[65] and the web of connections around him consisted mainly of businessmen and politicians from the Ga areas around Accra, with some Ashantis. The second informal network, suspected around Commissioner Harlley, was predominantly Ewe and notably included K. Gbedemah, Nkrumah's former finance minister and a shrewd organizer and businessman. The connections between Brigadier Afrifa and K. A. Busia and his emerging Ashanti-based political bloc were the most straightforward of the three.

---

*From September 1967 until April 1969 it was meeting in E. N. Omaboe's office. From April 1969 until its dissolution in July 1969 General Afrifa chaired its sessions.

THE TRANSITION TO CIVILIAN
GOVERNMENT

The elimination from the junta of its chairman,
General J. A. Ankrah, and of another Ga, J. E. O.
Nunoo, eliminated the Ga-based coalition from competition and eventually gave a big advantage to Busia
(the move was staged jointly by Harlley's police and
Attorney-General V. Owusu, the second most powerful
figure in Busia's emerging political bloc). A deep
suspicion of the power concentrated in the hands of
the Ewes* led to a swift and thorough irregular re-
assignment of key army officers. The replacement of
Brigadier A. Kattah, commander of the First Brigade
in Accra, and his appointment as military attaché in
Washington were widely attributed to the fear of
another coup.**

A preliminary battle also was fought on the
question of disqualifying former CPP officials from
political activities. In January 1968 the NLC under
General Ankrah enacted a Disqualification Decree
banning many categories of persons associated with
the previous regime from assuming public office.[66]
On the other hand the decree established an Exemption
Commission with the power of review. This body
exempted K. Gbedemah and six other persons before its
activities were suspended on November 14, 1968.[67]
Brigadier Afrifa, although a signatory of the decree,
unilaterally took the issue of abolishing disqualifi-
cations to the press four days after Gbedemah was
exempted. Afrifa declared that it had never been
the intention of the NLC "to place any individuals

---

*In March 1969 a near coup-mutiny occurred in the
Burma camp. J. W. K. Harlley spent a night in the
camp and succeeded in dissuading the key Ewe members
of the plot.

**Several other senior Ewe officers also were re-
assigned, but not the commanders of the navy and air
force. The policy of removing Ewes from sensitive
jobs was intensified under the civilian regime of
Busia and spread to the police and security after the
resignations of J. W. K. Harlley and A. K. Deku, and
to the civil service and diplomacy.

or group . . . in positions of the administration of
this country."[68] By an amendment to the decree,
several categories of lower officials were dropped
from the ban, which exempted 950 out of the 1,170
from the ban to run and to occupy a public office.[69]
From the initial number of more than 5,000 the NLC
in February 1969 removed the ban on all but 152 senior
CPP officials. The ban was made broader for founders
and office-holders of new political parties and then
was reduced again.[70] However, the former opposition
created another legal loophole, eventually made the
campaigning of K. Gbedemah and his party difficult,
and barred Gbedemah from the parliament despite his
victory in his electoral district.

The junta had been concerned with the deleterious
effect of politics on the internal cohesion of the
army and on army-police relations.[71] Although there
was no immediate challenge in sight the junta accelerated transition to civilian government in late 1968
and particularly under General A. A. Afrifa.[72]

Justice E. Akufo-Addo, chairman of the Constitutional Commission and an unofficial contender for
presidency, presented a draft of the new constitution
on January 26, 1968.[73] The draft envisioned separate offices of president and prime minister, somewhat
similar to the arrangements of the Fifth Republic in
France, and greatly increased the powers of the judiciary. The draft had a distinct conservative and
gerontocratic bias with the flavor of Western liberalism.

Registration of voters started on September 1,
1968, with the target of electing a Constituent Assembly and lifting the ban on political parties by
May 1969 and holding the handing-over on December 30
of the same year.[74] Referring to the slow and unsatisfactory results of registration, the NLC ruled
on November 7, 1968, that 49 assembly members would
be delegated by the district administrative councils;
91 members would represent various organizations,
chiefs, corporate bodies, and so forth; and 10 would
be appointed directly by the NLC.[75]

The assembly met in January 1969 and one of the
first announcements of the new NLC chairman, General
Afrifa, was that the ban on political activities would
be lifted on May 1 while the assembly was still in

session in the Parliament House. The Executive Council confirmed the date of the handing-over, which earlier was shifted to September 30, 1969.[76] When most of the articles of the new constitution already had been adopted, the assembly was called into a special meeting to consider a new proposal creating an interim Presidential Commission. It was to consist, "for a period not exceeding three years," of the NLC chairman, NLC deputy chairman, and chief of the defense staff.[77] The motion was introduced by a paramount chief from Brong-Ahafo, and it is not entirely clear whether and to what extent Busia and his Progress Party (PP) were behind it. What is beyond doubt is that the junta applied pressure when the assembly rejected the proposal at the first reading.

The former opposition wrote into the constitution a provision barring from the National Assembly every person against whom a commission of inquiry made adverse findings.[78] In addition, the junta members and their associates were given constitutional guarantees that no Ghanaian court would ever take action on the account of their unlawful and unconstitutional activities from February 1966 on.[79] The NLC members also were granted handsome "gratuities . . . as a token mark of the Nation's gratitude" and suitable pensions.[80] The army and police were assured of their autonomy in face of possible political meddling through the institutions of the Armed Forces Council and the Police Council, upon whose advice the president, not the prime minister, would make appointments and grant commissions.[81]

With all these assurances the NLC gave the green light to the first competitive national elections since 1956. Although technically fair, they confirmed marked advantages built up on the side of Busia's Progress Party. The elections were held on August 29, and the Progress Party won 104 of 140 seats in the National Assembly. K. Gbedemah's National Alliance of Liberals (NAL), with a program similar to that of the Progress Party, was haunted by the stigma of its CPP associations and the Ewe predominance in its leadership. The NAL won 29 seats, and three small parties picked up the remaining 7 seats. The election demonstrated a return to regionally and ethnically polarized party politics al-

though the CPP heritage of unification, centraliza-
tion, and combating parochialism made the picture
more complex. The Progress Party swept the Akan-
speaking areas, while the NAL captured practically
all constituencies in the Volta Region and 8 seats
in the Northern and Upper Regions.[82]
On September 3, 1969, K. Busia was sworn in as
the first civilian prime minister of the Second Republic. Its official birthday was celebrated with a
military parade and Westernized African pageantry on
October 1. General A. A. Afrifa, chairman of the
Presidential Commission, pledged that the Army would
be the last to undermine "what it created with such
patience."[83]
The junta stepped down and a one-year period of
legal tutelage by the military began. The arrangement worked reasonably well and provided for the
more gradual withdrawal of the military from politics. On August 31, 1970, Justice E. Akufo-Addo was
elected the first civilian president of Ghana by the
Electoral College of 140 MPs and 24 paramount chiefs.[84]
The circle was thus complete. The new order was con-
solidated; power rested securely in the hands of the
former conservative and chiefly bourgeois opposition;
the economy was stabilized and made more orderly although it remained stagnant; and the forms and style
of corruption changed somewhat. The country's social
problems were still there, in certain respects worse
than before the coup. On the whole, national integration seems to have been set back. But the army
and police grew larger and better paid, and their
hierarchy became a recognized and more influential
part of the new establishment.

THE FALL OF THE SECOND REPUBLIC
AND THE RULE OF THE NATIONAL
REDEMPTION COUNCIL

The life span of the Second Republic of Ghana
proved to be much shorter than that of the First Republic, and its accomplishments much more modest than
its promises. After 27 months of existence it was
overthrown by yet another military coup. On the
night of January 13, 1972, the troops of the First

Brigade, stationed in and around Accra, occupied key buildings and installations in the capital, including the prime minister's office, the airport, and the radio station. It was a bloodless takeover, as the troops met practically no resistance.

The country heard the voice of its new military lord-protector over the state radio at 6 a.m. His name was Colonel Ignatius Kutu Acheampong, commander of the First Brigade. A 40-year-old Ashanti and a military governor under the previous military regime, Colonel Acheampong, according to his own words, had entertained seditious thoughts since 1970. He undoubtedly took into account the lessons of the narrowly successful coup in 1966, planned his enterprise alone, and brought in a very small group of trusted military officers only several days prior to its execution. As in 1966, the coup was to take place during the civilian leader's absence from the country. There was something symbolic in the fact that Busia, unlike Nkrumah six years earlier, was not on a noted diplomatic mission in Peking but was undergoing medical treatment in London. Everything about the 1972 takeover seemed to be more prosaic, ordinary, easier, and on a lower key.

On the whole the coup received public support, although it was less emotional and exuberant. Only in Kumasi, the Progress Party's stronghold, were there ineffective attempts to resist the change. The chief regional executive and the local military commander were promptly put under arrest. Several days later the new regime also detained Lieutenant-General Afrifa, Colonel Acheampong's onetime subordinate and a hero of the previous military takeover. Afrifa was accused of planning to assassinate the new leader and to stage a march on Accra.

As is often done, the new junta dismissed the president of the Republic, prime minister, cabinet, regional governors, and other high officials. Only the judiciary was spared. The parliament was dissolved, the constitution withdrawn, and all political parties banned. The police put into "protective custody" over a hundred prominent figures of the previous regime.

The manifest reasons that prompted the Ghanaian military to reenter the political arena were stated by Colonel Acheampong in his initial broadcast:

Every honest Ghanaian will agree with me
that the malpractices, corruption, arbitrary dismissals, economic mismanagement
and a host of other malpractices which char-
acterized the Nkrumah regime have come back
to stay with us. The first people which
Busia put his eyes on were the armed forces
and the police. Some army and police officers were dismissed under the pretext of
retirement. Some officers were put in certain positions to suit the whims of Busia
and his colleagues. Then he started taking
from us the few amenities and facilities,
which we in the armed forces and the police
enjoyed even under the Nkrumah regime. Having lowered morale in the armed forces and
the police to the extent that officers could
not exert any meaningful influence over
their men, so that by this strategy coming
together was to them impossible, he turned
on the civilians.[85]

Immediate corporate and material interests of
the military undoubtedly loomed large in the minds
of the coup-makers and those who rallied to their
cause. The new junta, however, has been careful not
to go beyond the restoration of old privileges. It
also drew from the experience of the previous military regime and thus far has refrained from promoting
and rewarding its own members.

The corporate interests of the military and a
disharmony in civil-military relations explain the
fall of the Second Republic only partially. Certainly
cutbacks in the defense budget caused dissatisfaction
and directly aggravated Busia's opponents in the services. Government policies helped to unite most of
the top brass behind the putschists and to bring out
the corporate solidarity of the military. But the
military leaders also had different political views
than the government, and Busia had unwisely and
naively disregarded them. Later he branded the January 13 takeover "an officer amenities' coup." There
was a strong element of political innuendo in this
charge.

The 1972 coup succeeded politically because the
military's real or alleged grievances coincided and

voiced the dissatisfaction of the wider segments of
the Ghanaian population. Busia, not altogether unlike Nkrumah before him, underrated the unarticulated
and uninstitutionalized "silent" opposition to his
policies. Deceived by his party's overwhelming electoral victory in 1969, he arrogantly and self-right-
eously undertook a number of dubious, injudicious,
and unpopular measures.

The policy of massive expulsion of African
aliens did not solve the grave problem of unemployment but, rather, hurt the economy of Ghana. This
move was criticized severely in other African countries. Internally, the Progress Party's policies not
infrequently had overtones of tribalism and thus undermined the sense of Ghanaian nationhood--perhaps
the greatest achievement of the CPP period. The
Busia government cut down the benefits and allowances
of the civil service and dismissed over a thousand
of its members. The government also rudely offended
the judiciary. A new Industrial Relations Act disbanded the Ghana Trade Union Congress. "For the
first time in the history of Ghana the Police opened
fire on striking miners . . . , resulting in deaths
and several casualties."[86] Busia lost many of his
supporters in the academic community, at least in
part because of the changes in the student loan system. The Busia regime did not reconcile with the
honest Nkrumahists, although this was necessary to
normalize the political life of the country. By
stubbornly advocating a dialogue with South Africa,
Busia offended the feelings of African dignity and
solidarity among many Ghanaians, including the military.

The Busia government was not capable of seriously
reducing foreign debts and carrying out its threat to
repudiate the most dubious among them. Moreover the
Busia government had incurred new financial liabilities. After the government's attempts to revitalize
the economy proved unsuccessful, Busia decided to
administer a drastic medicine to the country. A 44
percent devaluation of national currency in relation
to the U.S. dollar and new heavy taxes affected most
of the Ghanaian population, especially urban low-
income families and cocoa farmers. This was the social climate in which the 1972 coup took place.

It is also true that the underlying cause of all these austerity measures was well beyond the control of any Ghanaian government, civilian or military. Busia and his party won the 1969 election after a long depression on the world cocoa market ended. The average price had then risen to £ 422 per ton. By 1971 the cocoa price fell again to £ 250 without a compensating increase in Ghana's cocoa crop. In a sense, both the First and the Second republics of Ghana were ruined by depressions on the cocoa market.

In 1971 the serious decrease in export earnings called for an immediate and strong state intervention, for an equitable distribution of hardship among various social groups. For ideological and political reasons Busia made no serious move in either direction. Moreover the prime minister and his entourage had failed to project an image of austerity and civic solidarity, which they demanded from the country. Political patronage, favoritism in awarding government contracts, and politicians' self-enrichment were well on the way to flourishing again. The members of the government declined to disclose their private assets at the time stipulated by law and soon became a target of public criticism. In summary, by January 1972 there was a sufficiently wide range of social groups willing to support an unconstitutional change, but only the military possessed the real power necessary to carry it out.

Colonel Acheampong's coup was entirely an army affair. The other services of the Ghana armed forces played no active role, with the police coming into the picture only at the final stage. The takeover divided the top brass for a brief period, but now the split was not as bitter as in 1966 and also there were no casualties. The chief of the defense staff, the army commander, and several other officers were temporarily detained. The junta promptly replaced them and the inspector-general of police.

The new ruling body assumed the name of the National Redemption Council (NRC), which had a tinge of Nkrumahist phraseology. At the close of the first day it was announced that the NRC consisted of seven members: six military officers (one colonel, one commander, two lieutenant-colonels, and two

majors) and one civilian (attorney-general). Among
the military members the main criterion of selection
seemed to be close relations with Colonel Acheampong
and a role in the execution of the takeover. But
very soon other considerations were taken into account.
The junta's composition was broadened to include all
the services and to better satisfy the demands of
hierarchical propriety. The newcomers to the NRC
were the air force and the navy commanders, as well
as the newly appointed inspector-general of police.
They rallied around Colonel Acheampong at an early
stage. Two original lower-ranking officers and the
only civilian were dropped. Finally the size of the
ruling body was fixed at 12 members.

During the first several months the new junta
used a system of government that closely resembled
the one during the first period of NLC rule (1966-67).
The National Redemption Council collectively assumed
the powers of the highest legislative and executive
body. The NRC chairman was proclaimed the head of
state and commander-in-chief. Thus he combined the
prerogatives of the president and of the prime minister. The NRC chairman is responsible for the appointment and removal of the junta members at the advice
of not less than two-thirds of the members and may
himself be removed by a unanimous decision of the
other members.

The NRC acts as an "inner cabinet." It includes
members who kept the key positions in the services
(the chief of defense staff; army, navy, and air
force commanders; inspector-general of police; and
so forth). Several NRC members were appointed commissioners in charge of the ministries. Colonel
Acheampong leads in the multiple-hat arrangements:
in addition to the already mentioned titles he assumed the positions of commissioner for defense,
finance, and economics.

The second circle of the government officials
is made up of commissioners who are not NRC members.
Among them are three major-generals and one civilian
(E. N. Moore, attorney-general and commissioner for
justice). As the three top-ranking members of the
NRC are only brigadiers (or the equivalent), by
seconding the three major-generals to important non-
military appointments the junta eased the problems

of hierarchical order. The NRC and the commissioners constitute the Executive Council.

The junta appointed as regional commissioners nine area military commanders ranking from major to colonel. In most cases the new military governors were sent to their native regions. As under the previous military regime only a relatively small number of senior officers at a time (around 30) is directly involved in running the country. The most notable difference between the two setups is a clearly subordinated role of the police under the NRC. It was given only one seat in the junta, one ministry (internal affairs, and even there the police inspector-general is assisted by an important army member of the NRC), and no regional governorships.

The thin spread of military rulers has led in practice to a renewed system of moderately extensive military tutelage. It also has increased, once again, the role of principal secretaries and other top civil servants. Under these arrangements the military brass monopolizes vital areas of decision-making and has veto power in less important matters.

On the day of the coup Colonel Acheampong stated that he intended to associate eminent civilians and representatives of several corporate bodies with the new ruling junta. The NRC soon appointed a nine-member National Advisory Council headed by the former speaker of the assembly. Three days later the National Advisory Council was disbanded after strong criticism in the state-owned press. Its members were called "tired old men" and "representatives of vested interests." So far the junta has functioned with only one civilian associated with it in an official capacity and without permanent consultative bodies. However, civil servants were included in several ad hoc panels.

Despite the lack of formal representativeness the military oligarchs so far have shown themselves more responsive to the needs, feelings, and opinions of wide segments of the Ghanaian population than was the case under the parliamentarian Second Republic. The junta gained massive acclaim at home when it unilaterally repudiated debts totaling £ 35 million out of more than £ 400 million of public foreign debt. Most of the controversial credits were contracted in

Great Britain. The second popular measure was a re-
valuation of the Ghanaian cedi that halved the rate
of the previous devaluation. The government also
ordered a sizable subsidy for several staple commodities in order to keep the prices at the pre-devalua-
tion level. The NRC set up a state distribution organization and announced stiff penalties for raising
prices, hoarding scarce goods, speculation, and so
forth. The ban on trade unions was repealed, and
the assets of a number of companies and individuals
were frozen or declared forfeit. The government also
made known its intention to become a majority share-
holder in mining as well as to reactivate state farms
and Workers' Brigades.

Less ideologically colored than the first military regime, the National Redemption Council has concentrated its attention on pragmatically solving
pressing economic problems. In this the junta has
shown a discernible movement away from Busia's liberalism toward the strong state interventionism of
Nkrumah. The military seems to have stopped half-
way and opted for moderate statism, but without
ideological labels.

A corresponding shift has occurred in foreign
policy. Ghana under Colonel Acheampong has assumed
a more militant stand on colonialism and racism in
Africa, reestablished diplomatic relations with the
People's Republic of China, and expressed a desire
to strengthen ties with the East and become more active in the politics of the Third World. In general
Ghana's nonalighment has become more balanced and
less self-effacing in relations with the Western
powers. After the 1966 coup the military made a cor-
rection in the opposite direction.

Internally the changes under the NRC found symbolic expression in a guarded but unmistakable re-
habilitation of Nkrumah. The anger of 1966 faded,
and the passage of time enabled the country to appreciate better his place in the history of Ghana
and Africa, as well as the positive sides of CPP
rule. Nkrumah died of cancer on April 27, 1972, in
distant Romania without seeing his country again.
His first funeral took place in Guinea, which gave
him refuge in 1966. Prolonged and rather unseemly
negotiations with President Sékou Touré of Guinea

dragged on for more than two months. On July 7
Nkrumah's body finally was returned and laid in state
in Accra. Colonel Acheampong paid tribute to the
great Ghanaian but clearly upheld the coup that ended
Nkrumah's rule.

President Sékou Touré's stubbornness helped the
junta to bring the wave of emotional Nkrumahism under
control. By the time the ex-president's body was
lowered into the grave in his native village Nkroful,
the tide had subsided. Thus the NRC was helped to
preach national reconciliation and to maintain a
kind of balance between the two political camps--the
Nkrumahists and Busiists. When compelled, the military struck either side. Thus the NRC canceled the
extraordinary congress of trade unions when it appeared that the Nkrumahists might capture the organization. In July the junta suppressed a Busiist conspiracy to stage a counter-coup.

The NRC slogans of order, discipline, austerity,
self-reliance, and nationalism now do have wide public support. The questions, however, remain: how
long the country will take military authoritarianism,
what the military will be able to deliver, whether
the military will live up to the lofty precepts, and
whether it will preserve internal cohesion. It is
too early to form a definite judgment on the second
military regime in modern Ghana.

CHAPTER

4

SIERRA LEONE:
MARCH 1967-
APRIL 1968

THE BACKGROUND TO THE MILITARY
COUPS IN MARCH 1967

The first military intervention in the modern
history of Sierra Leone occurred on March 21, 1967,
four days after the country went to the polls to
elect a new parliament. The preliminary results of
the elections triggered the military-police action
and to a large extent motivated the engineer of the
coup, the Royal Sierra Leone Force commander, Brigadier David Lansana. The causes of this event, however, lay deeper in the fabric of Sierra Leone's
politics.[1]

Sierra Leone gained political independence in
1961, although still retaining the British queen as
head of state. This event marked the final stage of
the gradual reorganization and relinquishing of executive powers by the British begun in 1951. The country became independent under the leadership of Sir
Milton Margai and his Sierra Leone People's Party
(SLPP), dominated by relatives of chiefly families
from the Mende areas (the Mende, living mainly in
the southern province, represented over 30 percent
of the total population).

The pattern of economic development of Sierra
Leone's rather prosperous economy[2] reinforced the
considerable inequalities already existing between
the relatively more developed western area (around

64

the capital, Freetown) and the southern and eastern provinces on the one hand and the northern province on the other. SLPP political patronage, mostly dispensed in the southern and eastern provinces, and a pronounced Southern and Mende bias of all SLPP cabinets fed the grievances of the North and areas that felt neglected.

In an Africanized Westminster parliamentary system, this led to the development of a rival political coalition with its base eventually in the northern province, populated mostly by the Temne (who represented about 29 percent of the total population). This anti-SLPP coalition also was supported by a majority of the Creole, a peculiar sociocultural group started by liberated slaves of the British.[3] For a long time a privileged group, this tiny minority of about 1 percent of the population had (and still has) very considerable advantages and predominated in the civil service and liberal professions.

The Sierra Leone People's Party stayed in power from 1951 until the general elections in 1967, having managed to win the two previous elections in 1957 and 1962. Formerly the predominant party, it steadily had been losing political ground due to desertion from its ranks and the rising tide of opposition. Upon gaining political independence the SLPP government embarked upon an ambitious but not well-calculated program of economic development while preserving the existing social system and the strong influence of the chiefs. The virtual absence of effective institutions for economic administration in a basically laissez-faire and open economy, and the scarcity of managerial and technical skills, contributed to the serious mismanagement of the nation's resources by an inexperienced and narrow-minded elite. The growing malaise of the SLPP regime became only more visible with the passing from the scene in 1964 of the widely respected Sir Milton Margai. He was succeeded by his younger half-brother, Sir Albert Margai, who, according to an official commission of inquiry, turned out to be an extremely corrupt politician, even by West African standards.[4]

The corrupt group around Sir Albert could not swallow the very real possibility of being voted out of the office in the forthcoming elections. But the

trend clearly was in favor of the opposition, the most
important party of which was the more plebeian and
mildly radical All People's Congress (APC). The APC
was formed in 1960, and its leader, Siaka Stevens, a
prominent trade union leader, had been an SLPP MP
until 1957.[5] While the public image of the SLPP was
increasingly tarnished, its patronage power also decreased since the country was entering an economic
recession and a budgetary squeeze.[6]

To deal with the opposition, the SLPP leadership
applied practically the entire range of techniques
of dirty politics, short of terror and a wholesale
subversion of the parliamentarian competitive system.
Election-rigging was widespread, but the limited
powers of the central government, localism, and resistance in the civil service had kept it within certain
bounds. The government also extensively used material
incentives, corruption, withholding of development
funds, taking away of licenses, arrests, harassment,
destooling of unsympathetic chiefs, and other forms
of administrative coercion to entice independent and
opposition candidates to cross the floor. It also
made several politically important appointments in
the civil service and in the army. The opposition
representation in the parliament was reduced by ar-
resting four MPs and depriving them of their mandates.[7]

To further increase his legal powers, Sir Albert
proposed an introduction of a single-party state,
but in the face of widespread hostility on the part
of the opposition and in his own party he dropped
the idea. Unlike his new foreign allies, K. Nkrumah
of Ghana and Sékou Touré of Guinea in their earlier
days, Sir Albert lacked a viable political organization, wide popular support, and charisma. He used
all the tricks, but within the limits of the Africanized Westminster model. His control of the country
was limited, and so was his determination to subvert
the system altogether; hence his reluctance to use
the police, secret service, judiciary, and army to
drive the opposition completely underground. Unable
to outlaw the opposition, Sir Albert tried to increase
his power legally through a new constitution that was
to do away with the formal dependence of Sierra Leone
on the British Crown. It was only a nationalist
sugar-coating. The hastily prepared draft of the

new charter was published on December 22, 1966, and despite the uproar of the opposition was rushed through the parliament in two readings on January 24 and January 26, 1967.[8]

In his foreign policy Sir Albert adopted a strong verbal anti-British stand on Southern Rhodesia and drew closer to Ghana and Guinea.[9] Without consulting or even informing his own party and the parliament, he secretly concluded a mutual assistance agreement with Sékou Touré. In order to create a crisis atmosphere in the country before the general election, due not later than August 1967, and to intimidate the opposition, in February 1967 the government arrested eight military officers including Colonel John Bangura, deputy force commander.[10] They were accused publicly of conspiring with the opposition to stage a military coup and to murder Sir Albert. The officers were brought before a court-martial but the charges were never substantiated. With the opposition press effectively attacking the ruling SLPP leadership, all these measures did not help Sir Albert. His prestige also was harmed by the announcement that Sékou Touré had placed Guinean troops on alert along the frontier with Sierra Leone.[11]

Under the conditions of strong polarization in the country and a sharp regionally/ethnically colored division in the civilian elites, the government party suffered a resounding defeat in the March 17, 1967, election. It won only 22 contested seats (plus 6 unopposed), against the opposition's 32 seats and 6 independents.[12] The election-rigging, intimidation, and fraud were not sufficient to avert a strong swing in favor of the All People's Congress.[13]

Sir Albert did not dare to subvert the institution of elections wholesale, as K. Nkrumah did, but neither did he want to accept the adverse outcome. He and a group of his closest lieutenants used their powers to the last, delaying the announcement of the results, misinforming the public, and pressuring the independent MPs and paramount chiefs. The chiefs' election, nonpartisan by convention, was to take place in the second round on March 21. But all the maneuvers to prevent a creation of an APC-dominated government failed and at 3:15 p.m. on March 21, 1967, Siaka Stevens was duly sworn as prime minister by the

governor-general Sir H. Lightfoot Boston. A majority
of the population in the capital was jubilant, and
there was dancing in the streets.

THE MILITARY COUPS OF MARCH 21
AND MARCH 23, 1967

At this moment the Margai group, acting through
the force commander, staged a coup that was meant to
be preemptive. The initial purpose of the coup was
to use a limited period of martial law in order to
annul the governor-general's action and somehow to
create a majority in the parliament. The army was
to be used as an instrument of civilian politics,
but Sir Albert overestimated his ability to control
this weapon once it was unleashed.

There does not seem to have been any advance
planning specifically for this action, although Sir
Albert's personnel policies were in the direction of
consolidating his hold on the army. The force was
put on alert two days before the elections as Police
Commissioner W. L. Leigh expected disturbances out-
stripping his capabilities. The preparations for
the coup were made during approximately two days by
Sir Albert's closest associates, and on the military
side by Brigadier Lansana, his deputy, Major Blake,
Major Jumu, and Major Kai-Samba, with the cooperation
of and intelligence from W. L. Leigh. A small force
of about a hundred soldiers executed this very simple
operation: they blocked the governor-general's residence at about 3:45 p.m., placed him and Prime Minister Siaka Stevens under arrest, and took over the
radio station and control of the main thoroughfare
of the capital.[14] At 5:55 p.m. Brigadier Lansana
announced over the state radio the imposition of
martial law, couching his action in legalistic arguments. By doing so he _created_ a danger to law and
order, and the army used arms against unarmed and
embittered crowds. About 30 civilians were reported
killed.[15]

The new government party went underground and
Brigadier Lansana failed in his attempts to convene
the parliament and, counting on the newly elected
paramount chiefs, to bring Sir Albert into office

more or less legally. The force commander also lost
control of his immediate subordinates. On March 23,
1967, he was arrested by Major Blake and, together
with Sir Albert Margai and Siaka Stevens, was taken
into "protective custody."[16]

In a radio broadcast to the country, Major Blake
confirmed the quasi-constitutional justification for
the previous coup in which he and the two other members of the new junta, Major Jumu and Major Kai-
Samba, willingly participated. Nevertheless, Major
Blake shifted the stress to the danger of tribal division in the country. He accused Brigadier Lansana
of being partial to Sir Albert and came out as a
champion of a coalition government but refused to
recognize the APC victory.[17] The new junta represented the sentiments of a non-Margai faction within
the SLPP, which recognized his unpopularity and considered him a political liability. The overwhelming
pro-SLPP bias of the new rulers and their commitment
to the basic status quo were confirmed by the appointment of P. Tucker, former secretary to the prime
minister and one of the chief engineers of the Lansana coup, as secretary-general to the junta.

The first and second coups initially were a
continuation by other means of civilian party politics in which the purported nonpolitical and supra-
regional nature of the armed forces was used as a
cover and as expendable political currency to achieve
particularistic goals. Only about two days later
did the nature of military organization appear clearly
as an independent factor, unequivocally impressing
itself on the political process and significantly
contributing to a change in the course of the military rule. Three pledges in the junta's initial
declaration were soon dropped: to restore a civilian
government in the shortest possible time, not to engage in politics, and not to open inquiries into the
past record of the SLPP government. In addition to
civilian politics, the authors of the second coup
were prompted by internal tensions in the army, a
desire for self-promotion, and the influence of the
Nigerian and Ghanaian coups of 1966.[18]

THE ESTABLISHMENT OF MILITARY RULE:
THE PROBLEM OF LEADERSHIP

While Brigadier Lansana had only declared martial law, the new junta suspended the constitution, dissolved all political parties and parliament, prohibited all political activity, put the governor-general under house arrest, and imposed a dusk-to-dawn curfew.[19] The new ruling body, consisting of seven senior officers and called the National Reformation Council (NRC), was to be aided by a civilian National Advisory Council.

The junta kept Colonel John Bangura, second-ranking officer in the force, in custody for a while despite the unsubstantiated nature of the charges. It originally appointed as chairman of the NRC the formerly third-ranking officer, Lieutenant-Colonel A. Genda, 40, who in 1966 was retired from the force and sent abroad as second secretary of the Sierra Leone Mission to the United Nations.[20] For several political, regional, ethnic, and personal reasons, the junta rescinded this appointment before A. Genda reached Freetown. Having eliminated two possible candidates, the junta stopped at the fourth-ranking Lieutenant-Colonel A. Juxon-Smith, 35, who at the time of the coup happened to be in Britain. Later, when the coup-makers ran into sharp disagreements with the new leader, professional ethics and the concern for public image contributed to the fact that they did not sack A. Juxon-Smith.

When the problem of a chairmanship was finally resolved, the original National Reformation Council consisted of five army and two police officers.* The composition of the new ruling body reflected

---

*Lieutenant-Colonel A. T. Juxon-Smith, chairman; Police Commissioner W. L. Leigh, deputy chairman; Major A. C. Blake, acting force commander; Major S. B. Jumu, commander of the only battalion; Major B. I. Kai-Samba; Assistant Commissioner of Police A. Kamara; and Major A. R. Turay. The position of W. L. Leigh was in recognition of his contribution to the easy success of both coups, chiefly in terms of intelligence.

several distinct elements and considerations. At
the initial stage of plotting these were the community
of political interests and the partly accidental possession by the military and police establishments of
the elements vital for carrying out the coup. At
the second stage these were supplemented by the somewhat rigged procedures and norms of a modern bureaucratic organization and by political considerations
aimed at making the junta a more acceptable ruling
body to the public. To achieve the latter the junta
came close to having two officers from each of the
four administrative divisions of the country.[21]

THE SIERRA LEONE ARMY AND
POLICE ESTABLISHMENTS

The Royal Sierra Leone Force was a continuation
of the battalion of the Royal West Africa Frontier
Force (RWAFF), stationed in Freetown.[22] The total
strength of the force was estimated in 1966 at 1,360
men and defense expenditure at $2,585 million, or
about 5 percent of the budget. The army, totaling
1,300, consisted of one infantry battalion stationed
in Freetown and one company on the Guinean border.
There was a miniscule navy. The small size of the
force and its concentration permitted face-to-face
relations of a small group, among about 50 officers
and the NCOs.

The Sierra Leone Police was reported in 1966 as
2,055 men strong. It was obviously much more scat-
tered around the country than the army. The police
also was British-trained and unarmed, except for
several squads of riot police. Both services were
well-paid, although inflation took a bite in the real
purchasing power of their salaries.[23]

By 1967 the Africanization of the army and police was almost complete, but the accelerated training of the localized officer corps negatively affected
morale and in the future posed the problem of career
opportunities. At least three serious internal conflicts erupted in the army officer corps in 1966 and
1967 due to the maladjustments, value conflicts, and
personal clashes of a small and young bureaucratic
organization. Another source of cleavages was polit-

ical interference and the determined efforts of Sir
Albert Margai to use the forces as a tool of his
rule. By March 1967 he achieved a high degree of
control over them.[24]

The police seemed to be less faction-ridden and
to have better leadership. The lack of isolation of
the officer corps and latent internal cleavages made
the army susceptible to outside political influences
with ideological and regional-ethnic undertones.
Given the degree of Sierra Leone's dependence on the
former metropole it was not unnatural for a number
of army officers to pick up rather radical and natiol-
ist ideas and, with abundant leisure time, to be
keenly interested in politics. The politization
seems to have been lower in the police, which, with
the exception of its commissioner, did not show en-
thusiasm for the coup.

Since the supreme civilian authority was done
away with, the junta made itself legally responsible
for the force.[25] In order to enhance their standing,
out of vanity and reckless disregard for public relations, the junta members rapidly promoted themselves
in rank* and failed to project the image of austerity
that they demanded of the country. This undermined
the junta's position both with civilians and in the
ranks.

The junta refrained from employing the army and
police officer corps for running Sierra Leone so that
direct involvement in politics was limited to about
10 officers at a time. There were no regular procedures for debating issues of governance within the
army and police, but in a small and concentrated
force it could be done informally. The scarcity of
qualified manpower was an important factor limiting
the army's real impact on the country. It became
involved in only one area, the anti-corruption campaign. The Anti-Corruption Squad was established in
July 1967[26] and given very extensive powers of search
and arrest.[27] For a while it reduced absenteeism of
civil servants, but otherwise the results of its

---

*By July 1967 A. T. Juxon-Smith was already brig-
adier; A. C. Blake was made a full colonel; and S. B.
Jumu and B. I. Kai-Samba, lieutenant-colonels.

activities were petty and ridiculous. It could not,
without intelligence, training, and special skills,
uncover the most economically damaging forms of corruption related to such activities as diamond smuggling, customs evasion, and wholesale trade. Instead,
the Anti-Corruption Squad arrested, for example, on
one day in January, one person for stealing a bottle
of Cinzano, a bus conductor for, issuing a two-cent
ticket instead of a five-cent ticket, and a truck
driver for stealing 10 bags of onions.[28] It seems
that some members of the squad themselves committed
acts of extortion. On the other hand several army
and police officers sat in the commissions of inquiry.
     On the whole the impact of NRC rule on the two
services was outwardly insignificant until their breakdown, but internally it badly hurt the force. On
the other hand relative status deprivation of the
military and police professions practically disappeared.

              NATIONAL REFORMATION COUNCIL RULE:
                 PROBLEMS, MANIFEST GOALS,
                   DECISION-MAKING, AND
                     ECONOMIC POLICY

     From the outset the new rulers had to deal with
the problem of external and internal legitimacy.
The legal foundations of the new regime were provided
by the Administration (National Reformation Council)
Proclamation of 1967 and the Constitutional Provisions
(Suspension) Decree of 1964.[29] The office of the
governor-general was suspended, but the country remained formally a monarchy within the Commonwealth,
with the NRC exercising the executive authority of
the queen.[30] At least legally, the external continuity of the state was preserved and no country has
challenged it (Guinean President Sékou Touré welcomed
it).
     The new junta had no positive program at the
time of the coup. In a semblance of it, unveiled to
the press by Lieutenant-Colonel Juxon-Smith on March
29, 1967, the manifest goals of the NRC were as follows: the eradication of tribalism, corruption,
bribery, and nepotism; a policy of austerity; and an

indefinite period of martial law. The junta intended
to restore budgetary and fiscal stability through the
implementation of the agreement concluded by the previous government with the International Monetary
Fund.31

The National Reformation Council operated as an
eight-man cabinet. The procedural rules of the NRC
were elaborated in early April 1967 by P. Tucker,
first secretary-general of the NRC. Decisions were
to be reached by a simple majority vote and once
adopted they were binding on all members. All sessions were attended by the two secretaries-general
(one to the council and one to its chairman, with
the latter appointed somewhat later), sometimes by
the attorney-general and those officials whose presence was requested (those in the last category stayed
in the room only during the deliberation on their
particular topic, and even the secretaries-general
often were asked to leave the room for a while).

The junta reduced the number of ministries from
15 to 9 and named them "ministerial departments."32
The junta members divided, unevenly, the responsibilities over them.*

NRS meetings were held in the cabinet room of
the former prime minister's office at least once a
week. Discussions were free and rather orderly during the sessions, which often lasted a whole day.
The procedure of taking votes was not widely used, and
the chairman often expressed the sense of the meeting.
It seems that he was outvoted only once at the very
beginning. Rather neurotic, mentally immature, sometimes erratic, quarrelsome, and in a way cunning,
Juxon-Smith did not permit it to happen again.

The NRC chairman was in charge of the NRC Secretariat, whose functions comprised those of the for-

---

*Lieutenant-Colonel Juxon-Smith took over control
of the NRC Secretariat, finance, and interior, including responsibility for the mines, the judiciary,
defense, and internal security. He also was commander-in-chief. Police Commissioner W. L. Leigh became
the member responsible for foreign affairs, and Major
A. C. Blake was entrusted with trade, industry, and
agriculture.

mer prime minister's office, Cabinet Secretariat,
Office of the Clerk of the House of Representatives,
and the former Development Office.[33] It was staffed
by senior civil servants.

Likewise, in the nine new departments the junta
appointed former permanent secretaries as secretaries
with all conditions of service unchanged. It made
only very slight modifications in civil service and
provincial administration.[34]

A significant influence on the junta was exerted
from April 1967 by the Economic Advisory Committee
(EAC). It was chaired by G. Conrad, a West German
adviser in the NRC Secretariat, and included the
governor of the Bank of Sierra Leone, two other senior civil servants, and unofficially B. Quinn, a
Scotsman and the resident representative of the IMF.
The junta accepted practically all the EAC proposals,
but not automatically and without persuasion.

On April 26, 1967, the NRC solemnly inaugurated
the National Reformation Advisory Council (NRAC),
which was to prepare the country for a return to
civilian rule and to advise the junta on general
political matters. It consisted of 19 appointed
civilians and 6 paramount chiefs from all 4 administrative divisions of the country and representatives
of corporate bodies. S. T. Matturi, principal of
Njala University College, was elected its chairman.[35]
The NRAC wasted precious time at the beginning and
lost a chance to make an impact on military rule.
Its usefulness in terms of public relations for the
NRC was circumscribed by the junta's obsession with
secrecy and confidentiality. The result was that
the advisory body soon became a closed debating society, ignored by the rulers and by the public.

The entire system of government under the National Reformation Council could be presented in the
manner shown in Figure 4.

The most important positive legacy of the NRC
rule was the relative success of the program of economic recovery in 1967-68. The economic policies
adopted by the junta were a more energetic continuation of the policies imposed on Sierra Leone under
Sir Albert Margai as an explicit condition for a $7.5
million standby credit from the IMF. The deflationary
and austerity program called for drastic reductions

FIGURE 4

Schematic Representation of the Decision-Making Structure Under the National Reformation Council in Sierra Leone, April 1967-April 1968

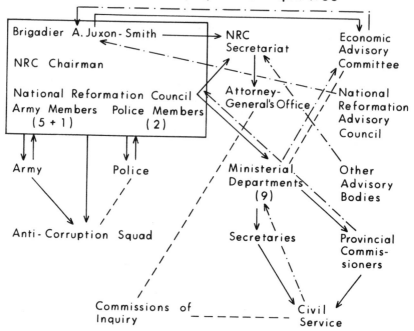

Key

——→ Relations of subordination

— — — Other types of power relations

——·→ Flow of information

in government development outlays. These were cut from Le 22.9 million* to Le 12.8 million under Sir Albert and further cut to Le 9.8 million under the NRC.[36] Unlike the Margai government the junta did not have to fear an approaching election. The NRC also reorganized the Sierra Leone Produce Marketing Board (SLPMB), which controlled exports of cash crops discontinued a subsidy to the Road Transport Corporation, and decided to phase out the Sierra Leone railroad.[37]

The drastic deflationary policy under the NRC represented a policy of substantial withdrawal of

---

*1 Leone = 1.2 dollars (1968).

the state from the area of economic development, initially externally imposed, but later eagerly accepted
by the new rulers. It was a reaction to the rather
imprudent, overly ambitious, poorly conceived and
executed economic policy of the SLPP government.
The military bureaucrats were aware that the task of
transforming society was beyond their capabilities,
even in straight technical and logistical terms. Imbued with the norms of financial accountability they
easily accepted conventional economic prescriptions.

The social cost of such policy was rather high
as a wide spectrum of social groups, mainly in urban
and mining areas, was hit by increased taxes, reduced
imports and public spending, rising unemployment,
and continuing inflation.[38] While real incomes of
wage earners declined, the situation in the countryside was less serious.

By the spring of 1968 the budget was stabilized
and the balance of foreign trade registered a substantial surplus,[39] but this improvement could be attributed only in part to the junta's policies.

THE ECLIPSE OF THE NATIONAL
REFORMATION COUNCIL

However, the political liabilities of the NRC
policies started to mount in the spring of 1968.
The autocratic military-police rule, supported by
threat of arms, and the ineptness and costly political mistakes created too many enemies of the NRC.
The number of people actually jailed was not significant, and many opponents were able to leave the country at will. On the other hand the junta's resources
for controlling and running the country were extremely
modest. Its coercive capacity was limited mainly to
the capital, and it had to rely on the civil service,
police, and traditional authorities. Its political
surveillance and information-gathering capabilities
were extremely weak, and the junta was not even informed about army morale. In practice the NRC re-
sorted to a paradoxical combination of brazen threats
and appeals for public support, with immature insensi-
tivity to public opinion in some areas and responsiveness in others.

The martial law decrees had driven the political parties and groups underground, and the muzzling of the press[40] forced opponents to use the already extremely well-developed channels of oral communication and publication of illegal tracts.

One of the most important and initially popular measures of the NRC was the creation of a number of commissions of inquiry dealing with various aspects of governmental activities under the previous civilian regime. It was consistent with the anti-corruption crusade announced by Juxon-Smith. The profound and lasting effect of these commissions on the politicized segments of population was the thorough and complete discrediting of Sir Albert Margai and his group in the SLPP leadership. It understandably antagonized many SLPP supporters, as well as senior civil servants who were forced to testify publicly in the presence of their subordinates.

The acute dissatisfaction and open opposition to the military rule among the APC sympathizers was understandable since the NRC continued to deprive the party of its electoral victory. The publishing of the report of the Dove-Edwin Commission of Inquiry on November 29, 1967, clearly established this fact, refuted a number of claims made by the NRC to justify its existence, and challenged the very foundations of NRC rule.[41] The university college in Fourah Bay became a center of opposition. Its indigenous faculty members and students staged a procession, clandestinely engaged in seditious activities, and maintained contacts across the border with Siaka Stevens and the APC leaders who received hospitality and help in neighboring Guinea.[42]

The relationship of the NRC with trade unions became tense after January 1968 when the workers felt the real pinch of the deflationary policies. The junta imprudently also offended several religious groups and the traditionalists when it abolished the secular powers of the tribal headmen[43] and expressed its intention to change the country's coat of arms. Gradually but surely the junta antagonized one section of the politicized population after another, particularly in the capital.

To counter the demands for a return to civilian rule the NRC adopted a delaying tactic. On February

21, 1968, it inaugurated the Civilian Rule Committee (CRC) as "a pro tem constituent assembly."[44] The CRC consisted of 75 members--15 appointed members of the National Advisory Council and elected representatives of various corporate bodies including the SLPP and APC.[45] Unexpectedly for Juxon-Smith, the formerly feuding civilian politicians swiftly reached an agreement and passed a recommendation for immediate return to civilian rule.[46] In early April Easmon, the CRC chairman, handed to Brigadier Juxon-Smith three memoranda and a document on the process of handing-over. Placed in an awkward position Juxon-Smith nevertheless had no intention of stepping down. While complicated maneuvering in the junta was going on, in the late evening of April 17, 1968, its members were arrested by mutinous soldiers and army NCOs.[47] All active indigenous army and police officers present in the country (about 90 in total) were stripped of their uniforms and jailed, often after having been mistreated by the mutineers. The coup claimed two deaths and six wounded.[48]

The inner core of the new junta, called the Anti-Corruption Revolutionary Movement (ACRM), included Sergeant-Major P. Conteh, Sergeant-Major A. Rogers, and four other NCOs and privates.[49] Colonel John Bangura, secretly present in Freetown, might have had something to do with it, but basically it was an internal pay strike of the ranks for better conditions of service and for self-promotion. Politicized regional-ethnic cleavages also played a role, many ACRM members being from the North. The ACRM could not run the country and the army, and it called on Colonel Bangura and Lieutenant-Colonel A. Genda. These two officers, together with the reactivated police officer, M. Parker, the new police commissioner, headed a seven-man National Interim Council (NIC).

The actions of the new ruling junta were swift, and they closely followed the recommendations of the Civilian Rule Committee. On April 23, 1968, Chief Justice Banje Tejan-Sie, who formerly belonged to the SLPP, was appointed acting governor-general. The House of Representatives was convened. On April 26, Siaka Stevens was sworn again as prime minister and formed a coalition government. Colonel Bangura dissolved the NIC and "retired" to the post of force

commander. The army and police were in shambles after 13 months of military-police rule.

Sierra Leone was the first African country to
try its former military rulers publicly. The government cunningly obtained from neighboring Liberia the
extradition of Brigadier Lansana. He and 17 other
officials were accused of high treason. In July 1970
a high court condemned David Lansana and nine others
to capital punishment. In August it was the fate of
former Brigadier Juxon-Smith. However, both verdicts
were quashed on technical grounds by the Court of Appeals. In October 1970 10 officers and NCOs were arrested and accused of seditious activities. In the
atmosphere of growing tension, division within the
ruling party, emergency measures, arrests of opposition leaders, and the post-effects of the Portuguese-
staged invasion of Guinea, the Sierra Leone House of
Representatives approved on December 22, 1970, agreements of mutual assistance with the neighboring countries of Guinea and Liberia. On March 23, 1971,
Brigadier John Bangura, the force commander, announced
to the nation the seizure of power. This time it
was premature, as history did not repeat itself: an
ill-executed attack on the prime minister's office
failed and Bangura was repudiated by other senior
officers, arrested, court-martialed, and promptly
executed. Guinean troops flew into Freetown at the
request of Siaka Stevens, who soon became president
and commander-in-chief of the newly proclaimed Republic of Sierra Leone.

The Sierra Leone Force by the summer of 1972
had regained much of the discipline and morale badly
hurt by the disastrous interventions in politics
since 1967. The APC government has not undertaken
any sweeping changes. Defense appropriations were
raised and a new battalion was organized and trained.
In this new unit former party and youth activists are
said to represent a sizable group. As a measure of
precaution, President Siaka Stevens retained the
Guinean detachment. Its presence, however reduced
and unobtrusive, testifies to still strained civil-
military relations, and hardly could be very popular
in the country.

THE UNION SOUDANAISE-RDA
REGIME

The Ghanaian coup that ousted Kwame Nkrumah had a strong echo in Mali. President Modibo Keita and the radical leaders of his single party, Union Souda-naise-RDA (US-RDA), felt directly threatened by it.* Despite pronounced differences arising from the pre-colonial and colonial past, as well as from the different levels of economic development of the two countries, the two regimes shared a number of outward features. The structure of ruling parties, the relationship between the party hierarchy and the state apparatus, and the preeminent positions of the leaders were similar. Their ideologies were influenced by several brands of Marxism, and the regimes extensively used charismatic symbols and techniques as a means for legitimation of power. The political lines of Ghana and Mali were in similar relation with the former colonial powers and the nonaligned, or close to it, posture in foreign affairs. The two regimes attempted to balance predominant economic dependence on the West with political ties in the East, and their

---

*Mali, Ghana, and Guinea were formally united as members of a federation, but it never really functioned.

leaders felt an affinity in perception of internal, continental, and extra-African problems.[1]

The Union Soudanaise started as a broad anti-colonialist coalition and developed its organization under the strong influence of the French Communist Party. Until the end it remained a mass party, formally encompassing in its ranks a majority of the adult population (a 1967 attempt to move in the direction of a party of "cadres" was not followed through). It achieved a predominant position before the country was granted independence by France and eliminated organized political opposition more thoroughly and easily than the CPP in Ghana.*

Alone in the political arena, the Union Soudanaise, despite its huge membership, had very serious internal weaknesses. With the very low level of literacy and education of the Milian population, adherence to the party was most often symbolic, formal and superficial. The paying of membership dues became a tax, and more substantial contributions by merchants represented a means of obtaining tangible favors from officialdom. The horizontal and vertical ties between party organizations were weak and so was control from the center.[2]

The party hierarchy had been inextricably intertwined with the government on the national level and underpinned by village councils and similar bodies on the local level. After independence, the US-RDA became predominantly the party of the state administration.[3]

The Malian leadership had adopted a "socialist orientation" in development in September 1962 and undertook several series of measures designed to change

---

*Two opposition leaders of the former Parti Soudanais de Progres (socialist party) favored before the independence by the French and supported by the chefs de cantons were jailed in 1962 after riots in Bamako and two years later died in the North. They seem to have been killed in an ambush by the Touareg rebels, but it was too embarrassing to the government to admit it. These are the only known victims of the monopolization of power by the Union Soudanaise. Other members of the opposition either joined the ruling party or left the country.

significantly the social and economic structure of the country.

However, the regime's ambitions and the strong statist strategy of development[4] were not supported by sufficient material resources and performance capabilities of the political system. The policy of enforced spread of cooperatives, the transformation of traditional flows of marketable surpluses of agricultural produce and a de facto internal state monopoly thereof, low purchasing prices for cash crops, and the state monopoly of foreign trade--all these means were intended to assure capital accumulation for industrialization, modernization of agriculture, and maintainence of a much more expensive sovereign state. On the other hand the regime failed to induce peasants to produce more and better goods for state purchases[5] and could not prevent the growing smuggling of exportable surplus across the borders, mainly to Senegal and the Ivory Coast. The results were adverse. Politically this strategy led to the rising dissatisfaction of the peasants, many merchants, and among the urban population. It also increased corruption of government and party officials.[6]

On the other hand the newly created, mostly on credit, infant light industries not only did not perform well to offset the losses in agriculture but in many instances drained scarce resources for development. The US-RDA did make progress in industrialization and improved the country's infrastructure.[7] However, advances were too costly relative to the very slim material base of the ambitious regime and its low absorption capacity. This was due to obstacles of an objective nature--very high transportation costs, the lack of known energy resource and raw materials, the small size of the Malian market, and strained relations with its wealthiest neighbors-- and perhaps most importantly, to glaring mistakes in the allocation of resources, incompetence, mismanagement, political interference, and nepotism. The scarcity of managerial and technical skills among the members of the civilian elite, the anti-capitalist and anti-profit ethos, intense nationalism and pride, and the priority given to "politics" over "economics" significantly contributed to the waste of resources.

The growth of state intervention had been accompanied by the burgeoning of the state bureaucracy:

from 13,337 persons on the public payroll in 1961 to 22,903 only seven years later.[8] The state budget was growing even faster, from FM (Malian francs) 6.7 billion in 1960 to FM 23.5 billion and a budgetary deficit of FM 5 billion in 1967-68.[9]

While the cost of bureaucracy in an underadministered country had risen in the post-independence period, Mali could no longer count on the "traditional" French budgetary subsidy of $7.5 million per annum. At the same time, the new state embarked in 1961 upon an ambitious--for Mali's resources--program of prestige construction and investment (including a presidential palace, a National Assembly building, establishments of higher learning, a 17-story hotel, a class A international airport, a national airline, and acquisitions for Malian embassies). The Malian leaders also conducted an active and relatively expensive foreign policy and overestimated their ability to benefit from the rivalries between the great powers and other states.

THE ROAD TO MILITARY
INTERVENTION

By the summer of 1966 the Malian leadership saw no other solution but to swallow its pride and approach Paris. In July 1966 President Modibo Keita presented a program of austerity designed to bring about an economic and financial recovery. In February 1967 the Malians accepted the harsh French demands. The devaluation of 50 percent was announced on May 6, 1967, and austerity measures stepped up. The combination of continuing inflation, blocked salaries, threatened layoffs, and a time lag between these and the conditional French aid turned the originally positive public reaction to reconciliation with France into disenchantment--and further, into strong opposition among state employees, party members, and large sections of the population.

It also contributed to a sharp polarization within the party-state leadership. Jockeying between two major factions, in 1966-67 Modibo Keita adopted a contradictory line. In economic and partly in foreign policy matters, he was reluctantly implementing

84

the platform of the "moderates" (US-RDA right wing) and the technocrats in the administration. On internal political matters the radical Marxist "hard-liners" were in ascendance. Feeling threatened by the adverse external climate highlighted by Nkrumah's downfall, Keita used the atmosphere of political crisis to expand his own powers at the expense of a kind of coalition collective leadership and to expand the prerogatives of the party national headquarters at the expense of the government. With the growing internal difficulties, he turned more and more toward the "radicals" who remained doubtful about the agreements with France. The radicals, instead of reorganizing the economy and making the regime viable, were stressing ideological anti-capitalist purity and stepping up the "class struggle." They also advocated increased coercion, militarization of the party, revision of the foreign policy of nonalignment, and going all the way into the Eastern socialist camp.[10]

The protracted latent political crisis--caused by the lower and middle state bureaucracy, state employees, workers, and other groups of the urban population joining the ranks of the dissatisfied--erupted in July 1967. On July 18 a street demonstration of members of the US-RDA youth wing, staged by the radicals in the party leadership, demanded that the president get rid of the moderates.[11] This open split in the party leadership was covered and justified by the demands for eradication of corruption and capitalist enrichment at the top. It was the end of the wide anti-colonialist coalition under the aegis of the Union Soudanaise. The radicals started an officially sanctioned arbitrary witch hunt, using as their main weapon the People's Militia.[12]

Founded in 1960 and officially sponsored by the High Commissariat for Youth and Sports (headed by Moussa Keita, the president's younger half-brother), the para-military People's Militia numbered 3,500 armed men in 1963-64 and by 1968 outnumbered the army by roughly three to one. Through rapid expansion, the People's Militia took over the policing function of another creation of the US-RDA youth wing, the Vigilance Brigades. The militia's functions came to include the mobilization and political indoctrination of the young, night patrols, limited control of traffic and market prices, as well as surveillance of the frontiers.[13]

When the intensity of the Malian "cultural revolution" reached its highest point, M. Keita joined the vocal and militant left and staged a small party palace coup. In clear violation of the party statute, he announced over the radio on August 22, 1967, his unilateral decision to disband the Political Bureau of the US-RDA, the highest executive body, and conferred all its prerogatives on the National Committee for the Defense of Revolution (Comité National pour la Défense de la Révolution, or CNDR[14]--the body notably included M. Diakité, minister of defense and security, and Colonel Sékou Traoré, army chief of staff). The most prominent moderates and centrists were dropped and replaced in key posts by radicals. Regional and local bodies of the US-RDA also were dissolved and replaced by committees for the defense of the revolution. The ensuing internal purge hurt the ruling party and also affected all levels of the administration[15] and weakened its ties with the US-RDA.

The excesses of the People's Militia, which slipped out of the effective control of the leadership, created new enemies of the regime. On January 17, 1968, Modibo Keita engineered a dissolution of the National Assembly and appointed instead a Legislative Delegation of 28 trusted members. Political agitation, unrest, and occasional strikes and outbursts of violence continued well through the summer of 1968.[16] Despite the virulence of the outspoken urban party youth, the "cultural revolution" failed to instigate public support for the regime or to arrest the disintegration of its popular base. The economic crisis persisted, and in a politically divided country the regime did not manage to recover from a strong shake-up. The legitimacy of the regime was seriously compromised, and its last-ditch attempt to secure increased Soviet aid and political support by approving the invasion of Czechoslovakia and repudiating the policy of nonalignment[17] was met with silent disapproval.

THE COUP OF NOVEMBER 19, 1968, AND ITS CAUSES

Heavily in debt only half-way through the austerity program, overwhelmed by the problems and the persistent silent dissatisfaction of most social groups, the divided Malian leadership was caught at a moment of great weakness and almost painlessly swept from the political scene by a military coup on November 19, 1968.

President Keita, accompanied by a large entourage, left Bamako by plane for neighboring Upper Volta on November 10, and on the way back attended a conference in Mopti, the main town of the Fifth Region. The first arrest of the coup was made on the afternoon of November 18--Colonel Sékou Traoré, army chief of staff, was kidnapped by the plotters at the Bamako airport.[18] Troop movements in Kati military base and in Bamako started soon after midnight and by 6 a.m. the presidential palace, the US-RDA headquarters, the radio station, the airport, the newly Soviet-built party school, and other important buildings and strategic points in Bamako were occupied or blocked. At 6 a.m. the soldiers easily disarmed the most credible center of potential armed resistance-- the People's Militia camp. Other possible centers of resistance--those around the party, trade unions, and youth organizations--did not materialize. The entire impressive structure collapsed without resistance.

The round-up of most important officials of the regime was almost complete when Modibo Keita and his entourage surrendered at about 11 a.m. on the road 25 miles from Bamako. Modibo, already on board a ship from Mopti, knew of the coup in Bamako and of the impending arrest. However, he did not address the population and made no attempt to escape. He was brought to the former party headquarters, and the head of the junta, Lieutenant Moussa Traoré, 32, declared to him that the Malian armed forces had decided to take over state power.

In a technically smooth, professionally planned, and well-executed bloodless coup, the regime of Modibo

Keita-UN-RDA was overthrown by a group of originally
four or five officers of the rank of captain and
lieutenant. During the day preceding the insurrection, the junta rose in membership by invitation to
the final number of 14. The plotting was initiated
by Captain Yoro Diakité, 36, director of the military
school, some time in 1966. Captain Diakité's deputy
in the school, Lieutenant Moussa Traoré,[19] became
the leader at the last meeting of the original nucleus
of the junta, at which the final date was fixed. It
was a preemptive coup, as the arrests of about 40
persons, including several officers, were imminent
as soon as the president arrived in the capital.
The corporate existence of the army itself was at
stake since Modibo Keita planned to replace it with
the People's Militia. The coup succeeded because of
the weakness of the regime, the effective operational
control of key army units by the plotters, good intelligence, and the professional qualities of the
Malian army. Public reaction to the coup was, on
the whole, very warm, but more moderate than in Ghana.

The motivations of the plotters were of a corporate, personal, and general political nature. The
growth of the People's Militia as a rival and even a
substitute, as well as the swelling security services,
posed a very real threat to the army. The militia's
abuses served as a focus of general discontent with
various aspects of government policies. The sense
of personal insecurity and the climate of purges also
contributed to the sedition. The officers also were
dissatisfied with the turn the regime took in the
course of the "cultural revolution," with the arbitrary disbanding of constitutional institutions and
elected party forums, and with the revision of foreign policy.

THE MALIAN ARMED FORCES

Prior to the coup there were in Mali armed formations placed under three state agencies. Under
the State Secretariat for Defense were the army and
the gendarmerie. The army, together with the elite
presidential guard, consisted essentially of four
battalions located in Bamako-Kati, Kayes, Ségou, and

Gao, totaling 4,500 men of whom about 100 were officers. The seven brigades of the gendarmerie counted
800 men. There was a small air force and a paratrooper company, both developed in response to armed
defiance of the central government by the Touareg
nomads. Almost half of the total territory of Mali,
mostly barren, was placed under direct military control. Military operations against the rebels and a
rather brief period of service in the Congo provided
substitute combat experience for the army, which had
virtually no traditions of its own.

The army was rather well-paid and -equipped although its standard of living had been slowly de-
clining. Apart from important internal security functions, the army had participated since its inception
in various para-military, civil, and political activities.[20] The US-RDA tried to penetrate the military, and a substantial number of membership cards
was distributed among members of the military. Nevertheless, the army had passively resisted the inroads and retained its separate and to a degree nonpolitical identity.

Two other formations, apart from the secret
police, were under the ministry of interior: the
Garde Républicaine, 1,900 men strong, and the police,
600 men strong. Under the High Commissariat for
Youth and Sports, and in fact under the youth wing
of the party, were the already mentioned People's
Militia, Vigilance Brigades, and the Service Civique
Rural, whose 3,500 members were given six months of
military training.[21] The official defense estimates
in 1966 were $8,825 million, and expenditures on all
types of armed formations totaled over 25 percent of
the state budget.[22]

RULE OF THE MILITARY COMMITTEE
OF NATIONAL LIBERATION

Composition

The new junta, called the Military Committee of
National Liberation (Comité Militaire de Libération
Nationale, or CMLN), came into existence on November

19, 1968. It consisted of four captains and ten
lieutenants. Lieutenant Moussa Traoré was made chief
of state while Captain Yoro Diakité occupied the position of first vice-chairman and also was appointed
to the newly created separate post of chairman of
the Council of Ministers. The junta contained the
original nucleus of the coup, members whose identi-
ties are a well-guarded secret, and invited members
with a slightly lower status. The ruling body basically was a group of close friends, colleagues, and
companions of roughly the same background, age,
status, experience, prominence, and intellectual
capacity.

The CMLN in its composition was influenced
largely by accidental factors, the personal relations
of former school and classmates and distant relatives,
and considerations to assure the success of the insurrection. One result was the predominance of officers from the First Region and the Third Region.*
The Sixth Region, covering almost half of Mali's territory and the source of the biggest internal threat
to the country's integrity, as well as the important
Fifth Region have not been represented on the CMLN.
In addition to the regional-ethnic imbalance, the
junta was created without due respect for other qualities of its members critical for rulers as opposed
to insurrectionists--such as intellectual capacity,
political skills, and public image and relations.
Because of the adopted rules of equality within the
CMLN, because of the desire to present an image of
internal unity and due to the new vested interests,

---

*The First Region accounted for six out of four-
teen members and later five out of thirteen, after
the accidental death of Lieutenant Mamadou Cissoko,
the new deputy chief of staff. Both Lieutenant
Moussa Traoré and Captain Yoro Diakité came from the
First Region. The First Region had been most severely hit by Keita's rupture with Senegal and felt
neglected by the US-RDA regime. It also used to be
the base of the major opposition party.

The Third Region accounted for five out of fourteen and later five out of thirteen CMLN members.

it proved impossible to alter the junta's composition later (see Table 2).

Contrary to its claim, the junta did not act on behalf of the entire army. Immediately before and on the day of the coup, the top brass remained either loyal to the civilian regime and tried to resist the insurrection or took a neutral wait-and-see attitude.[23] Problems with the NCOs and the troops were less serious. Nevertheless, the split in the army affected the junta both in its relations with the armed forces and internally.

TABLE 2

Composition of the Military Committee of National Liberation in Mali, 1968-70

Name	Rank	Position in the CMLN	Region of Origin
Moussa Traoré[a]	Lieutenant	Chairman	I
Yoro Diakité[a]	Captain	First vice-chairman	I
Baba Diarra	Lieutenant	Second vice-chairman	III
Filifing Cissoko[b]	Lieutenant	Permanent secretary	I
Youssouf Traoré	Lieutenant	Commissioner for settling conflicts	IV
Charles S. Cissoko[a]	Captain	Member	I
Malick Diallo[a]	Captain	Member	IV
Mamadou Cissoko[a,c]	Captain	Member	I
Karim Dembele[b]	Lieutenant	Member	III
Moussa Koné[b]	Lieutenant	Member	III
Mamadou Sanogo[b]	Lieutenant	Member	III
Tiecoro Bagayogo[b]	Lieutenant	Member	III
Kissiman Tounkara	Lieutenant	Member	II
Joseph Mara	Lieutenant	Member	I

[a]Attended military school in Fréjus (France).
[b]Had additional military training in the United States.
[c]Deceased.

Manifest Goals, Institutional
Framework, and Decision-Making

At the time of the coup the junta did not have
any clear political platform of positive action and
only reacted to what it felt was wrong in Mali under
Modibo Keita. It was a cleansing operation with limited objectives. The military technocrats tended to
view the two chief goals of economic recovery and national reconciliation [24] as "nonideological" and
"nonpolitical" ones. They hoped to achieve these
goals by streamlining the administration, improving
its efficiency and rationality, as well as by appeal-
ing to the patriotic feelings of Malians. The military rulers, less literate and eloquent than Modibo
Keita, cut down the speech-making and introduced a
more matter-of-fact style. On November 20 at 8 a.m.
sharp, Lieutenant Moussa Traoré addressed high officials with these sentences: "Gentlemen, I don't
want to talk long. You have heard enough long
speeches. This morning I simply want to tell you
that work should be normally resumed. I shall ab-
solutely appreciate frank collaboration with you,
so that all will benefit from the experience gained
so far. This is all I had to tell you."[25]
The first vague statements of the CMLN were limited to the expressed desire to reestablish liberties
and to abolish abuses of the previous regime. From
an emotional reaction to the style of its predecessors, the junta came out with a brief declaration of
intentions three days after the coup. It intended
to give top priority to economic recovery and to
budgetary balance. Trade would be reorganized and
there would be a shift toward more mixed public-pri-
vate and private sectors, while the state enterprises
occupying key sectors would enjoy the protection of
the state. Political institutions would be reconstructed on the basis of free democratic elections.[26]
Three days later, Captain Yoro Diakité made a more
detailed declaration for his government. He solemnly
declared that the army would return to barracks "in
the shortest possible time," "as soon as conditions
of real democracy are created." This statement included a timetable of the movement toward a civilian
regime. Moreover, a new parliament and a president
were to be elected by the end of 1969.

On the whole, the junta came out with a substantially modified but not radically different platform as compared with that of the US-RDA regime. The CMLN intended to liberalize internal and external trade, to dissolve unprofitable and heavily subsidized cooperatives, and to decrease public spending. It also announced a reorganization of state enterprises, honored the agreements with France, and took a more moderate stance in a foreign policy of "true nonalignment." Thus the junta essentially espoused the platform of the former right wing within the US-RDA.[27] The statist options were in a substantial part retained, and the policy of retrenchment was motivated by the desire to improve the efficiency and economic performance rather than by ideological considerations.[28] The junta coped with problems as they arose, on a day-to-day basis.

Once direct control of all regions was established, the junta had to establish the legitimacy of the new order. Using the state radio, the only local newspaper, L'Essor (which now became the mouthpiece of the CMLN), mass rallies, and tours in the regions by its individual members, the junta endeavored to affirm its legitimacy by stressing the negative aspects of the previous regimes.[29] Apart from the arrested ministers and prominent politicians, the junta did not touch the state administration, which continued to function as usual. All judges were retained. The new military-civilian government headed by Captain Diakité contained ministers and prominent figures of the previous government, notably J.-M. Koné, minister for foreign affairs and cooperation, and S. Coulibaly, minister-counsel to the CMLN.[30]

The evolution of the institutional framework and other essential characteristics of the new political order were started by the abolition of a number of institutions of the previous regime. There was a notable gradation in attitude toward them. The CMLN hesitated for a while on whether to retain the US-RDA after the party was purged and reconstructed (the CMLN was aware of this possibility, which was used in Algeria). Starting with the committees for defense of the revolution, the junta finally dissolved all bodies of the US-RDA, including the youth and women's wings, by November 29 and 10 days later ruled out a

93

single-party structure after a return to constitutional rule.[31] Two to three hundred persons of the
previous regime were arrested or detained. They seem
to have been treated correctly and with restraint.[32]
Only about 40 former officials eventually were retained
in custody,[33] the most illustrious among them being
the ex-president, who has been kept in the North
most of the time. The promised public trials of the
US-RDA officials never took place. The junta set
free political and other prisoners of the previous
regime, 130 in total,[34] and lifted administrative
restrictions on several well-known traditional leaders.[35]

Although the junta ordered most of the visible
symbols of the previous regime removed,* the break
with the past was not complete. The population,
state administration, politicized groups, and the
junta itself rejected only some manifestations of
the previous regime but not all of its instruments
and methods.

The trade unions, previously integrated in the
party, were treated differently from the US-RDA.
Two top trade union officers were arrested; the
junta dissolved all executive bodies and called for
the immediate election of new local trade union committees. A new Provisional Consultative Committee
was appointed,[36] and later a Provisional National
Bureau was set up. By the spring of 1970 this process of restructuring and recreating the labor movement reached the level of officially sanctioned national conferences of individual unions.

Within the state apparatus, primary attention
was given to the security services and to the High
Commissariat for Youth and Sports, the sources of
the recent threat to the army. The security services
were completely reorganized, partly purged, and subordinated to military intelligence. A CMLN member,

---

*For example, streets, squares, public buildings,
statues, and portraits bearing the name of Modibo
Keita or the US-RDA were changed. In this respect
the Malian military again was more rational than the
NLC in Ghana. For example, it did not change bank
notes that bore Keita's image.

Lieutenant T. Bagayogo, was appointed director of state security. The High Commissariat for Youth and Sports was depoliticized and downgraded to the level of General Inspectorate for Youth and Sports within the ministry of national education. About 10 national officers were replaced. Far fewer people were fired in other ministries. The main innovation was the stress on depolitization, but this did not necessarily increase the effectiveness of public services. One of the junta's proclaimed goals was the restoration of fundamental individual liberties,[37] and hence the upgrading of the judiciary.

The legal foundation of the new order was laid down by CMLN Ordinance No. 1 on provisional organization of public authority, published on December 9, 1968. The decree suspended in part the 1960 constitution and proclaimed as the highest institutions of the republic the Military Committee of National Liberation, the provisional government, and the Supreme Court. The chairman of the CMLN became the head of state.[38] In practice, there has been substantial intertwining between these three institutions, particularly the first two.[39] This has been even more obvious in the regions. In this respect the CMLN rule has been similar to the previous regime. The junta and military officers replaced the committees for defense of the revolution.

On the national level, the Military Committee of National Liberation became the highest extra-constitutional decision-making and controlling body with sweeping legislative and some adjudicative powers. The junta, more than the CNDR, had significant elements of collective leadership and institutionalized diffusion of power. The 14-member CMLN became a permanent institution about two months after the coup. The revoking of the earlier assurances of a speedy return to civilian rule was explained publicly by the very difficult economic situation and the lack of suitable civilian leaders.[40]

The CMLN and its secretariat inherited the headquarters of the former party. The only outside person allowed to attend the CMLN sessions has been S. Coulibaly, minister-counsel to the CMLN, and from September 1969 also minister for foreign affairs.

Other high officials, including the army chief of staff, can only be summoned to the junta meetings.*

After the reshuffle in September 1969 the number of officers holding simultaneous positions in the junta and in the Council of Ministers increased from two to four, an additional institutionalized link of communication between the two bodies being S. Coulibaly. The CMLN and the Council of Ministers have held from time to time "expanded (joint) meetings," particularly on economic matters to which high bureaucrats, general managers of state enterprises, and experts have been invited. Moreover at least five CMLN members have been in touch with high civilian officials in the course of their regular duties. The Council of Ministers, as under the previous regime, has been the policy-implementing and -administering body. However, the Council of Ministers and individual civilian ministers and ministries have remained important sources of initiative.

The junta created several ad hoc consultative bodies. One form was provided by the already mentioned "expanded meetings." The CMLN also formed in May 1969 a National Commission of Administrative Reform, chaired by B. Diallo, minister of labor, and comprised of senior civil servants and representatives of the trade unions.[41] In late July 1969 the junta convened a National Conference of Cadres at which it confronted 1,400 state officials and representatives of corporate bodies.[42] This ad hoc parliament of state bureaucracy disappointed the junta and did not produce constructive proposals. However, the criticisms raised at the conference indicated that the junta had a low degree of support in the civil bureaucracy, weakened the right wing within the CMLN and in the provisional government, and contributed to the downgrading of Captain Diakité and the elimi-

---

*The written internal regulations of the CMLN provided for taking votes. A decision on procedural matters requires a simple majority, while a question of substance necessitates a two-thirds majority. However, the junta reaches its decisions, if possible, by general consensus, the probable minority joining the probable majority.

nation from the government of two prominent ministers, J.-M. Koné and M. Aw.[43]

The junta also established two consultative bodies charged with the elaboration of a new three-year plan of economic recovery and stabilization.[44] To examine the plan the CMLN appointed an Economic and Social Commission made up of 10 senior civil servants, 10 representatives of the Chamber of Commerce, and 10 trade unionists. The commission worked effectively in February-March 1970 but was not dissolved after it presented a report. Some of its moderate recommendations were accepted by the junta.

The CMLN's own resources plus the available manpower from the officer corps have been sufficient, under these circumstances, to maintain the junta in control of the passively acquiescent country but not to carry out social and economic programs requiring mass participation. Mindful of the danger of the self-induced mutiny syndrome, the junta consciously limited the direct full-time administrative involvement of its members. All but five of thirteen CMLN members retained troop assignments. Several others added civilian responsibilities (mayor of Kati, minister of information, director of the cabinet of the chairman of the Council of Ministers) to their regular army load.

The entire formal structure of the CMLN rule can be presented schematically as shown in Figure 5.

THE JUNTA AND THE POLITY

By the spring of 1970 it became obvious that the majority within the CMLN had no intention of relinquishing power in the near future and that it contemplated the continuation of essentially the same system of government for the next four to five years. The splintered and unarmed, although at times vociferous, civilian opposition did not represent a serious challenge. The most active opposition groups were among students,[45] younger civil servants, intellectuals, former activists of the US-RDA, and probably most importantly in trade unions. The junta has treated persistent opponents with restraint on the whole, but at times has moved swiftly from liberal

FIGURE 5

Schematic Representation of the Decision-Making Structure Under the Military Committee of National Liberation in Mali

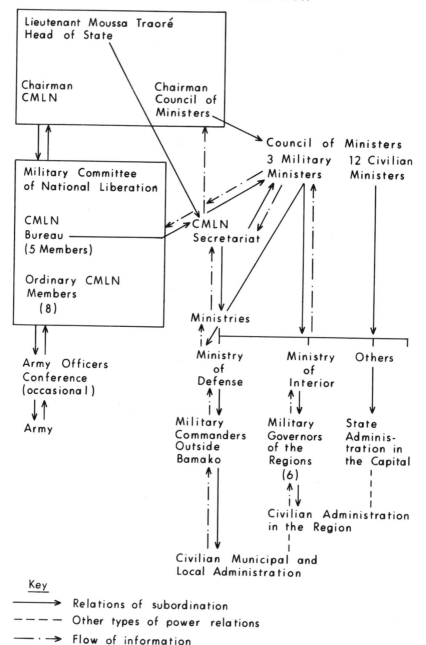

Key

⟶ Relations of subordination

— — — Other types of power relations

— · ⟶ Flow of information

tolerance to intimidation and even to individual cases of physical mistreatment.*

Throughout the first 18 months the CMLN enjoyed the passive support of peasants and of most merchants and tradesmen who were the main beneficiaries of partial liberalization in agriculture and commerce. Less secure than the Ghanaian junta, unwilling and unable to try an abrupt departure from the previous civilian order, less experienced and determined, and with less skillful civilian allies, the Malian junta vacillated during the period of its greatest popularity and missed the opportunity to resolutely implement unpopular but necessary measures in the state sector and in the administration. Some excessive labor was laid off, but fewer and with more timidity than in Ghana.[46]

The partial reorganization of the state sector, contraction of public expenditure, particularly of development outlays,[47] and attempts to increase financial discipline and to improve tax collection, coupled with unfavorable weather conditions and cattle diseases, soon began to hurt the peasant and urban population. Unemployment in urban areas climbed. The thorough liberalization of internal trade, advocated by the right wing of the ruling military-civilian coalition, dramatically increased the smuggling of grain to neighboring states and almost caused a crisis in the towns.[48]

Faced with the strong residues of the Union Soudanaise in the administration and trade unions, among students and intellectuals, as well as in the army, the junta itself underwent a change. The shift strengthened the centrist and slightly left-of-center group around Lieutenant Moussa Traoré at the expense of the group around Captain Diakité, who was close to the pro-French right. The CMLN reintroduced and reinforced administrative controls of internal trade in the autumn of 1969, refused to bow to French pres-

---

*For example, one delegate to the national conference of the Syndicat National de l'Education at de la Culture was beaten by soldiers in April 1970 on his way home. He was too vocal in criticizing the military regime.

sure to close unprofitable state enterprises, and by
the spring of 1970 became active in foreign affairs
on a platform very similar to Modibo Keita's in 1961-
62.*

On the other hand the junta suppressed an alleged
attempt to stage a coup on August 12, 1969, by Captain Diby Sillas Diarra, the popular governor and
military commander of the Fifth Region.[49] Called a
"true socialist" by local officials, Captain Diarra
not only represented a cleavage between the junta
and a part of the officer corps, who felt left out
of power and its privileges, but also espoused and
implemented more leftist policies in his region.
During Lieutenant Traoré's first official visit to
the Fifth Region, Captain Diarra never attacked the
deposed president in his speeches and consistently
and conspicuously called the new chief of state and
his entourage "comrades." Lieutenant Traoré kept
answering "Mister Governor, ladies, and gentlemen."
These were not insignificant symbols.[50]

The Captain Diarra affair once again reinforced
the internal cohesion of the junta. Handicapped by
the lack of political instruments of persuasion and
organized popular support, the junta has been learning only slowly the complexity of forging a consensus
among politicized groups and of creating and sustain-
ing a positive commitment to action on the part of
larger segments of the population. Having abolished
the only political party in the country, imbued with
an anti-political ethos and mistrust of "politicians"
and continuing to pretend to be apolitical and supra-
political, the junta attempted to supplement the only
instrument it nominally had, the state administration.
Internal dissent and disagreement with the CMLN made
the civilian bureaucracy an unreliable tool. The
junta tried to lure the trade union leadership to become a transmission belt for the regime and a substitute for the political party. With this in view the
junta gave a green light to a complete reconstruction

---

*Characteristically, Lieutenant Moussa Traoré's
first visit beyond the circle of immediate neighbors,
in May 1970, was made to President Nasser of the
U.A.R.

of the trade union structures in December 1969. Politically inexperienced, the junta made no preparations, and instead of gaining an ally it allowed
many of the trade unions to become hotbeds of opposition.[51]

On the whole the half-hearted and inept attempts
of the junta to create a popular base among the politicized social groups were not successful. The CMLN
has operated in an atomized political environment,
with no identifiable and coherent group of civilians
able to inspire reasonable confidence from the junta.
The CMLN itself has been divided behind the facade
of corporate unity, with its unpopular majority hang-
ing onto power for as long as it could. The period
of military rule gave the CMLN self-confidence in
the ability of its members to replace more civilian
ministers.* On the other hand the shift in the coalition of military officers and some civilian bureaucrats was counterbalanced by the growth of networks
of informal civilian influentials around the key members of the junta.

In November 1971 the Malian junta entered the
fourth year of its rule. Internal disagreements behind the facade of corporate unity continued to plague
the CLMN during the third year of its existence.
These were reflected in several shifts in the Council
of Ministers. Captain Yoro Diakité, in addition to
the position of the first vice-chairman of the CMLN,
became minister of national defense, interior, and
security in September 1970. Supported by Captain
Malik Diallo, he often was at odds with the dominant
group of younger CMLN members around Moussa Traoré.
Finally in April 1971 the latent rivalry broke into
an open clash. The chief of state publicly accused
Diakité and Diallo of "immoderate ambitions, egocen-
trism," and of plotting to overthrow the CMLN after
having failed to make the junta accept "their anti-
national, anti-African and retrograde positions."

---

*This trend, started in 1969, was confirmed dur-
ing another reshuffle of the Council of Ministers in
September 1970 when three civilian ministers were
dropped and replaced by junta members.

Diakité's political elimination removed but one, although probably the most dangerous, source of conflicts within the junta. The event probably reduced the previously sizable majority within the CMLN that was determined to hang on at least until implementation of the new three-year plan of economic stabilization.

In the 1972 New Year message, the now Colonel Moussa Traoré declared that the return to constitutional rule was "at the center of the preoccupations of the government and the CMLN." By then the junta had partly overcome the crisis in the relations with the National Union of Malian Workers, which lasted from the autumn of 1970 until January 1971.

On July 4-5, 1972, yet another abortive attempt to stage a coup was reported. The move apparently originated within the junta itself and was directed against its leader.

6

THE INTERRELATIONSHIP BETWEEN THE SOCIOPOLITICAL ENVIRONMENT AND MILITARY INTERVENTION

Having reviewed separately the relevant developments in Dahomey, Ghana, Sierra Leone, and Mali throughout the 1960s we shall now attempt to analyze the interrelationship between the social environment, in its historic, social, and economic dimensions, and the political system on the one hand and military intervention on the other.

A more or less profound malaise of the civilian political order and of the regimes in power was present in Dahomey, Ghana, Sierra Leone, and Mali at the time of the military seizures of power. But this also might be true of those African countries that have not experienced military takeovers. The sample of this study was not designed to test theoretical propositions related to the causes of military intervention. However, it seems useful to analyze the differences between the crisis symptoms present in the four countries prior to the coups. The factors that were operative during the pre-independence period will be examined first.

FRAGMENTATION OF CIVILIAN ELITES

The broad anti-colonial movement coalitions already varied in strength and fragmentation at the time political independence was attained.

The Union Soudanaise-RDA in Mali and the Convention People's Party in Ghana had achieved the greatest

size, coherence, and relative advantage over local
political opposition that was more conciliatory towar
the outgoing colonial power. In the very appreciably
less developed environment (economic, social, cultural, political), the US-RDA gained in Mali a great
monopoly and, it seems, also a greater internal coherence than Nkrumah's CPP. The US-RDA was distinctl
less a vote-getting machine than the CPP and it, unlike the Ghanaian party, succeeded in dispersing and
eliminating organized opposition. In Ghana the opposition largely went underground, and abroad and preserved most of its leaders and network of alliances
until the coup.

In Sierra Leone the early predominance of the
Sierra Leone People's Party (SLPP) already had been
seriously challenged in the pre-independence period,
particularly after the establishment in 1960 of the
major opposition party, the All People's Congress
(APC). The pre-independence movement, if one may
use this term for Dahomey, was badly splintered
throughout the modern history of Dahomey, except for
brief periods in 1946, 1958, and November-December
1960. After independence Dahomey oscillated between
formally unified but internally fragmented single official parties and mosaics of old political clubs
that appeared every time the single party was legally
or illegally dissolved.[1] Thus in Dahomey heavy factionalism was only a continuation of pre-independence
politics and hardly changed as a result of the presumed stresses of separate statehood (we are referring
to a common assumption in the literature on the African military).

Variation in relative strength and internal coherence does not seem to result in appreciably different susceptibility of the chosen civilian regimes
to military coups. But, not unexpectedly, the sample
indicates that less fragmented civilian coalitions
stay in power longer. The ages of the Ghana and
Mali civilian regimes at the time they were ousted
were 9.9 and 8.2 years, respectively, compared with
5.3 years in Dahomey and 5.8 years in Sierra Leone
(see Table 1 in Chapter 1). It is true that the
more coherent anti-colonial movements attained independence somewhat earlier, and if there is something
about the period of late 1965-68 (for instance, the

influence of the world market coup contagion) that
affected <u>all</u> civilian regimes, then this factor loses
in importance.

SOCIAL-CLASS AND INTRA-ELITE CLEAVAGES

What are the most salient cleavages that brought
about the decline and disintegration of the former
broadly based movements?

Along the lines of social, income, and occupational stratification of the politically conscious
and active segments and groups of population, Ghana
presents the most clearcut case. There the military
intervention coincided with and to a certain extent
represented sharp opposition to the Nkrumah-CPP rule
on the part of the pre-independence indigenous bour-
geois-chiefly coalition. The former United Party,
whose leaders played a noticeable political role
throughout the period of military rule, had a well-
articulated platform and consistently opposed the
populist Nkrumahist coalition, whose most dynamic ingredient originally and for quite some time afterward was the new indigenous semi-literate Ghanaian
entrepreneur. The CPP nationalist and "socialist"
statist intervention,[2] not always at the expense of
the expatriate economic interests, well served
Nkrumah's purposes, and the "political kingdom"
(Nkrumah's favorite phrase) was a sure way to get a
place "under the sun." The Nkrumahist coalition
started cracking under the stresses of economic recession and the ever-growing isolation of the group
around the "Supreme Leader" from its natural social
base.

In Mali the situation by 1967-68 was similar to
that in Ghana of 1965-66, with several important differences. A much poorer and economically stagnant
country, Mali has not developed even the rudiments
of a new private entrepreneurial class. The traditionalist indigenous merchants, although sometimes
hurt by excessive nationalization and bureaucratic
controls, adjusted rather well to the US-RDA regime
and turned to their advantage even such evils as a
disorganized internal market, smuggling, and small-

scale corruption. The pre-independence intelligent-
sia and modern better-educated middle class were so
small, undeveloped, and/or nonexistent that there
was no place for a well-entrenched, articulate, and
sophisticated bourgeois opposition of the type
Nkrumah had to contend with.

As in Ghana, the military in Mali reflected the
widespread discontent of the population, but the
Malian military probably was closest in its attitudes
to the vague feelings of the peasantry. Unlike Ghana,
in Mali it was basically a contest between two groups
within the state bureaucracy--one in military uniforms and well-armed and the second in civilian dress
and supported by secret police and the so-called
People's Militia. In the absence of a coherent and
politically conscious opposition to the Modibo Keita
Union Soudanaise regime, the Malian army acted on
November 19, 1968, in almost a political vacuum, and
this action only imperfectly reflected the social
cleavages of Malian society.

In Dahomey, the civilian political order was
brought to a complete legal deadlock by three quarreling clans of the irresponsible, spoiled, and short-
sighted elite. Two of these political clubs, headed
by H. Maga and S. M. Apithy, had a distinct regional
base but did not significantly differ in social composition. The Apithy group had perhaps a higher percentage of traders and some rudiments of what may
later become an indigenous bourgeoisie. The Dahomeyan
trade unions, a privileged minority of about 2 percent of the total working population, representing
mostly civil servants, were more frequently allied
with the third political club, headed by J. Ahomadegbé
However, the basic ingredient of all three traditional
political clubs was provided by politicized and volatile civil servants and semi-employed intellectuals
who were scrambling for the spoils of public office.
At first the Dahomeyan military was unwillingly
dragged into politics as simply another, albeit armed,
interest group.[3]

In Sierra Leone the initial military coup, staged
by Brigadier D. Lansana, was in substantial part a
continuation by other means of struggle for power between two civilian political parties or blocs. Both
parties were amalgamations of numerous, often over-

lapping, social groups. The opposition (APC) was less conservative, had fewer paramount chiefs and their close relatives in the leadership, and had closer ties with trade unions, students, and the academic community in Freetown and among the urban unemployed. It also included a mildly radical youth wing, absent in the ruling SLPP. But these were not the issues. As in Dahomey the struggle was for the spoils and power of public offices, between two alliances of politicians with comparable programs and social clienteles.

It seems that, at least in this group of countries, military intervention in politics did not, in the most direct sense, result from cleavages between social classes. In Ghana it coincided and to a degree represented the conflicts between the upper and upper-middle indigenous strata in the most developed, stratified, and complex society of the sample. Mali is the lowest on the scale of social complexity, yet it ranks second in terms of reflecting social cleavages of the Malian society, however imperfectly and partially. In the middle of the scale--Dahomey and Sierra Leone--this relationship is least convincing, as other social cleavages tend to play more prominent roles.

REGIONAL-ETHNIC CLEAVAGES

The most talked-about among these other social cleavages are regional-ethnic ("tribal") conflicts. The two nationally unifying and centralizing regimes in Mali and Ghana seem to have reduced the relevance of these conflicts during the gestation period and at the initial stage of military intervention.[4] But in Ghana prolonged military rule brought them to the fore again, and the same might happen in Mali as well, although so far regional grievances and cleavages have been inconspicuous and without overt ethnic coloration.

In Sierra Leone and Dahomey the alleged danger of a bloody ethnic-communal confrontation was used extensively as a manifest justification after the Dahomey coup of December 22, 1965, and in Sierra Leone after the first and particularly after the

second coup on March 23, 1967. Taken in a direct
sense, these claims seem to have been largely exaggerated by the military in order to bolster the legit
imacy of military rule. In a wider social context
the blockage of civilian constitutional order was
provoked by clashes of the three (in Dahomey) and
two (in Sierra Leone) political blocs, which, althoug
in part ethnically overlapping, did have a rather
distinct regional base (this is not true only in regard to the third political bloc in Dahomey, represented by J. Ahomadegbé). It is difficult to disentangle clearly the various components of an essentially political struggle for scarce resources between the more or less privileged regions in Dahomey
and Sierra Leone. However, the ethnic-cultural coloration of these conflicts appears to me secondary
(and historically accidental).

As far as the military establishments themselves
were concerned, their ethnic composition largely distorted the lines of conflicts in the society at
large. If one can generalize about them, in the absence of recent reliable ethnic breakdowns, a compo-
site picture would be that the enlisted men come predominantly from the less developed regions while the
officer corps from more privileged (chiefly in terms
of education) and advanced areas. Ethnically influenced alignments among the officers did have political significance from time to time (notably in
the Dahomeyan coup of December 17, 1967), but even
there they tended to trail in importance behind corporate grievances and internal conflicts based on
other grounds (such as rank, age, and professional
background).

It seems that the relationship between regional-
ethnical cleavages and military intervention is rathe
weak, being influenced by other factors, and that it
is less important than is popularly believed.

SOCIAL ENGINEERING AND
DISEQUILIBRIUM

A much more salient factor seems to be the pattern and intensity of social engineering undertaken
prior to the coups by civilian elites. In three of

the four cases in this sample (Ghana, Sierra Leone, Mali) the initial military interventions were brought about at least in part and indirectly by the failures of such attempts. The "radical" Nkrumah-CPP regime in Ghana and the Modibo Keita-Union Soudanaise regime in Mali were the most ambitious in their intentions and less so in real attempts to transform the respective societies, to industrialize them, to reduce dependence on the former metropoles and on the West, as well as to achieve international influence and the goals of assertive Pan-Africanism.

The Ghanaian military in principle was agreeable to some of the nationalist goals (industrialization, greater self-reliance, international prestige). But as time passed its mute disagreement with other objectives, often only implicitly understood, and particularly with the methods used to achieve them, grew to reach the level of rejection and silent but bitter opposition. A substantial body in the officer corps contested in private the virtues of several radical departures from the social order that prevailed during the terminal years of British rule.[5] They opposed the downgrading of traditional authorities and of the established indigenous elite. They also criticized, both on practical and on more general grounds, what they considered to be excessive socialization in the economy, the cutting off of Ghana from the "traditional" (i.e., British, Anglo-Saxon) sources of capital, expertise, and markets. A separate but related chapter was their resentment of the subversion of the Africanized Westminster model with British-inspired norms and rules of the game, as well as their criticism of foreign policy moves deemed hostile to Britain and to the West.

However, despite these disagreements, determined plotting in the army started only after the Nkrumah-CPP tinkering with the social, economic, and political system directly and unmistakably affected the military's corporate interests. Grave miscalculations and mismanagement of the Ghanaian economy by the civilian elite, combined with the deteriorating world cocoa market, had direct repercussions on the budgetary allocations for defense; and inflation had eaten up a substantial part of the professional soldier's pay.

Furthermore the spread of the party and centralized government control jeopardized the traditional corporate autonomy of the army through political interference, secret police surveillance, and attempted indoctrination. The civilian authority also tried to divide the army internally and to change the traditional patterns of supplies and foreign technical assistance to the Ghanaian armed forces.

In addition, the growth of the presidential guard, security services, and the attempts to create para-military brigades posed a direct threat to the corporate existence of the army. When these consequences of social engineering and the consolidation of Nkrumah's dictatorial powers appeared obvious, attempted military intervention became inevitable and only a matter of time.

In Mali, the civilian elite had been more prudent. Even at the time of severe financial distress it did its utmost to avoid inflicting a serious decline in the material standards of the army personnel. In part this was due to an internal security threat and to armed defiance of the central government by the Touareg nomads in the North. Besides, Malian traditions of corporate autonomy and political noninvolvement were less pronounced than in Ghana, and the army chief of staff, Colonel Sékou Traoré, was made a member of the supreme political decision-making body.

The party-army symbiosis in Mali was more advanced and less resented than in Ghana as the officer corps, even the plotters, did not reject the fundamentals of the party platform. Yet the policy of radical transformation of Malian society inevitably led Modibo Keita to suppress all potential hotbeds of internal opposition and to step up secret police surveillance, including that of the army. It is debatable whether he had to threaten its existence by beefing up the armed People's Militia. Personal and corporate insecurity of the officer corps became sufficiently strong to outweigh all alleviating circumstances, and at the moment of the greatest weakness of the civilian regime the army moved in.

In Sierra Leone the failure of the SLPP policies of economic development had not really affected the army and did not reduce its material standards. Po-

litical meddling with the commissions and assignments
of senior officers in the Sierra Leone Force was
sporadic and had not deviated significantly from what
was permissible under the British system of civil-
military relations. The corporate security of the
army had never been in question. The ruling party
leadership relied on personal connections and the
allegiance of senior officers and did not try overt
politicization and indoctrination. The policies of
the Sierra Leone People's Party had been confined
almost exclusively to economic development within a
framework of an open, laissez-faire economy and did
not seriously and deliberately affect the existing
social system. Thus there were few grounds that
would have directly stimulated military intervention.
Instead it followed an electoral defeat of the ruling
party, caused fundamentally by the SLPP failure in
economic development and in limited and partial social change, with the military hierarchy initially
defending the discredited and corrupt regime.

In Dahomey none of the civilian governments
preceding the Soglo military-civilian coalition had
seriously tried or was capable of introducing radical
changes in Dahomeyan society. The civilian elites
were too busy scrambling for the spoils of the public
services payroll and for the side benefits of state
offices, while the country stagnated. The issue of
social disequilibrium introduced by the civilian
elite as a causal or contributing factor for military
intervention has not been relevant in Dahomey. More
important was the failure of the civilian elites to
do anything about the pressing problems of the country.

It seems that the pattern and intensity of social engineering undertaken by a civilian elite, and
the deliberate social disequilibrium caused by it,
has a direct bearing on the probability of overt
military intervention. The armies in Tropical Africa
have a separate and very different origin from the
ruling political parties (compare this, for example,
with China, Yugoslavia, Algeria); they were acculturated in the British and French norms of corporate
autonomy; and they inherited modified British and
French pay scales, which made them a very expensive
institution and a privileged well-armed minority.

Under the prevailing conditions a clash seems inevitable between a civilian regime effecting radical social change and expanding its power on the one hand and the army with a vested interest in preservin the fundamental ingredients of the social order that existed at the time independence was attained on the other.

Theoretically this could be avoided if such a civilian regime possesses extraordinary material resources that permit it to advance rapidly economically, have a generous patronage windfall, and pay off both the military and the formerly privileged social groups being displaced by the new elites (President K. Kaunda's regime in Zambia might be close to this in certain respects).

Another possibility is the strong political and military backing of an outside power, which has the effect of a credible deterrent. Former colonial powers generally accept this role only when social change reinforces their economic and strategic positions or is advantageous to them in some other important respects (for example, France in the Ivory Coast, Cameroun, and Gabon). This combination did not occur in the countries in this sample, and other outside powers were not sufficiently interested in underwriting and actively defending the radical regimes of Modibo Keita and Kwame Nkrumah.

ECONOMIC DIFFICULTIES

As was noted earlier the civilian regimes in Ghana, Mali, and in a less acute form Sierra Leone faced grave economic problems as a result of serious miscalculations, poor planning and execution in economic development, and waste of resources due to the lack of managerial and technical skills of the inexperienced ruling political elite. These regimes occasionally or often disregarded the profitability and viability of state enterprises, using them as tools of welfare and nepotism. Politically motivated and costly schemes of patronage and preoccupation with "politics" as opposed to "economics" also contributed to the economic difficulties.

112

The radical regimes, particularly that of Nkrumah, engaged themselves in excessive and unrealistic international prestige projects such as national airlines, airports, sumptuous public buildings, and presidential residences. They also conducted costly and ambitious foreign policy activities exceeding the financial resources of a given country and made serious foreign aid miscalculations.

To this one should add the waste of public funds through straightforward corruption, present in all four countries but particularly gross in Ghana and Sierra Leone. In Dahomey funds that otherwise could have been earmarked for developing the stagnant economy were consumed by the unreasonably large and costly but well-organized and volatile state administration. About 13,000 state employees and their families consumed 65 percent of the national budget and enjoyed an average monthly income of about $80 per employee, compared with the estimated average annual per capita income of about $60.[6] Mali has been less affected by this legally sanctioned parasitism.

The internal economic and social problems were combined in some instances with the deterioration of the terms of trade in several commodities prominently represented in the exports of Ghana and Dahomey. Ghana was badly hit by and did not react in time to the rapidly falling price of its main export commodity, cocoa. This downward movement started in the second half of 1960 and did not reverse until mid-1966. In Dahomey the falling prices of palm oil and palm products, the stagnant volume of agricultural production, and rising imports caused the steady decline of the export-import ratio from 71.8 percent under the French in 1959 to 31.2 percent by 1966.[7] The substantial foreign trade deficit of Sierra Leone (Le 12.6 million in 1966 and Le 14.7 million in 1967) and subsequent budgetary difficulties were only in a very small part caused by terms of trade. Most important was a drop in legally registered diamond exports and adverse weather conditions, which hurt agricultural exports.

The locally accumulated resources of the Malian state were reduced only insignificantly by the falling price of peanuts. They were more than compensated by a dramatic increase in exports of cotton, mainly

through the French company SFDT.[8] The actual drop
in officially recorded exports of the main export
commodities--cattle, grain, dried fish--was due to
the injudicious agricultural policies of the Malian
leadership. These policies resulted in a vastly increased smuggling and tax evasion.[9] The magnitude
of smuggling was approximately calculated by experts
of the World Bank as shown in Table 3.

To sum up, in two of the four cases (Sierra
Leone, Mali) financial and budgetary crises were
caused basically by internal developments. In one
case (Dahomey) there was a combination of adverse
conditions on the world market, domestic stagnation
in agricultural production, and the absence of any
significant progress in industrial development. In

TABLE 3

Recorded and Unrecorded Foreign Trade of Mali,
1965-68
(in millions of Malian francs)

	1965/66	1966/67	1967/68
Imports			
Recorded	9.41	7.80	12.63
Unrecorded	3.65	3.48	4.87
Total	13.06	11.28	17.50
Exports			
Recorded	3.05	4.14	5.06
Unrecorded	6.41	5.60	8.64
Total	9.46	9.74	13.70
Balance of trade			
Recorded	-6.36	-3.66	-7.57
Unrecorded	2.76	2.12	4.77
Total	-3.60	-1.54	-2.80

Source: International Bank of Reconstruction
and Development, International Development Association, Economic Development in Mali, Evolution, Problems and Prospects, Vol. I, Main Report (Washington,
D.C.: IDA, May 1970), Table 25.

one case (Ghana) the country did not offset the falling price of its main export commodity by increased
agricultural production, or alternatively by gaining
headway in industrial development and diversifying
exports. In two out of four cases (Ghana, Dahomey)
the high dependence on a single item of agricultural
export and the high vulnerability of the domestic
economy significantly contributed to economic crises.
     In all four cases military intervention followed
within a time span varying from several days (Ghana)
to several months of the announcement and implementation of new austerity measures by civilian governments. However, the total time lag between the beginning of the most recent phase of austerity could be
so long (in Ghana between 1961 and 1966; in Mali between 1963 and 1968; Dahomey has been in a perpetual
economic crisis since independence) that no direct
relation could be established between economic difficulties and military intervention, except for a
general statement that acute shortages in the resource allocation system could contribute to military
intervention. The staying power of a given regime
and the quality of civilian leadership and its ability
to guide, persuade, and control are critical factors.
     Military coups also occur in the absence of
economic difficulties (Libya) and could be avoided
for long periods of time under the most severe economic stress (Guinea, Haiti).
     The mistakes in economic development made by the
leaders of Ghana, Mali, and Sierra Leone were not
uniquely African.* But under the conditions of
scarcity, these mistakes had much more severe social
and political consequences than would have been the
case in richer, more diversified and developed econ-
omies and in better integrated societies. In a dif-

---

     *Grave miscalculations, mismanagement, incompe-
tence, and colossal waste of resources have been known
to most developed countries and to great powers having very divergent social and political systems: the
TFX fighter plane and the SST projects in the United
States; the "virgin lands" and the Great Turkmenian
Canal projects in the USSR; and "The Great Leap Forward" in China are only a few examples.

ferent geopolitical context--i.e., if they were more
important to the USSR or to the People's Republic of
China, and given massive foreign aid--the Ghanaian
and Malian regimes might have gotten away even with
those mistakes.*

CORRUPTION

Conspicuous and large-scale corruption can seriously hamper economic development. It also represents an important aspect and a side effect of the
degeneration and decline of a civilian regime and
reduces its ability to resist a military coup. The
extent of the most visible forms and allegations of
corruption certainly provided an impetus to military
intervention in Ghana in 1966. The abortive counter-
coup of April 17, 1967, also was justified by its
author, Lieutenant S. Arthur, in part on the grounds
of corruption, but this time as practiced by the military rulers themselves. In Dahomey junior officers,
who staged the coup on December 17, 1967, were motivated in part by continuing misappropriations and
self-enrichment under the military-civilian govern-·
ment of General Soglo and by the complicity in it of
several senior officers.
In Sierra Leone corruption was not an issue during the March 21 and March 23, 1967, coups as far as
the military leaders were concerned. However, very
credible accusations of government corruption, misappropriation, and misspending previously leveled by
the opposition strongly compromised the ruling party
and the prime minister, Sir Albert Margai. Corruption contributed to the ensuing electoral defeat of
the Sierra Leone People's Party, but on the other
hand the fear of prosecution strengthened the determination of the group around Sir Albert to block the
constitutional system and to stage a military coup.
Hence corruption indirectly prompted military inter-

---

*One could speculate on whether the Cuban, Mon-
golian, or Albanian solutions of social engineering
and economic development could have been applicable
in West Africa.

vention. Once the second military junta was in power
it changed its stand and made the struggle against
corruption an important part of the government program. And like Lieutenant Arthur in Ghana, the mutineers on April 17, 1968, accused the National Reformation Council of the same sin and called the new
junta the Anti-Corruption Revolutionary Movement.
However, that was basically a pay strike for better
material and other conditions of the service, with
corruption used as a popular political slogan.

In Mali corruption played no noticeable role as
a factor motivating the leaders of the successful
coup on November 19, 1968. The same also was true
of the alleged abortive attempted coup in August
1969. It seems that poverty and certain puritanical
traditions in Mali made conspicuous large-scale corruption difficult and reduced the importance of this
issue.[10]

This review indicates that nowhere in the countries in the sample, even in Ghana under Nkrumah and
Sierra Leone under Sir Albert Margai, did corruption
reach such proportions as to directly affect budgetary
allocations for defense and to cause inflation, and
hence to push the military into action to defend its
material interests. The criticism of corruption was
important, primarily in Ghana and to a lesser extent
in Sierra Leone, as a manifest justification for
military rule and as a legitimizing symbol, but it
clearly was secondary in the military's motivation
to intervene. The strength of the issue of corruption naturally declines when the coup-makers themselves are not very different in this respect from
the previous elite.

THE COMPETITIVENESS OF THE
CIVILIAN POLITICAL ORDER

Turning to the organization of political power
under civilian regimes prior to military intervention,
one can conditionally use the distinction competitive-
noncompetitive. The application of this tool requires
a clear understanding of the existence of several
dimensions of competitiveness and the willingness to
anticipate possible strong intervening variables.

117

The relativity of this dichotomy is well-known. Moreover the political systems of the four countries in the sample all had been competitive up to a point and on a certain level of analysis.

However, the selection of two closely related features of the political process--the legally sanctioned and in fact existing periodic or regularized competition of political parties at the ballot box and the tolerance of the centers of political activity and of influence outside and contrary to the wishes and preferences of the regime--permits us to place the four polities on a continuum. The contrasts relevant to the purposes of this inquiry are particularly visible when one looks at the two pair within the English-speaking and the French-speaking halves of the sample: Ghana versus Sierra Leone and Mali versus Dahomey. The still remaining, although eroded, prevalence of the Western norms of electoral political games in Sierra Leone and Dahomey produced a sufficiently different political climate that affected military intervention. Without dwelling any longer on the real meaning of the dichotomy under conditions of bloc voting and of a more direct impact of economic patronage than elsewhere, I shall divide the four countries--for the limited purposes of this inquiry--into legally competitive or semicompetitive (Dahomey and Sierra Leone) and noncompetitive (Ghana and Mali).

The erosion of political ballot box competition can be related to or followed by the development of internal intelligence, political surveillance, and control of the politicized population. If the resources of the police establishment are to a significant extent channeled in this direction as opposed to the conventional maintenance of law and order, this instrument of political control can, up to a point, inhibit and make difficult seditious activities. In Africa, however, they can hardly prevent an insurrection in the long run, if not accompanied by other--economic and political--means of removing or mediating social tensions.

The capacity of police to control internal dangers to the regimes is limited even in the most "policed" states of Tropical Africa, if compared with police establishments elsewhere. As there are no

reliable figures on the actual size of the internal
security personnel in the strict sense, it is difficult to make valid comparisons between Tropical Africa and other groups of poor countries. It seems,
however, that this side of governmental effectiveness remains relatively rudimentary in West Africa
both in quality and quantity.* Among the countries
in the sample Ghana and Mali seem to have more developed systems of internal political surveillance.

It appears that "noncompetitiveness" as such,
and taken in the specific sense, does not inhibit
military intervention but can make it more violent.
The competitiveness of civilian politics in Dahomey
and Sierra Leone produced several situations of stalemate in the constitutional system, which in turn were
used by the military as a justification for the coups.
On the other hand the military in Ghana and in Mali
justified their own insurrection against the established civilian authority by the lack of competitiveness and by the concentration of state power in the
hands of the single-party leadership. In other
words, both "competitive" and "noncompetitive" political systems contain in themselves important sources

---

*The only available, although unsatisfactory,
computation of the total internal security forces per
10,000 adults was made by Ted Gurr for the period
around 1962. The figures for the four countries in
the sample and several selected countries of similar
size from other regions are as follows:

Ghana	24.1	Libya	135.9
Sierra Leone	16.3	Albania	107.0
Dahomey	12.6	Nicaragua	83.8
Mali	4.6	Bulgaria	75.2
		Haiti	59.6

Source: Ted Gurr, New Error-Compensated Measures of Comparing Nations: Some Correlates of
Civil Violence, Center of International Studies Research Monograph No. 25 (Princeton, N.J.: Princeton
University, 1966), pp. 118-23. To obtain more realistic figures for Dahomey and Mali, Gurr should have
included the Gendarmerie in internal security forces.

of latent instability conducive to military intervention.

This is not to say that the competitiveness of the civilian regime is without consequences for the genesis of the military rule that supplants it. Police control, more pronounced in noncompetitive political systems, makes plotting very difficult and dangerous. The top appointments in the armies of Ghana and Mali (for example, those of Major-General C. M. Barwah, chief of army staff in Ghana, and Colonel Sékou Traoré, chief of staff in Mali) were made in view of assuring both political or personal loyalty to the president and the regime.

Political manipulation at the top and close secret police surveillance made the participation of the highest ranking officers in the plotting and in the execution very difficult.

In both noncompetitive cases (Ghana and Mali) the coups were executed by officers in intermediary positions of direct operative control of military units. In both cases the plotters used almost exclusively oral face-to-face communications during the gestation period and with the troops at the initial stages of insurrection. These two coups were directed against the civilian regimes and at the same time against the top brass, even though a number of the latter (particularly in Ghana) had sympathies for the cause of the insurrection.*

One should not, however, overstate the case (Uganda, for instance, recently provided a conflicting example[11]). A sufficiently long tenure of a noncompetitive regime in Tropical Africa seems to promote, up to a point, divisiveness within the military establishment during the gestation period and at the time of the execution of a coup. It is theoretically possible in a noncompetitive situation to recreate

---

*Furthermore the "secondary" or follow-up military coups in Ghana (abortive coup of April 17, 1967), Dahomey (December 17, 1967), and Sierra Leone (April 17, 1968) all happened in noncompetitive situations, all originated in intermediary and/or lower echelons of the army, and painfully divided the military establishment.

the army and to make it almost homogeneous in terms
of norms, training, and ethnic background, but there
are almost no countries where one could easily envision, in practical terms, such a departure from
the status quo. Besides, certain cleavages in the
army (functional, organizational, age) cannot be
eliminated even if the government succeeds in bringing it entirely under control and incorporating the
army into the regime.

The difficulties of plotting in noncompetitive
systems tend to eliminate political preparations for
the coup and the subsequent period of military rule.
The nucleus of the incipient junta usually is very
small, for security reasons. In Ghana it consisted
of two active organizers plus at the final stage the
chief of police, in Mali of four to five, as against
at least ten top officers of the Dahomeyan army, who
for weeks carried on consultations with civilians
and foreigners before moving in on December 22, 1965.
Similar preparations could have been carried out in
Sierra Leone too, were it not for the fact that the
March 21, 1967, coup was decided upon only about two
days earlier. The lack of thinking and preparation
has multiple effects depending on such factors as
the composition of the junta, the political and intellectual caliber of its leading and most influential members, the relative strength of the civil service, and the influence of civilian opposition groups
to the ousted regime.

The noncompetitiveness and strong police surveillance accompanying it also affected the composition of the junta. Preoccupied with the security aspects of the plotting and with sheer survival, the
seditious officers hardly could apply rational principles of selecting a good and viable ruling body for
the country once the coup succeeded. They typically
approached and recruited close friends and those officers who, often by accident, happened to occupy
critical positions in the military establishment (intelligence, ammunition depots, signal corps) from
the standpoint of the purely technical success of
the coup. The result of all these circumstances in
Mali was a regionally/ethnically imbalanced ruling
body, lacking in intellectual qualities, general education, and political skills. In Ghana this situation

was alleviated by the higher educational standards
of the top brass, the political skills of the police
members of the National Liberation Council, and
sheer luck.

Briefly, the noncompetitiveness of the preceding
civilian political order tends to divide the military
establishment and to weaken rational elements in
selecting a viable and appropriate military junta for
the country and, from this point of view, has a negative effect on military rule. On the other hand if
noncompetitiveness and other accompanying features
produce deep hostility in the military establishment
and in the polity at large, this opposition enhances
the internal cohesion of the junta and strengthens
military rule by assuring it substantial initial
popularity. In other words, very strong and repre-
hensible "noncompetitiveness," accompanied by what
are considered brutalities, is likely to produce
beneficial effects for military rule that outweigh
its negative effects (divisiveness and irrationality).
Milder and more socially acceptable noncompetitiveness
seems to have mainly negative effects on the incipient military rule.

MASS MOBILIZATION AND ITS
PARA-MILITARY EXPRESSION

Neither political scientists nor African rulers
have reliable instruments to measure correctly the
degree of real mass mobilization and population participation, or to distinguish the docile acquiesence
of cheering crowds at official ceremonies from internally motivated adherence to the regime. The African
rulers certainly are aware that it is less than total,
but their own tools of consolidating power prevent
them from assessing it realistically.

It appears that there is a direct link between
one facet of mass mobilization and military intervention. In Mali and Ghana the attempts by Keita and
Nkrumah to give mass mobilization a para-military expression served as important stimulants of military
intervention since they directly touched on the corporate security of the military establishment. The
Mali (particularly) and Ghana coups represented a

122

strong armed preemptive reaction to these attempts.
The existence of para-military formations of the
ruling party in Mali was taken into consideration
very seriously by the military plotters at the time
of the preparations. The Malian military junta directed the main punch against the People's Militia
and, as it turned out, overrated it. In Ghana the
Workers' Brigades were unarmed and the threat to the
army came instead from the presidential guard, a
privileged and isolated part of the regular armed
forces. In Dahomey and Sierra Leone there had been
little mass mobilization and participation in politics anyway.

In brief, it seems that only the para-military
aspect of mass mobilization and participation through
the mechanism of the mass party has significant bearing on military intervention. Depending upon their
credibility and real coercive strength, para-military
auxiliaries of the ruling political movements can
either deter military intervention or, when these
two qualities are lacking but the para-military force
still represents a potential danger to the army,
serve as a strong stimulant.

EXTERNAL ENVIRONMENT

In the discussion of economic difficulties the
question was raised of the interrelationship between
the external (to the polity) environment and military
intervention. This question has four main aspects:
external general political climate, external economic
climate, direct foreign intervention or subversion,
and the contagion of military groups.

The first two of these dimensions have been
brought to the fore by those who claim that the military coups against Nkrumah and Keita were staged
and/or teleguided by the Western powers and were a
part of a much wider intercontinental conspiracy
against radical and leftist regimes.[12]

In the present group of countries the military
coups in Dahomey (December 1967) and in Sierra Leone
(March 21 and March 23, 1967) happened in strategically and politically unimportant countries and from
the standpoint of the former colonial powers were

exclusively internal political affairs. The coups
changed nothing or next to nothing in the relations
of the two African countries with their former metropoles. These relations were not even a minor issue
of military intervention.

There are some indications that the French mildly
favored the advent of General Soglo, chief of staff.
They and the U.S. ambassador, who had been interested
for some time in reversing President Apithy's decision to establish diplomatic relations with the People's Republic of China, might have contacted the
general prior to the coup. It has been asserted in
Dahomey that the previous Apithy government already
had a standing American offer of a $5 million loan
if Dahomey changed its position.* The Soglo government did precisely that, but has not received the
loan. The French, however, had nothing to do with
the ousting a month earlier of President Apithy, who
was as pro-French as General Soglo, which finally led
to the establishment of a military-civilian government.

The external environment of Dahomey in December
1965 was mildly favorable to a coup, but the coup's
immediate cuases--fragmentation and quarreling among
the three blocs of civilian politicians and a deadlock of the constitutional system--were hardly affected by it. Of course, one could go much further
back into the modern political history of Dahomey
and argue that the fragmentation of the elite on a
regional-ethnic basis closely followed the uneven
overlay of French colonization and Western education
or were due to divisive policies of the colonizer.
But this also is true of practically all countries
of Tropical Africa, and no one has shown that the inequalities and cleavages did not exist in Dahomey
before the colonization and/or would not have occurred without it. On the other hand the Dahomeyan
elites could not unite even during the anti-colonial
ferment, and since independence have not faced an

-----

*This might have been a misunderstanding on the
Dahomeyan side, as the United States seems to have
been ready to finance a joint Dahomeyan-Togolese
road project.

external threat or challenge that might have driven them together.

Substantial autonomy of military intervention was manifested in Dahomey in December 1967 when otherwise pro-French military officers of the intermediary and lower ranks ousted General Soglo, who clearly was favored and politically and economically supported by the French government and by General de Gaulle personally. Even in the face of Dahomey's overwhelming dependence on France, the new junta dared to disobey and to stage what it knew in advance would meet with disapproval in Paris. However, the junta hoped to get away with it and to retain the budgetary support promised to General Soglo by De Gaulle about two weeks earlier. Nevertheless, this support was withheld by the affronted French government. Despite the lack of any appreciable public support for the coup at home and in the face of serious economic difficulties, the military junta of the young cadres carried out its program and stayed in power for eight months.

As far as Sierra Leone is concerned, the British had some reasons to be dissatisfied with Prime Minister Sir Albert Margai, who had sharply attacked them on the question of Southern Rhodesia. Despite his verbal radicalism in foreign relations, Sir Albert and his government had not undermined British economic interests in Sierra Leone. Contrary to the claims in the Guinean press and to some nationalist hints in his party's propaganda, the British have not opposed the severing of ties between Sierra Leone and the British Crown. It has been a legal fiction anyway. On the contrary, the strongest pressure against the republic has come from inside the country, and the operation presented very complicated problems not to Britain but to Sierra Leone. Even if the frictions between the two countries had caused some displeasure in London, the coup staged by Brigadier Lansana on March 21, 1967, was in support of the defeated Sir Albert, not against him; and the two subsequent coups (March 23, 1967, and April 17, 1968) had no appreciable bearing on Sierra Leone's relations with Great Britain and the West.

All three coups in Sierra Leone met with the approval, in varying degrees, of the government of neighboring Guinea. President Sékou Touré rendered political support to Sir Albert Margai, who subsequently was defeated in the general election, and concluded with him a secret agreement of mutual assistance in the event of an external or internal threat to their respective regimes. From the late autumn of 1967 President Sékou Touré had offered hospitality, material, and technical assistance in Guinea, this time to Siaka Stevens, Sir Albert's rival, and to his party. With Guinean help Stevens and other leaders of the APC maintained contacts with the internal opposition to the military junta, carried out hostile propaganda in Sierra Leone, and trained a small number of "freedom fighters." But the coup-mutiny of April 17, 1968, occurred almost exclusively because of internal corporate reasons of the army, was basically a pay strike, and initially did not have a pro-APC political coloration.

In Mali the Union Soudanaise regime had taken since independence a number of steps that limited or almost eliminated French interests and influence in several areas. French troops left the bases in Mali. The regime introduced Malian national currency on July 1, 1962, and left the West African (French) Monetary Union but not the zone of the French franc. The Malians also nationalized foreign trade, which used to be dominated in imports chiefly by French private capital, and diversified the pattern of foreign trade and foreign aid, mainly in the direction of socialist countries. Malian leadership and diplomacy had helped the Algerian rebels and had sharply criticized and condemned several French actions, such as nuclear explosions in the Sahara desert.

On the other side the break between Mali and its former colonial metropole was never complete and bitter. The Malians continued to receive French technical assistance and to use French establishments of higher learning. There were some common grounds in the Malian policy of nonalignment and De Gaulle's foreign posture. Mali, a landlocked and poor country without known mineral endowment or other resources, with almost negligible French private investments and a few French residents, has been and now is of little economic, strategic, or political interest to France. The traditional pattern of Malian trade consisted of exporting agricultural produce (cattle, grain, dried fish) to neighboring French-dominated African territories and importing processed goods and some agricultural produce from the same countries (mostly Senegal, later also from the Ivory Coast) and/or from France, directly or indirectly.

The change in the state-controlled foreign trade in practice meant importing industrial equipment and services on credit from the East without realistic prospects of repayment. Because the Malian state could not enforce its monopoly of foreign trade and could not stop the rise of smuggling, actual sales in Mali of goods produced in France or by French-owned companies in Senegal and the Ivory Coast probably had not seriously decreased in value. The French lost some potential exports of industrial equipment and other goods and services that would have necessitated state subsidies and increased foreign aid. But the change, barely noticed in Paris, severely damaged Mali. It caused a heavy outflow of private Malian capital, disorganized the internal market, and reduced government receipts from export duties (one of the main sources of revenue). The shortages forced the government to import grain to feed the urban population, while private traders continued to export Malian grain illegally. The government policies made officially recorded exports and imports even more expensive than before because the Malians had refused to use the only railroad (Bamako-Dakar) available to them. The role of foreign assistance and the accompanying rise in Mali's indebtedness can be seen in Table 4.

Finally, four years after the proud announcement of a national currency, it was the Malian leadership, not the French, who asked to be taken back. In late 1966 they were on the verge of bankruptcy and admitted a political defeat. In February 1967 Mali accepted the conditions for French backing of the Malian currency, which was thus to become convertible again, for renewed French credits and expanded economic, technical, and cultural assistance. The conditions were harsh: French control of monetary emission, curbed inflation, reduced budgetary spending, reorganization of the public sector, and eventually the closing of hopelessly unprofitable state enterprises.

TABLE 4

Selected Indicators Related to External Financing of
Economic Development in Mali

	1959	1964/65	1965/66	1966/67
GDP (in millions of U.S. dollars)	269.4	366.2	383.2	421.3
Per capita income (in U.S. dollars)	60	80	82	89
Estimated gross disbursement of foreign assistance (in billions of MF)				
France		2.4	2.0	1.5
EEC		2.1	2.4	1.5
People's Republic of China		1.8	1.1	1.4
USSR		2.7	1.8	2.2
Other		4.3	5.8	4.0
Total		13.3	13.1	10.6

External Public Debt (in millions of U.S. dollars)		1966	1967	1968
Total debt outstanding, including undisbursed		193.1	213.0	211.2
Total debt service		9.2	8.0	5.4

Source: International Bank of Reconstruction
and Development, International Development Association, Economic Development in Mali, Evolution, Problems and Prospects, Vol. I, Main Report (Washington, D.C.: IDA, May 1970), basic data.

But at least in principle these conditions did not foreclose the continuity of the Malian socialist experiment and the Malian leadership, including its Marxist hardliners, still had hopes in this respect. Modibo Keita's downfall, in immediate political terms, resulted from the fact that he was caught between the negative popular reaction to the harsh austerity measures and his unwillingness and inability to go all the way through a painful reappraisal of strategy and policies.

We know of no indication that the French government negotiated the Franco-Malian agreements of 1967 in bad faith and laid a trap for the Malian radicals. It seems that the Malian leadership shortly before the coup seriously considered renouncing the agreements,* but this does not change the fact that Mali, regardless of who was in power, needed France more than vice versa. The new military regime, presumably pro-French, long has resisted the French demands to close the unprofitable state enterprises and in certain respects has displayed more nationalism and pride in relations with the former metropole than did the previous radical regime.

Despite the ex post facto sympathy for the military coup in the West and the conjectures concerning the French training of the future junta, Lieutenant Moussa Traoré's stay in France in 1968, and several others, we came to the conclusion that as of today there is no evidence to support the charges of foreign conspiracy. French intelligence might have had fragmentary knowledge that something was in the offing, as the question of a possible coup had been in wide circulation in Bamako for months. But it is doubtful that the French knew the identity of the plotters and had contacted them.

It seems certain that high French officials and the embassy in Bamako were in the dark. More important, the accumulated internal problems and cleavages were more than ample to hasten Modibo Keita's downfall. Opposition to his rule in Mali was sufficiently

---

*We see no immediate connection between the vacillation of the Malian leadership and the coup of November 19, 1968.

129

widespread and potent to support an unconstitutional
change for the lack of an institutionalized alternative. Any outside assistance to the coup or interference with it would have been unnecessary--even
detrimental to it.

In Ghana the Nkrumah-CPP regime had made many
steps deemed prejudicial to the West throughout the
years and particularly after 1961. Nkrumah spent
most of the substantial sterling reserves in Britain
and undermined the almost exclusive position of Britain and British-American private capital in the modern sector of the Ghanaian economy. The CPP leadership also diversified Ghanaian foreign trade, foreign
relations, foreign aid, and other ties, thus opening
Ghana, formerly an exclusive preserve of the West,
to the Eastern powers, smaller socialist countries,
Arab countries more or less hostile to the West,
and so forth. Ghana conducted an activist and ambitious foreign policy both in Africa and elsewhere,
loudly attacking Western imperialism and neocolonial-
ism on numerous issues (South Africa, the Congo,
Southern Rhodesia, nuclear tests, Vietnam) and thereby
sometimes annoying the Western powers. Nkrumah's
regime had lent political, organizational, and financial support to various political groups and individuals in Africa who claimed to be or were in fact
openly or clandestinely struggling against the remnants of Western colonialism, apartheid, white racism,
or against regimes directly supported by the Western
powers or strongly pro-Western. Nkrumah also had
enlisted Soviet, Chinese, East German, and Czechoslo-
vak security and military assistance in order to dis-
rupt in numerous ways Western positions and influence
in Africa. This list of Nkrumah's "sins" is not complete, but sufficient to understand, to put it mildly,
the unfriendly feelings in the West toward his regime.

On the other hand Nkrumah had never severed all
his ties with Great Britain, the United States, West
Germany, the Commonwealth, and smaller Western nations, and until the last moment tried to maneuver
between the West and the East. Although the USSR
and East European countries had become important foreign trade partners of Ghana, economically the country remained largely within the Western zone of influence. Despite serious frictions in foreign policy,

the West remained the main source of capital and
know-how for the developing Ghanaian economy and provided over 80 percent of all credits. The biggest
industrial project, the Akosombo High Dam, the alumi-
num smelter, and related installations were built by
an American concern with U.S. public funds backing
it. During his last months in office, Nkrumah un-
successfully tried to obtain a Western loan of $1
billion.

Nkrumah's position was contradictory but not
unmanageable. He did not overcome the reservations
toward him in the Soviet and Chinese leadership.
Despite difficult and unpleasant relations with him,
the Western powers, primarily the United States, did
not consider Ghana important enough strategically,
economically, and politically to undertake a direct
action against Nkrumah. Their displeasure undoubtedly
was known to the silent opposition in Ghana, encouraged it, and possibly resulted in some contributions
to the opposition groups abroad.

So far there has been no evidence that the West
went any further.* Above all it was unnecessary.
Internal opposition to Nkrumah in the army, police,

---

*One of the most knowledgeable sources of the ex-
ternal conspiracy allegations, Geoffrey Bing, Nkrumah's
former attorney-general and the author of Reap the
Whirlwind (London: McGibbon and Kee, 1968), could
not give me any convincing evidence on this score.
My personal conclusion, after carefully looking into
the matter, was that in 1965-66 the British and U.S.
embassies could expect a coup. Probably the only
Ghanaian in a position to throw a new light on the
"Western conspiracy theory," J. W. K. Harlley, is
not likely to do so, thereby inflicting damage on
his former British superiors, mentors, and friends.
The argument that Nkrumah in the long run was ousted
through hideously manipulated cocoa prices on the
world market cannot stand up to serious criticism.
Even if it were possible, in 1966 Ghana's share of
the world market amounted to about 35 percent, and
the depression affected other producers as well, including those with strongly pro-Western governments
(Nigeria, for example).

131

university, civil service, and among most of the groups of urban and rural population was sufficiently widespread and strong enough to destroy the regime once its security force was neutralized. It is unlikely that the engineer of the coup, Colonel E. Kotoka, had plotted with foreign interests or with their agents. This would have been too dangerous and probably fatal. Besides, he did not need friendly foreign interference. The expected jubilant reaction in the West was important not for the staging of the coup but to assure economic and political support after it was over. Even without it the military regime probably would have survived anyway.

If to this day there is no available evidence of direct interference, could not it be that the general political climate and the high degree of economic cultural, and, less frequently, direct political dependence on the West somehow promotes or influences military intervention, at least in West Africa?

The evidence in the sample suggests the existence of relative autonomy of political processes in the four states, despite a high degree of economic and cultural dependence of the modern sector and the urban areas in them on Western markets, sources of capital, education, and know-how. The relative autonomy of political change, including here military intervention, has been observed elsewhere. In the four countries in the sample it is helped by the near self-sufficiency in basic food products, coupled with the fact that up to 90 percent of the population (in Mali) lives under conditions of subsistence agriculture. Besides, even small and weak African polities to a certain extent could take advantage of modest rivalries between the great powers and conflicting interests of other countries (Israel versus the Arab states, for example). The region as a whole and the countries in the sample were not sufficiently important to the great powers to warrant outright or thinly veiled intervention as occurred in Iran, Guatemala, Suez (U.A.R.), the Bay of Pigs (Cuba), and in Czechoslovakia.* Selective African sensitivity

---

*The clouds of not completely improbable French and/or entente intervention passed over the Dahomeyan

to such undertakings on the continent and what is left of Pan-Africanism and African-Asian solidarity probably contributed to it and made similar interventions politically costly compared to conceivable gains.

Not included in the sample are the African countries and regimes deemed to be strategically, economically, and politically important to France. This former colonial metropole is the only outside power that maintains regular military forces on the soil of politically independent countries of Tropical Africa. These units, plus the specially trained airborne forces of intervention based in southern France, constitute a credible deterrent to domestic military intervention, sedition, and insurrection, and actually have been used in Senegal, Cameroun, Gabon, and Chad. Thus the "French-speaking" half of the sample could be viewed as representative only of African countries less important to France.[13]

Unlike any other great power in Africa, France has treaty rights and obligations to intervene militarily in the cases of immediate external or internal danger to the governments of a majority of its former

---

scene on two or three occasions, notably in December 1967. But in our sample the most explicit threat of foreign intervention after a coup was made not by a great power but by militarily weak Guinea when President Sékou Touré declared publicly that he would send the Guinean army to Ghana, across the territory and despite the immediate protests and rebuttal of the Ivory Coast. The plotters in Ghana and Mali seem to have been not quite sure whether Nkrumah and Keita had some secret arrangements or agreements with the Soviet Union. Several pronouncements of the Malian leadership in 1968, the Soviet-Malian negotiations in July, and Malian support for the Warsaw Pact Soviet-led invasion of Czechoslovakia in August 1968 were thought to indicate the desire of Modibo Keita and the Union Soudanaise radicals to obtain the status of a full-fledged "socialist country" and an associate of the Soviet bloc, coupled with guarantees similar to those enjoyed by Cuba. The Soviets have denied that they had given any military guarantees to Mali.

colonies. "Mutually" binding "bilateral" agreements in the area of defense and security were not concluded only with a few former French colonies (Guinea, Mali, Upper Volta).

Despite these rights and obligations, and despite explicit demands by the governments involved, France did not intervene in a number of cases. The first was in August 1963 in Congo-Brazzaville, where the French changed their mind at the last moment, did not use the paratroopers who had already arrived from Dakar, and let fall the strongly pro-French, conservative, and unpopular regime of F. Youlou. De Gaulle initially rejected a similar demand by President Tombalbaye of Chad and only with reluctance sent French reinforcements (chiefly the Foreign Legion paratroopers from Corsica) in 1969.

It is believed that France is firmly committed and would intervene almost automatically in Senegal, the Ivory Coast, Cameroun, and Gabon, and somewhat less certainly in Niger and on Madagascar. The major criteria are strategic importance (air and naval bases in Dakar, Senegal, and Diégo-Suarez on Madagascar), political and economic importance (Senegal, the Ivory Coast, Cameroun), substantial French private investments and French enclaves (Senegal, the Ivory Coast, Cameroun), and deposits of uranium (Gabon, Niger). The French intervened in Chad mainly because of Niger uranium and the important air base in Fort Lamy. President Tombalbaye also used a sentimental argument with De Gaulle--the importance of Chad in the first successful military operation by Free French troops during World War II under the future Marshal Leclerc.

The certainty of French military intervention in recent years has been one of the chief and effective deterrents of internal military coups in the countries covered by firm French guarantees. It ought to be added that Paris, exposed to domestic and international pressures, is more tolerant, flexible, and relatively less "neocolonialist" than the French colons, who are most numerous in the richest and climatically more agreeable "French-speaking" countries.

The British no longer have a comparable lobby in the independent tropical African countries undomi-

nated by white minorities of European extraction.
The bulk of British investments and English-speaking
whites are elsewhere on the continent, i.e., in the
South African Republic and Southern Rhodesia. These
circumstances have an appreciable bearing on the very
low probability of direct British military intervention in tropical Africa.

The British have "decolonized" their relations
with Africa much more thoroughly than the French.
Instead of strong paternalism supplemented by the
instruments of tight political, military, and economic
control, they rely primarily on the self-interest of
local elites. These elites have been substantially
acculturated into Afro-British traditions and have a
very real stake in the continuing junior partnership
with British and Anglo-American capital and in basically retaining the traditional pattern of trade relations, markets, sources of capital, and technology.
In these respects the "English-speaking" half of the
sample appears sufficiently representative.

It seems that if the conditions for special
French interests are not operative, there is no significant variation in the military intervention-re-
lated vulnerability of the four countries in the sample, according to the level of economic development,
degree of monetization of the economy, level of ur-
banization, percentage of exports in the GNP, and
other socioeconomic indicators. However, the margin
between a healthy and sufficiently rapid economic
development and an economic crisis is very narrow,
depending primarily on the qualities of elites and
leadership.

Finally, the phenomenon of contagion certainly
influenced military intervention in all four cases.
The Dahomeyan coup of December 22, 1965, was
the second intervention of the Dahomeyan military in
politics, and by that time the relative strength of
external stimulants already had lost its potency compared with internal Dahomeyan and intra-army causes
and motivations. But the first coup on October 28,
1963 certainly was influenced by the assassination
of President Sylvanus Olympio and a military takeover
on January 13, 1963, in next-door Togo. The distance
from the Dahomeyan capitals (Cotonou and Porto-Novo)
to the Togolese border is only about 40 miles, and

there are many family and other close ties across the frontier. The coup in Congo-Brazzaville on August 15, 1963, in which a coalition of the army and the trade unions ousted the regime of Abbot Filbert Youlou,[14] also had an impact, and the Dahomeyan coup of October 1963 took a similar form.

This Dahomeyan coup influenced in turn the thinking of Captain Yoro Diakité of the Malian army, the chief architect of the coup against the regime of Modibo Keita and the Union Soudanaise in Mali on November 19, 1968. The Malian plotters undoubtedly keenly followed the coups that occurred elsewhere in Africa, particularly in Ghana and Algeria.

The Ghanaian coup on February 24, 1966, was influenced in part by the unsuccessful coup of January 15, 1966, in Nigeria. It was led by Major Chukwuma Nzeogwu of the Nigerian army,[15] a former schoolmate at Sandhurst of Major A. A. Afrifa, the secondary architect and executor of the anti-Nkrumah coup. Other Ghanaian officers who at one point or another contemplated an insurrection were well aware of the military coups that occurred in other Commonwealth Afro-Asian countries, particularly in Pakistan and the Sudan.

The Sierra Leone coup-makers were impressed with the examples of Ghana and Nigeria, which by then had experienced another violetn change. H. Fisher comments:

> In Sierra Leone this contagion affected not only Army officers. One of the most prominent and respected civilians in the country told the NRC [the junta; Fisher apparently had in mind Dr. Davidson Nicol, principal of Fourah Bay College] the day after they took power, that he had been in touch with General Ankrah [of Ghana] and the Nigerian regime for the previous six months, and that Sierra Leone could profit from their experience. These views apparently carried considerable weight with Juxon-Smith at this stage. Even the political opposition had toyed with such ideas: on October 22, 1966, an article in We Yone had suggested that it might be a good thing, in order to

avert financial disaster, to suspend the
constitution and have a period of Army direction.[16]

It appears that external contagion plays an appreciable role particularly during the gestation period of the first military coup in a given country.
Later its importance diminishes for the makers of
the original coup but not necessarily for the new
pretenders to supreme state power. The pattern of
contagion shows the still strong influence of colonial
heritage, as the impact seems stronger within each
of the two major groups of the African states--French-
speaking and English-speaking. In the latter group,
the stimulants coming from another Commonwealth country out of the region, or even out of Africa, could
be stronger than an example of a geographically much
closer French-speaking country. A similar situation
still seems to prevail among the French-speaking
countries of Tropical and North Africa. This phenomenon of clustering has its natural underpinning in
the buddy relationship the African officers have developed during military training and previously,
during active service, in the former metropole. It
is reinforced by the pattern of communications and
the still prevailing economic and cultural ties to
and via London and Paris. Other important variables
are geographic proximity and cultural closeness
(Ghana-Togo-Dahomey, for example), the similarity of
the civilian regimes (Ghana-Mali), and the prominence
of the potential target of a coup (Nkrumah). Finally
there is a phenomenon of negative contagion or of
deterrent by example.
It appears from the comparative review of sociopolitical factors influencing military intervention
in West Africa that at least one group existed as a
"given" even prior to the gaining of independence.
This group includes internal divisions and the lack
of cohesion among civilian elites and politicized
groups of the population as well as general economic
vulnerability and external dependence.
This writer is of the opinion that regional-
ethnic cleavage, although of importance, has been
overplayed in the literature and particularly in
popular press. This is particularly true if the

137

issue is treated as isolated from the basically economic competition for scarce resources. Due to the still low level of "modern" class differentiation in the region, and in most of Tropical Africa, the corresponding type of social conflict does not seem to have appreciable bearing on the incidence and other characteristics of military intervention in African politics.

The review of possible economic factors seems to lead to conclusions that tally with the thesis of general vulnerability of the independent African states. However, the concrete manifestation of praetorianism appears to be more closely related to the strategy, tactics, quality, and behavior of the civilian elites and policy-makers during periods of economic duress. There seems to be no economic inevitability of military intervention.

The factors related to the qualities of political system appear the strongest of all aspects of the sociopolitical environment. The common denominator of the features of political systems that tends to provoke military coups is the danger to personal and corporate security, as well as to the privileged position of the military in society. The most potent explanatory variables, at least as far as West Africa is concerned, seem to be found in the area of civil-military relations themselves, rather than in the realm of general social conditions.

The limited sample points to the objectively most probable situation leading, but still not inevitably, to a military coup--namely, the combination of a regime attempting to change the social status quo, internally and externally, with serious economic and financial difficulties. Due to their origin, mode of aculturation, and material standards, the armed forces in Tropical Africa in most cases are directly interested in the preservation of the system inherited from the former colonial power. These characteristics of the West African military will be discussed in the following chapter.

And finally, external contagion also contributes to the proliferation of direct military intervention in politics, while the theories of great power conspiracies so far have lacked convincing supporting evidence.

7

THE IMPACT OF THE
SOCIOPOLITICAL
ENVIRONMENT ON
THE MILITARY

It has been argued that the phenomenon of military intervention in the politics of Tropical Africa cannot be fully explained before we have identified and isolated the interrelationships between the wider societal factors and the military organization.[1] This line of analysis seems to us as indispensable as the preceding discussion of the direct impact of the sociopolitical setting on the phenomenon of praetorianism. Our intention is to take various properties of military organization in Tropical Africa not as a given but as a result of interplay between external impulses and domestic factors.

EXTERNAL IMPULSES

The British Military Legacy

The army and police establishments in Ghana and Sierra Leone were founded and developed until independence by the British.[2] A high degree of British influence has persisted in varying degrees in these army and police establishments ever since, despite Nkrumah's attempts between 1961 and 1966 to reduce

and to diversify the sources of equipment, supplies,
training, and external aid. These efforts affected
only the new services of the Ghana armed forces. By
1967 the officer and the NCO corps of the Royal
Sierra Leone Force had been thoroughly although not
completely Africanized. In addition to the still
predominant reliance upon the British the force had
received modest aid from Nigeria and Israel. This,
however, did not change the essential character of
the force as an imported and imperfectly integrated
institution. The Royal West Africa Frontier Force
(RWAFF), the predecessor of the armies of Ghana and
Sierra Leone, was developed not in response to the
defense requirements of what later became independent
African states but to the projected contingency needs
of the British empire in other parts of the relatively
demilitarized continent[3] and outside Africa.

With the termination of colonial rule these external needs disappeared, without thus far being replaced by credible external threats to Ghana or
Sierra Leone.* The colonial heritage had several
politically relevant repercussions.

It left behind professional military establish-·
ments that, despite their relatively small size compared to Europe and other continents,[4] were still
excessively large in terms of defense and internal
security requirements. But Nkrumah, guided by foreign
policy ambitions on the continental scale and having
misjudged the resource base at his disposal, decided
to further expand the Ghanaian army.

Second, the pay scales and other material privileges of army personnel have not basically changed
from the standards of the colonial army. The new
African officers, like senior civil servants, inherited the pay scale of the British predecessors,
which was geared to a standard of living in the in-
dustrially developed metropole. In the class- and
color-stratified colonial army, the pay of NCOs and

---

*The repercussions of the anti-colonial guerrilla
movement in Portuguese Guinea--and the Portuguese-
staged invasion of Conakry, capital of the Republic
of Guinea--might have changed this situation as far
as Sierra Leone is concerned.

enlisted men was closer to the prevailing pay of
civilians in the underdeveloped Gold Coast and Sierra
Leone, but still several times higher than the GNP
per capita. The best organized and armed "trade
union" in these countries, the army not only opposed
any scaling down of the nominal pay after independence
but in private even demanded upward revision to offset inflation. The army's vested interests in preserving its effectiveness and morale were officially
justified as compensating for the almost nonexistent
professional hazard of what was only a glorified
super-police.

Third, the Ghana and Sierra Leone armies inherited military installations that were located predominantly in the already relatively developed areas
on the coast and close to the largest harbor and
airport, which were near the capital. It was a log-
ical consequence of the projected employment of the
forces by the imperial power, but in the new independent polities such location minimized the beneficial
side effects of considerable budgetary outlays for
defense. Not only did this spending not contribute
significantly to the development of an infrastructure and production and services in the less fortunate parts of the country but it also did not promote
the development of civilian interest groups supporting the military and made the army a potential
Praetorian Guard conveniently located in and close
to the capital.

Fourth, the timetable for relinquishing executive
power by Britain put defense and internal security
at the bottom of the list. Even four years after
the proclamation of independence, the Ghanaian army
still was commanded by a British general, H. T. Alexander, assisted by 200 expatriate officers and NCOs.
In Sierra Leone at the time of the first military
coup, i.e., six years after independence, there were
still 20 British officers and NCOs.[5] The pattern of
decolonization promoted separation between the African political elite and the indigenous officers.
This separation in Ghana was rationalized by the
British in terms of their own model of civil-military
relations ("Army out of politics, politics out of
the Army"). In the short run the presence of the
British had the effect of a protective shield for

the CPP regime. At the same time, the community of
origin, values, and perceptions among British civilian
and military elites that underpinned the transplanted
model of civil-military relations was conspicuously
absent in the former colony. The prolongation of
the British presence, however convenient it might
have been in certain respects, only delayed the forging of such consensus. The pattern of decolonization
made the civilian political elite the least aware of
the problems of the Ghanaian military as compared to
other areas of governance. In conjunction with the
lack of interest groups supporting the military, it
produced understandable pressures on the government
to reduce the force and the defense outlays.

Fifth, the uneven tempo of decolonization and
the rapid promotion of African officers during the
terminal years of colonial rule had a destabilizing
effect on the military organizations of Ghana and
even more strongly on that of Sierra Leone. Several
profiles of officers appeared, with varying careers,
past exposure to the British norms, general educational background, involvement in domestic politics,
and so forth. In Sierra Leone particularly, a substantial gap in age and duration of service appeared
between the most senior indigenous officers (Brigadier
D. Lansana and Colonel J. Bangura) and the group of
substantially younger and probably better-educated
and -trained officers (Lieutenant-Colonel A. Juxon-
Smith, Major Blake, Major Jumu, Major Kai-Samba).
The accelerated promotion of African officers, often
from close age groups, created a potential problem
of career blockage several years later.[6] In Ghana,
internal cohesion and discipline also were affected
negatively by the pattern of transition and the subsequent rapid expansion of the army in 1962-65.
These destabilizing features did not produce immediate
mutinies, as happened in East Africa, but nevertheless
made the armies vulnerable to internal conflicts and
self-induced internal coups. The colonial heritage
also was responsible for a lower status of policemen
as compared to the position of army officers.[7] This
factor became relevant at the time of military-police
intervention in Ghana and Sierra Leone and had an appreciable impact on the functioning of the respective
military-police juntas.

Sixth, the military and police establishments
in Ghana and Sierra Leone inherited the patterns of
recruitment practiced under the British. Although
in Ghana there were some attempts to diversify them,
the predominance of the coastal and southern areas
(particularly the Ewe, also the Ga and Fanti) in the
officer corps remained, with relatively few Ashantis,
for historical reasons.[8] Among the enlisted men a
high percentage still came from the least developed
North. There still were traces of relatively low
social status of the military under colonial rule,[9]
which contributed to the isolation of the army from
the civilian elites.

In Sierra Leone the colonial practice of re-
cruiting for the army and the police up to 40 percent
Mende due to their relative educational advantages[10]
not only persisted but was reinforced by the predominance of the Mende politicians within the ruling
party. The SLPP governments encouraged the enlist-
ment and promotion of Mende officers, aiming to make
the army a reliable tool of their rule. It brought
their number to about 70 out of the total of about
110 officers in the army and police. The insignificant percentage of Creoles reflected, as in Ghana,
the low social prestige of the military in the colonial time. The pattern of recruitment inherited
from the British helped in particular to align the officer corps, where the Mende share was around 60 percent, to the ruling political party, while the still
high percentage in the lower ranks from the North
and from among the Kono made them susceptible to the
political propaganda and influences of the rival political coalition, the All People's Congress. Thus
a combination of ethnic-cultural heterogeneity, an
uneven pattern of economic development, an uneven
spread of education, and, to a significant extent
influenced by the above-stated circumstances, the
British-initiated pattern of recruitment seems to
have contributed in varying degrees to promoting the
cleavages within the army among the officers, among
the NCOs, among the soldiers, and among the above-
mentioned groups.

Seventh, the armies of Ghana and Sierra Leone
inherited the organizational format of the colonial
army with the colonial infantry battalion as the

basic unit.[11] Not only did they inherit the language
of command of the former colonial master but also
the division of labor with the internal security
forces, internal regulations, terminology, ranks
structure, the already mentioned pay structure, uniforms (with few modifications), arms, equipment, and
so forth. The size of the military establishment
had something to do with the colony's importance and
its economic potential, but only imperfectly.[12]

The post-colonial development of the military
establishments in Ghana and Sierra Leone in terms of
their expansion and development of services other
than infantry (under colonial rule these were supposed to be exclusively or predominantly British)
was only in part a function of the country's size.
More important seem to have been the expected economic power, the available cash and credit resources,
and the ambitions of the civilian rulers. Thus Ghana
developed an expensive air force and navy and made
significant investments in the corresponding infrastructure (an air base in Tamale and a naval base in
Secondi-Takoradi in particular), while Sierra Leone
has not appreciably advanced in the direction of
technical modernization, mechanization, and the ac-
quisition of modern arms.

Eighth, the military and police establishments
of Ghana and Sierra Leone, and particularly their
officer corps, inherited an Africanized but basically
British structure of norms and military traditions
that have little in common with the pre-colonial heritage of the African societies.* One ought to be
careful in extrapolating the relevance of a foreign
reference group as a determinant of the social and
political behavior of the military in Ghana and
Sierra Leone.[13] Nevertheless, the overall importance
of normative impact is unmistakably present.[14] The
political relevance of this norms structure and the
close personal ties with the British Commonwealth

---

*It suffices to see the Ghana Army Museum in
Kumasi to conclude that the source of inspiration for
the Ghana military is still the former colonial con-
queror of the Ashantis and not those native forces
that resisted the British conquest.

144

and Anglo-Saxon military among the most senior officers lies in the possible incongruence of the norms
with the norm structure and aspirations of a civilian
elite. The incongruence becomes critical if and
when the civilian elite tries to reduce dramatically
the dependence of the country on the former colonial
metropole. This aspect of the British heritage was
clearly relevant in Ghana under Nkrumah, despite the
dicta of the British "apolitical" military code of
behavior. The movement toward establishing social
closeness as well as norm and aspiration congruence
between the civilian and military elites was under
way in Ghana after the 1966 coup, but it occurred on
the basis of the norms espoused by the politically
and socially conservative older established bourgeois-
chiefly elite, which is as pro-British as the army
top brass.

The French Military Legacy

Most of what has been said about the British-
created military establishments of Ghana and Sierra
Leone applies to the armies and internal security
forces in Dahomey and Mali. There were several differences between the British and French systems of
colonial rule that affected the future armed forces
of the new independent states. As did the British,
the French looked on Black Africa as a source of
military infantry manpower, and they used the predominantly African units commanded by French officers
and NCOs longer than did the British.[15] But unlike
the RWAFF, the French troops were not localized.
The manpower was recruited in many parts of the
French colonial empire in Africa and subsequently
mixed in the units. This meant that at the time of
independence the new armies were completely recreated,
using manpower from many, often disbanded, units.
This reduced the modern traditions of the new armies
almost to zero.
However, the influence of the French colonial
troops has been as strong in Dahomey and Mali as
British influence was in Ghana and Sierra Leone.
Most of the enlisted men and NCOs of the two relatively small professional armies came from the French

army, as did the many African officers who were rapidly promoted and trained. The Dahomeyan and Malian armed forces inherited the installations (i.e., the location and roughly the size of the former French colonial units); much of the equipment, internal regulations, organization, and terminology; French as the predominant language of internal communication and almost exclusive language of command; the ranks and the relations between them; and the uniforms (with slight modifications).

The Dahomeyan and Malian armed and internal security forces also retained the French system, which consists of the army, Gendarmerie, Garde Ré-publicaine, Sûreté, and civilian police.[16] In most of the French-speaking African countries the Gendarmerie is placed under the ministries of defense and in important respects carries out functions roughly equivalent to some of the functions of police in English-speaking countries. As a result the civilian police and Garde Républicaine subsequently played an insignificant role in the execution of military coups and in running Dahomey and Mali. The place of police officers in the Ghanaian and Sierra Leonean juntas has been "taken" occasionally by Dahomeyan and Malian Gendarmerie officers.

Dahomey and Mali also inherited the basic pay structure of the French colonial troops, which was reinforced by the willingness of the French government to pay at full rate all officers, including French officers of African origin, serving in Africa after independence. The French ministry of defense has continued to this day payments to African officers with long service in the French army and with combat experience and decorations for, among other things, helping the French to suppress the anti-colonial movements for independence in Indochina and Algeria.[17]

Despite the French budgetary support, which was more important in Dahomey than in Mali, there have been pressures from civilian politicians in both countries to reduce the financial load of the inherited military establishments, by slashing the manpower or by bringing the pay structure closer to the prevailing economic conditions of the underdeveloped

146

countries or by both means. The Malians did effect
a reduction of defense allocations in 1960 after the
French troops were withdrawn from the bases in Mali.
However, between 1961 and 1966 the allocations were
increased from $5 million to $10 million (at 1960
prices and exchange rates).[18] In response mainly to
internal security needs Mali developed with U.S.
and Soviet aid a small air force, a paratroop company,
and a mobile engineer unit.[19]

Dahomey has not faced such challenges; nevertheless, the staying power of an armed bureaucratic organization was sufficient to prevent any budgetary
cuts after the proclamation of independence.[20] Whatever the mechanism, the military establishments in
both Dahomey and Mali--in their size, cost, location,
organization, technical level--still bore a greater
imprint of the French colonial heritage than influence
or determination by the indigenous factors of the
new independent polities.

As in the English-speaking half of the sample,
the dynamics and the pattern of transition from the
colonial state to independent statehood had destabilizing effects on both internal military organization and the relationship between the military and
the civilian elites. Accelerated and politically
motivated promotions of junior officers and NCOs
with long service in the French army, coupled with
crash training of young and better-educated graduates
of civilian or military schools, produced a rather
heterogeneous officer corps. These officer corps
contained several distinct types of officers with
varying general educational and professional backgrounds and different exposure (in duration and
quality) to the norms of the French army, to combat
experience, and to domestic unrest and formative political influences. These variations tended to be
related to the officers' age and rank, thus creating
sources of future internal cleavages. Externally,
the almost abrupt transfer of responsibility for
defense and internal security, unlike the gradual
process in other areas, made relations and mutual
understanding with the civilian elites more difficult.
As in the English-speaking countries this was more
true of the army than it was of the police.

THE PERSISTENCE AND PRESERVATION
OF THE COLONIAL HERITAGE

It is obvious from the preceding review that a
number of fundamental characteristics of the armies
and police establishments of Dahomey, Ghana, Sierra
Leone, and Mali were influenced only marginally by
the domestic sociopolitical environment. These organizations were in the mid-1960s, and in many respects
still are, the partly Africanized extensions of the
defense and security establishments of Great Britain
and France. These links and external influence have
been maintained in the name of efficiency, basically
through four channels:

1. At the time of the proclamation of independence and for several years afterward, the colonial
metropoles maintained (the British on contract and
the French by direct assignments) a large number of
their officers in the armed forces of independent
African states. With the progress of Africanization,
or more precisely of the localization* of the officer
and NCO corps, this number has been decreasing.

The radical regimes of Mali and Ghana had gone
the furthest in replacing the expatriate officers
and in relying on other powers. But even they could
not fully extricate the technically most complex and
advanced services such as the air force, engineering
units, armored units, and signal corps. In Sierra
Leone and Dahomey, despite the lack of noticeable
modernization of the armies, the British and French
officers and advisers remained important**; and in

---

*I.e., the replacement of Europeans and Africans
from other territories by indigenous officers and
NCOs.

**The most recent example occurred in Dahomey.
On December 12, 1969, Major M. Kouandété, chief of
staff, staged a palace coup and had President E.-D.
Zinsou arrested as he was entering the presidential
palace. Major Kouandété allegedly ordered that Zinsou be flown to Kouandété's native North, but the
French pilots of the miniscule Dahomeyan air force,
presumably his subordinates, refused to carry out the
order. Zinsou was transported in a military vehicle.

Dahomey there were even individual cases of a reverse process.*

2. Another channel, present only in Dahomey, has been tight surveillance by the French embassy, the office of the military attaché, and the French intelligence of all important developments in the country and the army, making it virtually impossible to deviate from the already established and patterned organization of the armed and security forces. No change could occur without the blessing and material and political support of the French embassy and of Paris.[21] The heavy dependence on the French budgetary subsidy might have restrained the expansion of the Dahomeyan army as the French embassy can resist such pressures better than local civilian politicians.

3. Furthermore the continuity of the inherited organizational patterns in the military establishments of the four countries increasingly relies on the system of training the officers, and less significantly the NCOs, in military school located in France and Britain. Again, Mali and Ghana are more self-reliant than Sierra Leone and Dahomey in terms of available local military schools, but even there-- in the army schools in Kati and Teshie--methods of training, materials, regulations, and naturally the language reflect the colonial experience. Officers above junior ranks and particularly in technically advanced services and branches still are sent mostly to the former metropole for training. Junior officers also are sent because of such reasons as shorter courses and medical treatment.

The radical regimes in Ghana and Mali tried to reduce this dependence, but their efforts met with resistance and disapproval among both the British advisers and the top brass in Ghana and with silent disagreement in a part of the Malian officer corps. Training of cadets and officers in the USSR had not

---

*After it was found that the opportunity for malfeasance in the post of the army intendant had been an irresistible temptation for Dahomeyan officers, a French military adviser was appointed to fill it, under the theory that what is bad for national pride might be good for the state treasury.

149

advanced far before the coups, and the Ghanaian attempt proved a failure. The critics of this diversification, taking the status quo for granted, had a point when they argued that it would lower the effectiveness of the respective armies and divide the officer corps.* After the coup the National Liberation Council in Ghana introduced exchange visits of entire Ghanaian and British units.[22]

Dahomey and Sierra Leone rely almost entirely on French and British schools for officers, and to a lesser extent for the training of NCOs. Many military officers of all four countries also maintain social contacts with their former buddies, colleagues, and acquaintances among the military officers of the metropole or of other African and Commonwealth countries dependent on Paris and London.

4. In addition, the continuity has been perpetuated by the continuing dependence of the four armies on France and Britain for arms, equipment, supplies, services and aid. The radical regimes in Ghana and Mali had done the most in diversifying these sources. Some arms and equipment were bought or received as aid from the United States, USSR, Czechoslovakia, Commonwealth countries, U.A.R., Israel, and Yugoslavia, but these shipments affected only a fraction of the total supplies and stock. After the coups in Ghana and Mali, there has been a reversal of this trend. The diversification of equipment and arms supplies has been minimal in Dahomey and Sierra Leone.

THE IMPACT OF THE DOMESTIC
SOCIOPOLITICAL ENVIRONMENT

While the size, complexity, organizational format, physical location, technical level, and a number

---

*There is some evidence that this factor contributed to the alleged abortive coup in Mali in August 1969. Its presumed leader, Captain D. S. Diarra, had undergone training in the USSR in addition to training in France. The Soviet experience may have reinforced his ideological preference for radical socialist options.

of other important features of the armed forces of
the four countries were influenced predominantly by
factors external to the new polities, or by a combination of external impulses and internal limitations and considerations, at the time of independence
there was still some room for various aspects of the
domestic sociopolitical environment to impress themselves upon the army and police establishments. Besides, not all external impulses came from the former colonial metropole. The predominant super-police
functional orientation of the four military establishments, for example, resulted from the low level
of modern militarization in Tropical Africa. This
factor is still operative.

Although the recruitment policies of the British
distorted the ethnic composition of these services
as compared to the populations at large, the regional-
ethnic heterogeneity and possible conflicts within
the Ghanaian and Sierra Leonean military stemmed
from and reflected the heterogeneity of and cleavages
within the civilian population. Despite the colonial
heritage, there also has been a correlation, however
imperfect, between such factors as the size, technical level, location, and cost of these establishments
on the one hand and the economic base, geographic
position, climate, level of education, availability
of technical skills, and so forth on the other. Some
of these links are of consequence for the phenomenon
of military intervention in the post-independence
politics of a given territory.

For instance, the general cultural level, education, and the supply of managerial skills in the lower
strata of the population seem to have set a lower
limit on the rank of coup members until the mutiny
syndrome within the army could result in the establishment of stable juntas. As noted earlier, in
all four countries the military takeovers directed
against civilian regimes were followed by successful
or abortive internal coups* whose leaders were equal

---

*In our view, it is not quite correct to call all
these recurrent insurrections counter-coups as Ruth
First does in Power in Africa (New York: Pantheon,
1970), p. 20. It seems appropriate to distinguish
at least three types: (1) against the titulary

to or lower in rank than those in the ruling juntas.
In Dahomey on December 17, 1967, these respective
(highest) ranks were general (junta) and major
(counter-junta); in Ghana on April 17, 1967, lieutenant-general and lieutenant; in Sierra Leone on
March 23, 1967, brigadier and major and on April 17,
1968, brigadier and sergeant-major; in Mali on August
12, 1969, captain and captain. The authors of the
Sierra Leonean coup-mutiny on April 17, 1968, were
able to seize power and arrest all active officers
but could not run the country and, in the long run,
also the army and police forces. They themselves
recognized this and appealed for help to the two
senior retired officers, a colonel and a lieutenant-
colonel. The two leading mutineers in Sierra Leone
were from the signal corps and apparently possessed
certain conspiratorial and organizational skills
that allowed them to stage a coup. But in Mali the
ineptness of poorly educated infantry NCOs seems to
have contributed in large part to poor planning of
a conspiratorial meeting and easy detection of plotting by military intelligence, which was headed by
a leading conspirator from the previous coup. It
appears that at the present level of general educational, cultural, and economic development a successful military junta must be effectively led by at
least a junior officer, sufficiently educated, trained
and skillful.

We do not possess sufficient data to answer
thoroughly the question to what extent and in what
way the organizational and internal relations within
the military and police establishments mirror social
divisions (other than regional-ethnic) and cleavages
in the four polities.[23] As was noted earlier, the
formal hierarchical structure of these establishments
was transplanted from the former metropoles. The
structure has reflected, up to a point, the internal
social stratification of the British and French societies (for instance, the relations between officers
and the rest of the troops was inherited historically

───────────────

leader of the junta, (2) against the entire junta,
and (3) against military rule as such. We call only
the latter a counter-coup.

from European feudal society) and the more complex multilayer pattern of stratification that was later created in the British and French colonial empires. The present pay structure in African armies, for instance, reflects the latter--with a huge gap between the pay of the officer (i.e., former white officer) and that of the enlisted (i.e., African) man. The same is true of a number of features of internal army life: separate dining and recreation facilities for officers, NCOs, and enlisted soldiers; very different housing conditions, officers' servants; the officer's style of life, which imitates British, and to a lesser extent French, gentlemen.

These para-class differences are artificial and have little underpinning in the present-day societies of Dahomey, Ghana, Sierra Leone, and Mali. This is due mainly to the still rudimentary, fluid, and porous modern class stratification in most of the countries of tropical Africa. Officers in these armies most often come from families that are socially very close to those of the soldiers. The only difference between the families is that the former could send their children, or at least one male child, to school. Once commissioned, most African officers feel obliged to help out numerous relatives, to maintain their younger brothers in school, and so forth. They themselves in time become members of the elite, but the difference in income is somewhat minimized by a larger number of claimants on higher incomes. In a certain sense, however, the class stratification of the colonial societies spills over into the new independent polity through military hierarchy as privileges, access to secondary and high schools, capital accumulation in the forms of savings invested into real estate and business ventures, and so forth are passed on to the next generation.[24] Viewed from this perspective the military and police establishments very distantly reflect existing social class divisions in society. At present the flow from the army to the society at large seems to be more important as it contributes to the creation and hardening of class distinctions.

On the other hand some of the potential or real cleavages within the military establishments have been actively promoted by civilian politicians who

were reacting to the colonial dependence and/or
guided by domestic power considerations and foreign
policy aspirations.* In Chapter 3, dealing with
Ghana, we examined the divisive techniques used by
Nkrumah to weaken the interventionist potential of
the military. Some of these operations led to organizational changes within the armed forces, e.g.,
the separation of the presidential guard from the
army proper and the accelerated development of the
former as an elite coup-deterrent. For similar reason the Gendarmerie in Dahomey at one stage was separated from the army. Nkrumah tried to promote
cleavages among the top brass. The internal power
considerations in Ghana and Mali had considerable impact on material standards of the armies, their position vis-à-vis and their relations with the civilian
security establishments. Power considerations of
the rulers and the character of mass parties at their
disposal led to the creation or attempted creation
of para-military forces as a deterrent to military
coups and as a potential replacement for the professional armies.

THE INTERNAL ENVIRONMENT: THE POLITIZATION OF THE ARMY

The civilian elites in all four cases, although
by different methods and with varying intensity,
initiated or sped up the process of politization of
the armed forces. These encroachments on the autonomy
and the presumed apolitical nature of the military
establishment in varying degrees conflicted with the

---

*For instance, domestic power considerations in-
clude the increase in the number of officers from
particular ethnic groups occupying sensitive positions: the Mende in Sierra Leone, the Nzima and Moslem Northerners in Ghana under Nkrumah.

In regard to foreign policy aspirations, Nkrumah's and M. Keita's maneuvering between West and
East led them to attempt a diversification of training and supplies of the respective armies, which had
divisive effects on the officer corps.

154

norm structure and with the notions of professionalism inherited from the British and French armies. Given the fact that the apolitical ethos is more developed in the British armed forces, and that there has been no organizational continuity between the French colonial army and the African national armies, this conflict was less pronounced and acutely felt by the officers in Dahomey and Mali. In Dahomey the resistance to politization lasted only several months. In August 1963 Colonel Soglo, chief of the general staff, when invited to a party congress stated: "We have nothing to declare, the Army does not make politics!" In October of the same year Soglo let the army be dragged onto the political stage,[25] and the Dahomeyan officer corps has remained willingly politicized ever since.

In Mali the ruling party, US-RDA, had formally penetrated the army and made it a tool of political education and of spreading party directives within and outside the barracks. In 1966 Modibo Keita made the next step. By including Colonel Sékou Traoré, chief of staff, in the highest decision-making body in the country, he tried to give the army a real stake in the preservation of his regime.

In Sierra Leone the deliberate politization visibly affected primarily the top brass. In the absence of a coherent ideology and organization on the part of the ruling Sierra Leone People's Party, the civilian elite cultivated the personal loyalty of the top officers and made them privy to some political problems and to other issues of governance. Politization of the Royal Sierra Leone Force has been the most limited and discrete of the four cases.

In Ghana, Nkrumah's intentions to penetrate and politically conquer the army were clear and manifest, but the results were much more modest than in Mali. The drive to have all Ghanaian officers enrolled in the party was initiated by Minister of Defense Kofi Baako at the annual army conference in 1963. However, the degree of acculturation of the Ghanaian officer and NCO to British norms was so strong that Nkrumah listened to the advice given to him by his confidant Brigadier Barwah and quietly shelved the idea. A modest number of membership cards seems to have been actually distributed before the 1966 coup, chiefly in the privileged presidential guard and among junior officers looking for promotions.

In at least three out of four cases (Dahomey, Mali, Ghana), the deliberate attempts to politicize the army were prompted or reinforced by the fear of military coups, which had occurred elsewhere on the continent. This was clearly the case in Dahomey in 1963. President Maga could not but be disturbed by the fate of President Sylvanus Olympio, who was murdered by Togolese veterans of the French army on January 13, 1963. President Maga saw a solution in limited and controlled politization of the military, but this delicate operation, as it turned out, exceeded the manipulative capabilities of the Dahomeyan political elite. Hence the civilian elites of Dahomey have experienced the fate of the sorcerer's apprentice for at least seven years. At least in part this also was the lot of the Ghanaian and Malian civilian regimes because the ruling parties could not in fact assure the loyalty of the officer corps. Figuratively the CPP and the US-RDA regimes opened the gates but let the silent opposition occupy the fortress. The difference between the Dahomeyan coup in 1965 on the one hand and the Ghanaian and Malian ones on the other was that in the latter two cases of military intervention (in 1966 and 1968) one of the manifest corporate objectives was to regain corporate "apolitical" and "supra-partisan" autonomy.

CHAPTER

8

MILITARY RULE
AND ITS IMPACT
ON THE POLITY

The mode of operation, duration, and several
other qualities of military rule in Dahomey, Ghana,
Sierra Leone, and Mali seem to have been influenced
by the circumstances under which the seizures of
power occurred and the manner in which they were carried out. Therefore, before discussing the issue of
military rule it is pertinent to identify dimensions
of the coups that seem to have been important for
the evolution of military rule.

THE RELEVANCE OF THE COUPS FOR
THE SUBSEQUENT MILITARY RULE

There have been numerous attempts to classify
military coups on all continents and more specifically
in Africa.[1] The analysis of the nine military coups
in our sample will be centered around four groups of
facts: the circumstances of plotting, the direction
of the coups, motivations of the coup-makers, and
the general social environment in which the coups
took place. In dissecting the coups we shall go further than has been done in the literature. The number of possible combinations of component characteristics is so large that labeling the combinations
does not seem useful.

We discussed earlier the broad sociopolitical
context within which military intervention takes

place and some possible cause-and-effect links between the two. At this juncture we shall point out only what seems to be insufficient clarity in a number of works on military intervention when it comes to differentiating probable or presumed social causes of intervention from internal motivations of the military. Obviously these two sets are not identical, although some elements could be related to one another.

The motivation for political change through military intervention is closely linked to political, social, corporate, and personal perceptions of the most relevant social groups and corporate bodies. Of primary importance, of course, is the inner motivation of the active agents of political change, i.e. (in this study), of the military. Going one step further, we can distinguish the complexity and heterogeneity of even small professional armies and the complexity relevant to their coup potential. Within these structures we can recognize several interrelated yet distinct sets of perceptions that could be related schematically to four hierarchically interposed groups of ranks: top brass, intermediate and junior officers, NCOs, and enlisted men. The relative weight of these four groups, and hence the relevance of the respective stimulants, varies according to the general social and internal corporate environment as well as the place of the army in the polity (see Table 5).

THE PROBLEM OF LEGITIMACY

As we have seen in the case studies the engineers of the six coups that led to the installation of military governments immediately encountered the problem of legitimizing the new rule.* The real or

---

*We shall omit the problems of legitimacy for the unsuccessful coups, IV and IX, and the counter-coup in Sierra Leone, VII, whose proclaimed goal was to return to a legitimate civilian government. The legitimacy of the abortive insurrections is not without theoretical interest per se but is not di-

feared potential challenges to the legitimacy of the
new political orders and/or governments were of external and internal nature.

As far as the external legitimacy was concerned,
none of the military governments in our group faced
critical or insurmountable problems of potential political isolation on the international scene. For
all four countries the most important factors economically and politically were the attitudes of Western powers: for Dahomey and less so for Mali, the
attitude of France; for Sierra Leone, that of Britain;
and for Ghana, those of Britain, the United States,
and the Federal Republic of Germany. The two most
important coups internationally--against Nkrumah in
Ghana and M. Keita in Mali--understandably were well
received in the West, and the only concern of the
diplomacy of the Western powers was not to betray
too much delight and exuberance. So they waited until the new regimes were duly recognized by "moderate"
pro-Western political regimes in Africa, and in individual cases they even may have encouraged and sped
up this process. The new rulers, particularly in
Ghana, were privately assured of moral, political,
and financial support very soon after the coups.

The 1965 coup in Dahomey did not change anything
in relations with the former metropole and was rather
benevolently looked on by the French. In December
1967 Paris was annoyed and felt affronted by the anti-
Soglo coup but not strongly enough to raise the question of the continuation of diplomatic relations.
On the other hand Major Kouandété did his best to
assure the French government of his loyalty and in
order to enhance the legitimacy of the new junta
ceded the position of president to Lieutenant-Colonel
A. Alley in whom Paris had more confidence and trust.

The Sierra Leonean coup in March 1967 posed a
technical constitutional question of the relationship
between the military government and the British Crown
because the junta suspended the post of governor-
general, the Crown's respresentative, and de facto
abolished the monarchy. On the other hand politically

---

rectly related to the central concern of this study--
effective military rule.

159

TABLE 5

Comparative Characteristics of Overt Military Intervention in Dahomey, Ghana, Sierra Leone, and Mali, 1965-70

Variables	Dahomey		Ghana		Sierra Leone			Mali	
	December 22, 1965	December 17, 1967	February 24, 1966	April 17, 1967	March 21, 1967	March 23, 1967	April 17, 1968	November 19, 1968	August 12, 1969
	I	II	III	IV	V	VI	VII	VIII	IX
Success	+	+	+	-	+	+	+	+	-
Highest rank among the plotters	general	major	colonel	lieutenant	brigadier	major	sergeant-major	captain	captain
Size of the original nucleus of the plot	~10	3-4	3	1	~10	4	2-3	4-5	10-12
Civilian participation in plotting	+	i	-	-	+	-	i	-	-
Police participation in plotting	-	-	+	-	+	+	-	-	-
Duration of plotting (roughly)	5 mo	4 mo	6 mo	1.5 w	3 d	2 d	4 mo	1.5-2 y	2-3 w
Size of the subsequent junta	5-6 (fl)	10 (fl)	8	4 (pl)	4	8	3	14	unknown
Of which, police officers	-	-	4	-	1	2	1	-	-
Motivations of:									
plotters	HF	FD	ABCDF	DEF	HF	DFE	AD	BCF	FDE
top brass	HF	-	BCF	-	HF	DFE	wkFH	wkD	-
intermediary and junior officers	HF	FD	CDFB	DEF	-	-	-	wkD	FDE
NCOs	-	-	ACF	D	-	-	wkFH	ACDF	D,wkF
enlisted men	-	-	AC	-	-	-	wkFH	ACF	-
Division within the military establishment during the coup	-	+	+	+	-	+	+	+	-
Direction:									
against regime	-	-	+	+	-	+	+	+	+
against government	+	+	+	+	+	+	+	+	+
against military leaders	-	+	+	+	-	+	+	+	+
against military junta	-	+	-	-	-	-	+	-	-
against military rule	-	-	-	-	-	-	+	-	-

The following data table is printed in landscape orientation on the page (rotated 90°). Columns represent individual coups; the bottom row gives the duration of the subsequent military junta.

Existence of widespread latent or overt civilian dissatisfaction with the government at the time of the coup	–	–	++	–	–	–	+	+	++
Existence of organized civilian opposition to the government at the time of the coup	+	–	+	–	–	+	+	+	–
Legal competitiveness of the political system at the time of the coup	+	–	–	+	+	–	–	–	–
Violence accompanying the coup: rough estimate of deaths	–	–	30 M	+	30 C*	–	4 M	2 MC*	–
Public reaction:									
in capital	+0	0	+++	0	–	0	– –	+	?
in provinces	0	0	+++	0	0	0	– –	0	0
Manifest justification of the coup:									
tyranny			+	+			+	+	+
illegitimacy of the previous government		+	+	+	+		+	+	+
internal security, law and order	+			+	+	+			
mismanagement, inefficiency, and corruption		+	+	+			+	+	
other political disagreements	+	+	+				+		+
agreements	+	+	+	–			+	+	+
Duration of the subsequent military junta	2y	7 mo	3.6 y	–	2 d	1.1 y	2 d	9 d	3.5 y*

Key: A: conditions of service (pay strikes); B: corporate autonomy; C: corporate and personal security; D: self-promotion; E: other personal; F: general political disagreements; H: overt civilian pressure; M: predominantly military casualties; C*: predominantly civilian casualties; MC*: mixed casualties; O: indifferent.

Explanation of symbols used: i: insignificant; ~: approximately; mo: month; y: year; w: week; d: day; pl: planned; fl: fluid; inf: informal; wk: weak; +: presence, positive; –: absence, negative.

the coups did not change the nature of bilateral relations. British flexibility and pragmatism were displayed once again, and in the absence of any other external challenge the Sierra Leonean junta set out to deal with internal problems of its rule.

Relations with the Eastern powers, notably with the USSR and the People's Republic of China, were of some concern to Ghana and more so to Mali. The Soviet Union had become the biggest single buyer of Ghanaian cocoa by 1966 and had a sizable program of technical assistance in the country. For Mali, China and the USSR were the biggest single sources of credits--FM 20 billion and FM 17 billion respectively[2]--and of technical and cultural assistance. Both Ghana and Mali had a substantial number of students in the USSR,* and in addition Moscow offered restrained hospitality to Nkrumah on his way back from Peking and facilitated his trip to Conakry. The antecedent Soviet and East German aid to Nkrumah's security apparatus and his meddling in the affairs of other African states burdened the situation further, as did the vociferous anti-Communism of the new Ghanaian rulers.**

However, both Ghana and the USSR had real stakes in continuing economic and political relations. By 1966 the Soviets had sufficiently advanced from the manifest posture of supporting "revolutionary," "progressive," and radical movements and groups toward a policy of "peaceful coexistence" with the effective regimes in independent African states not dominated by minorities of European extraction. This also included the most conservative, oppressive, and pro-Western regimes. As a result of all these circum-

---

*The organizations of Ghanaian and Malian students in socialist countries promptly denounced the military takeovers, verbally challenged the legitimacy of military rule, and thus complicated the relations of these two countries with socialist states.

**On the other hand the Ghanaian junta, despite its emotional pronouncements, seems to have played down and concealed from its own public the deaths of a dozen Soviet and East German security advisers killed in Flagstaff House on the day of the coup.

stances, the USSR has not challenged the legitimacy
of the military government,* and the junta directed
its anti-Communist wrath against the less politically
and economically important Chinese, Cubans, and East
Germans.

The Malian junta was much more moderate. It
tried to minimize any anti-Communist and anti-so-
cialist undertones of the coup and almost immediately
set out to allay the potential fears and misgivings
of the Eastern powers. It effectively used the Eastern connections of several officials of the previous
regime who joined the military-civilian coalition
and sent abroad a large number of high ranking "goodwill" delegations.

In Dahomey and Sierra Leone the problem of recognition by Eastern powers was of no consequence.
On the contrary, the Dahomeyan military regime unilaterally and without any provocation broke off
diplomatic relations with the People's Republic of
China.

As far as recognition by African states was concerned, the most acute problem arose when the "radical" African regimes refused to accept the military
government of Ghana and tried to bar its representative
from meetings of the Organization of African Unity.
The latter move collapsed due to the timely defection of Nkrumah's delegate and foreign minister, A.
Quaison-Sackey, the overwhelming warm reaction to
the coup inside Ghana, and the effective control of
the country exercised by the NLC. It took the radical regimes some time to reconcile themselves to the
unpleasant reality. President Sékou Touré of Guinea
proved to be the most acrimonious and hostile and
publicly threatened to invade Ghana via and despite
the protests of the Ivory Coast. He not only extended hospitality to Nkrumah and verbally conferred
various honorific but meaningless titles on him but
also to a certain extent placed Radio Conakry[3] and

---

*Although the Soviets might have helped Nkrumah's
activities from Conakry, as the NLC implied on several occasions. On the other hand the Soviets sto-
ically withstood several serious provocations and
humiliations by the military regime.

Guinean diplomatic machinery at Nkrumah's disposal
to enable him to carry out subversive activities
against the military government. The breakdown of
diplomatic relations between Ghana and Guinea was
followed by serious diplomatic incidents and emotional
intolerance on both sides, and the first public mes-
sages of goodwill were exchanged only after the NLC
gave way to a civilian government. The reaction of
the African radical regimes, mainly Guinea and Algeria, toward the Malian coup was milder, and their
apprehensions were soon soothed.

On the whole, the external environment has been
either favorable or neutral to the new military governments, and the spirit of noninterference prevailing in the Organization of African Unity helped them
to obtain a measure of international respectability
that was important in order to consolidate their rule
internally.

The military rulers used a number of techniques
to bolster their legitimacy internally and externally. One of these was a stress on the unconstitutionality and illegitimacy of the previous civilian
regime. The Ghanaian junta kept repeating the charges
of tyranny, subversion of the norms of parliamen-
tarianism, repression, and violations of human and
individual rights. Due to Nkrumah's refusal to hold
parliamentary elections in 1965 the CPP regime was
labeled unconstitutional. Nkrumah also was accused
of corruption, misspending, and mismanagement, as
well as conducting foreign policy prejudicial to
Ghana's national interests and contrary to the spirit
of African unity.

The Malian junta in its public relations and
propaganda campaign used accusations of Modibo Keita's
dictatorial rule, "cult of personality," repression,
lawlessness, and violations of the constitution and
the party statute. The previous regime ruled through
extra legal bodies like the CNDR and dissolved the
National Assembly. The US-RDA rulers allegedly had
continuously improvised, were concerned with pseudo-
prestige, and had mismanaged national resources.
They also were accused of deviating from a foreign
policy of "nonalignment," renouncing the principle
of national sovereignty and noninterference into the
internal affairs of other states, and so forth.

In Sierra Leone, Brigadier Lansana justified
his imposition of martial law by the false argument
of the unconstitutionality of the appointment of a
new APC-dominated government and intentionally lied
to the country by pretending that Siaka Stevens was
not yet sworn as the new prime minister. The succeeding junta led by Major Blake repeated Brigadier
Lansana's contentions, using them as a legitimizing
symbol. In Dahomey, General Soglo could not utilize
the same argument but he indirectly used the lack of
prestige enjoyed in the country by the provisional
government of T. Congacou. The weakness of this
negative tact and in part the accompanying circumstances led the Dahomeyan and Sierra Leonean juntas
to play on the dangers of internal disorder and
bloody regional-ethnic clashes if the military coups
had not occurred. This claim was of debatable value
in Dahomey and admittedly false in Sierra Leone.

Since nothing succeeds like success, the military
regimes in Ghana and Mali derived their initial legitimacy from their warm public reaction and their
effective control of the respective countries. To
enhance their legitimacy they used the state-owned
mass media--radio, television, and newspapers--as
well as mass rallies and meetings held throughout
the country. These instruments also served with
varying effectiveness the military regimes that were
met either with hostility (the first coup in Sierra
Leone) or with indifference (the December 1967 coup
in Dahomey and the March 23, 1967, coup in Sierra
Leone). Typically, soon after the takeovers the
members of the new juntas visited their native towns
or villages and places where they had served previously
or were known through relatives, wives, or personal
connections. On such occasions public meetings were
held and the population saw the new rulers with local
dignitaries and power-brokers. New ties, patronage
and interest group articulation, and a modified net
of power relations between local, regional, and national political levels were established.

The military rulers in all four countries were
anxious to gain prestige through association with
more or less traditional sources of power and with
religion: the chiefs and clergy in Ghana, leaders
of religious communities in Mali, traditional rulers

and denominational leaders in Dahomey. The Sierra Leonean junta was the least successful in trying to benefit from the association with paramount chiefs (who were included in two advisory bodies) and religious life. The stress on neotraditionalism and religion seemed particularly appropriate as a legitimizing device in contrast with the radical regimes in Ghana and Mali, which had been influenced by Marxism and atheism. The differences between the two cases in this respect were substantial.

In Mali the institution of chef de canton, created by the French and later abolished by the US-RDA regime, had no great importance, and the remnants of the pre-colonial power structures either were fragmented or continued to function informally on the local level through the US-RDA period.[4] Traditional authorities were left intact only among the Touareg nomads in the North until the insurrection broke out. Modibo Keita, unlike Nkrumah, has been a devout Moslem believer and although in this respect he was not typical of the inner circle of the Malian leadership, this personal trait and corresponding religious tolerance in Mali eased tensions between the regime and the traditionalist majority of the population.[5] The party's newspaper on many occasions has affirmed the compatibility of socialism and Islam.[6] The new military rulers were still closer to those groups of the population that were least affected by the materialist and atheist strain in the US-RDA ideology, for whom appearances in mosques and Catholic churches served as a legitimizing symbol.

In Ghana the persisting social, and to a lesser extent political, influence of the chiefs is still appreciable. The actual degradation of many of them under the CPP, coupled with what was considered undue politization and exploitation of these officers for political purposes, had alienated from the CPP regime the traditionalist segments of the population, particularly in rural areas. The opposition to Nkrumah himself attempted to utilize some of the traditional trappings and symbols for its own purposes and to capitalize on the fact that his policies and suspected intentions were resented by a substantial part of the population. Nkrumah's attempt to place all corporate and other organized bodies under the party's control and his adoption, at least in words, of a strong anti-Western posture led to conflicts with Protestant denominations and the Roman Catholic Church over the separate and "apolitical" children's, women's, youth, and other organizations connected with Western Christian churches (YMCA, YWCA, Boy Scouts, Girl Scouts). A superstitious nonchurchgoer, Nkrumah also offended the urban Christian elite that has been a willing and conscious pipeline of British and Western influence into Ghana.

The military junta on the other hand used both its sympathies and ties with the chiefs and its Christian churchgoing fervor as an instrument to forge popular support. The NLC upgraded the institutions of the traditional rulers and improved their financial situation without fully reversing the clock. NLC members took a keen interest in chiefly affairs and appeared in national dress at traditional ceremonies. Their church attendance also was well-recorded by the government-owned mass media.

Another ex-post facto symbol of legitimation used by the Ghanaian and Malian juntas has been the conscious effort to adhere as closely as possible to the Western liberal norms of political tolerance and presumably to the political doctrine of laissez-faire. The juntas were reluctant to interfere in the internal affairs of those institutions and corporate bodies borrowed from Britain and France that are considered nongovernmental and nonpartisan in the former colonial metropole (schools, universities, trade unions, various voluntary associations, women's, children's, and youth groups). The abolished political parties and most of their members, with the exception of relatively few leaders, have been treated with restraint. This has been done, particularly in Mali, at significant political cost, yet the juntas were determined to show that they were different and better than the regime they illegally ousted. This also was useful for public relations in the West, East, and within Africa.

If the junta accused the previous regime of conspicuous spending of public money and an obsession with prestige, then the junta members have tried to project and manipulate the dual images of modesty and austerity: they drive in jeeps instead of limou-

sines; they also reduce conspicuous spending, i.e.,
travel abroad and other forms of nonproductive visible spending. The Malian junta, and to a lesser extent the regime of young cadres in Dahomey, has done
this. The military also tries to enhance its legitimacy by negating the existence of any selfish motives
for plotting. The Sierra Leonean junta, the CRN,
pledged not to enhance the material standards of the
army, and the members of the CMLN in Mali avoided
promoting themselves in rank despite the many vacan-
cies in the top grades. Nor were there such promotions under the government of young cadres in Dahomey.
This feature seems to be associated with insecurity
and lack of self-confidence or possibly might result
from the influence of puritanism (there is an element
of the latter in the Malian case).

In all five cases of successful coups followed
by prolonged periods of military rule (coups I, II,
IV, VI, and VII in Table 5 above) the new military
juntas used the continuity of administration--civil
service, particularly judiciary, and, if possible,
ministers of the ousted government (the latter happened in Dahomey, Sierra Leone, and Mali). The
juntas also made declarations of basic continuity in
regard to foreign affairs and international commitments as a legitimizing device for internal and external consumption.

We conclude that several types of methods to
achieve legitimacy are recurrent in most situations.
The two most frequent are as follows: (1) "legitimation in the negative," i.e., playing on the real
or pretended illegitimacy and unconstitutionality of
the previous regime or on its unpopular traits and
(2) "legitimation through association" with various
symbols of social and para-political prestige. The
tools at the juntas' disposal are almost identical,
i.e., travel in the countryside, mass rallies, visible presence and display of the attributes of state
power, the government-controlled mass media, and
patronage power. The use of particular devices seems
to be determined by the reaction to accusations
leveled against the ousted regime. The particular
mix of such devices, its variation over time, and
the duration of determined efforts depend on public
reaction to the military regime, the strength of the

residues of the previous order, and the junta's life
style, norms structure, and commitments.

THE COMPOSITION AND INTERNAL
ORGANIZATION OF THE JUNTAS

It was noted earlier that the size of the initial nucleus of plotters tends to be smaller under
conditions of tight secret police surveillance and
when the plotters are not in the highest ranks and
are not plotting together with those who hold effective control over the state apparatus. The eventual
size of the junta, or more precisely the number of
members invited or coopted by the original nucleus,
depends to a large extent on the exigencies at the
time the junta is enlarged. If the expansion occurs
while the military outcome of the coup is still un-
certain (as happened in Mali) then the criteria used
are related primarily or exclusively to considerations of assuring success in pure military terms,
and possibly to preserving the army's corporate
unity. As the expansion in Mali seems to have occurred after the initial success of the insurrection
(the kidnapping of the army chief of staff) and as
the plotters decided to play for all or nothing, the
resulting body was the largest in the sample. The
original nucleus desired to include as many reliable
holders of critical elements in the military establishment as possible. The first full meeting of the
CMLN did not take place until after the consummation
of the coup. Hence the consideration of a feasible
working size probably was not considered of great
importance since the decision to rule the country
for an extended period of time was taken one to two
months later.
In Ghana the expansion was agreed upon by two
out of three members of the nucleus* after Colonel

---

*Colonel Kotoka and Inspector-General of Police
J. W. K. Harlley. The third member, Major A. A. Afrifa, was then in the field, and although more important militarily than Harlley, his political and intellectual influence at that stage seems to have been
negligible.

Kotoka's proclamation over the radio and after military success became certain. Therefore the criteria for expansion were a combination of prominence in plotting, internal corporate considerations, and political needs. Three members of the nucleus were there, but of the two military and police officers most active in the preparations, Major Coker-Appiah and A. Deku, director of the Criminal Investigation Department, the former was not considered and the second got in only with great difficulty.

On the army side, the nucleus was expanded by the inclusion of the second-ranking general fired by Nkrumah seven months earlier from the position of chief of army staff. He was invited to become chairman of the junta in order to restore and preserve corporate unity and hierarchical order. Next to be coopted was the commander of the First (and most important) Brigade, Colonel Ocran, who at that moment was eliminating the last pockets of resistance. Inspector Harlley's political skills and the fact that Colonel Kotoka was enjoying his hospitality in police headquarters probably contributed to the near parity in representation of the police. Harlley seems to have been content to bring along only two of his subordinates--J. E. O. Nunoo, a Ga, and B. A. Yakubu, the only Northerner in the future junta--and to obtain a four-to-three army-police ratio. He was reluctant to have A. Deku on the council, apart from personal reasons because with Deku the number of Ewe members rose to three out of eight, an excessive ratio.

Once a coup is over, the formation of a junta, even if it is fluid and informal as was the junta headed by General Soglo in Dahomey, cannot be postponed indefinitely. In the three cases where the juntas were established _after_ the consummation of a successful coup--the March 23, 1967, and December 17, 1967, coups in Sierra Leone and the December 17, 1967, coup in Dahomey--expansion from the original nucleus occurred several days later. The mechanisms in these two cases were somewhat different: by strict invitation in Sierra Leone and as a result of blurred, undeclared, Byzantine, and behind-the-scenes bargaining and sizing up of the relative weight of various factions of junior officers and some NCOs in Dahomey. In both cases corporate propriety and the concern for rank hierarchy were present, but, in comparison to the cases dealt with previously, there was a clear concern for politically, as opposed to militarily, relevant criteria of selection. The Sierra Leone nucleus went so far as to manipulate the selection of the invited chairman in order to, among other things, achieve equal representation in the junta of all four administrative divisions of the country. In Dahomey there was a strong concern to have an equal number of Northerners and Southerners. Apart from the ethnic background, there are some indications that the public images of several candidates were taken into account.

Such criteria for subsequent successful rule as intellectual caliber and relevant experience do not appear to have been operative. The range of possible choices along these dimensions in the numerically rather small and organizationally simple officer corps seems to have been very limited, if it existed at all.

We conclude that the later the expansion of the original nucleus of plotters takes place the greater is the relative weight of political criteria for the selection of the coopted members of the military junta. This phenomenon can be explained by the process of eventual removal of strong anxieties for personal and corporate security, as well as by the replacement of the original concern for technical success of the coup by considerations related to the junta's ability to rule the country.

We discussed previously the differences in patterns of the army and police organizations along the British and French lines. As a result of one of these differences, the civilian police in French-speaking countries plays a negligible role in coup situations while the Gendarmerie's importance is similar in certain respects or sometimes even greater than that of police in English-speaking countries. This contrast resulted in the presence of a small number of Gendarmerie officers (but no police officers) in or close to the military juntas of Dahomey and Mali. The commander of the Malian Gendarmerie, Major Bala Koné, was not a member of the nucleus but supported the coup and in recognition was made minis-

ter of information. Other high Gendarmerie officers,
Major Adandédjan and Captain F. Johnson, were members
of the first and second juntas respectively in Dahomey. The police in Ghana and Sierra Leone on the
other hand--despite their impressive numbers and importance in terms of intelligence, communications,
and ability to control the countryside and watch
the borders--were unarmed. Hence the coups in both
countries were almost exclusively army affairs, with
the police coming into the picture only after the
ousted government was neutralized. The upshot of
this was the lower status of police representatives
in the juntas and, in Sierra Leone, a distinct minority participation (two out of eight members). Thus
the organization of the army and police establishments
in the sample clearly led to distinct patterns of
junta composition, to a French-speaking versus English-
speaking dichotomy, and to peculiar stratification
within the juntas in the English-speaking half of
the sample.

The inclusion of police officers in the Ghanaian
and Sierra Leonean juntas introduced a potential
source of cleavages along army versus police lines.
In the NRC in Sierra Leone this cleavage took the
form of a mild antagonism between A. Juxon-Smith
and W. L. Leigh,* and NRC Chairman Juxon-Smith on
several occasions expressed his preference for an
all-army junta. In the Ghanaian case, the problem
was not so much personal relations between the army
and police members in the council. Moreover, the
police officers, particularly Inspector-General Harlley, contributed significantly to the preservation
of the body, which was on the brink of total collapse
on at least two occasions--thanks to its army members,
A. A. Afrifa in particular and later J. A. Ankrah.
What burdened army-police relations was the rather
low esteem in which the Ghanaian police were held by
the army personnel. In the army's mind, the police
were associated with corruption, low professionalism,
and repressive measures under Nkrumah,[7] and this pro-

---

*The second police member, Deputy Commissioner
A. Kamara, did not assert himself and participated
in the NRC out of loyalty to Commissioner Leigh.

duced not so much cleavages within the junta as between the junta and junior officers in the army.

There seems to exist some correlation between
the degree of insecurity and tension under which
seditious activities and plotting are carried out
and the stability of the subsequent junta. The
juntas whose nuclei were formed under the tension
and stress of insecurity (Ghana, Mali, second coup
in Sierra Leone) turned out to be rather well-struc-
tured and stable in this sense. The two coups that
were preceded by almost open plotting with participation of a number of civilians (the Soglo coup in
Dahomey in December 1965 and the Lansana coup in
Sierra Leone in 1967) led to the formation of fluid
and unstructured juntas. The December 1967 coup in
Dahomey seems to support the notion of a minimal
threshold of tension and insecurity above which seditious activities produce internally stable, structured, and more coherent bodies. In 1967 the stress
during several months of plotting among Dahomeyan
officers was rather low and barely above a postulated
minimum. The resulting junta was structured but
lasted in this form for less than a month. A common
sense explanation of the noticed regularity is that
above a certain level the risks and anxieties of
plotting contribute to the creation of bonds of loyalty and community as well as bonds of certain divisions of labor and a "feel" of the other members in
the group.

Not all the juntas that had operated over an extended period of time* evolved their own internal
rules and procedures. Both Dahomeyan juntas were
fluid or ill-structured, informal and policentric, and
competing institutions: the presidency, Council of
Ministers, Military Vigilance Committee, Military
Revolutionary Committee, Military Tribunal, and so
forth. There were no clear and stated rules on how

---

*In Dahomey, the Soglo junta for two years and
the government of young cadres for eight months; in
Ghana, the NLC for three and one-half years; in
Sierra Leone, the NRC for almost 13 months; and in
Mali, the CMLN for three and one-half years to date
(by summer 1972).

these groups should go about reaching at least a
semblance of consensus and concert of action.

In Ghana and particularly in Sierra Leone the
influence of the procedural practice of the British
cabinet was distinct. The internal rules for the
Sierra Leonean NRC were elaborated by a British-
trained top civil servant and an official of the
previous government who consciously selected from
British practice those elements that seemed to be
appropriate for the military rulers. The Ghanaian
NLC worked during the first 16 months as a military
version of a cabinet and from July 1967 on became
an inner cabinet whose three members also participated
in the work of the 17-member military-civilian Executive Council.

The Ghanaian and Sierra Leonean juntas deviated
in their actual practice, as opposed to the written
norms, from the British model. The principle of collective responsibility, one of the central elements
of British practice and a cornerstone of political
discipline, was violated on a number of occasions by
prominent junta members, notably by Juxon-Smith of
the NRC and Afrifa of the NLC. Both were almost arrested but eventually went unpunished. In the juntas'
deliberations there was an appreciable element of
African palaver, or arriving at a consensus after a
long parley. Although the procedural rules stipulated
the procedures for taking a vote, the juntas tried
to avoid clear confrontations and preferred to debate
controversial issues several times over rather than
to see their ranks divided. It was in a large part
due to this concern that the chairman of the two
bodies wielded considerable power when they formulated
a common platform and used the prerogative of closure.

Although operating within a framework of different modern bureaucratic traditions basically inherited
from the French, the Malian junta in its internal
practice was very close to the actual mode of operation of the Ghanaian and Sierra Leonean juntas. One
member of the CMLN, Captain Diakité, did not thoroughly follow the principle of collective responsibility, and although his transgressions were not as
blatant as those of Juxon-Smith and Afrifa they were
nevertheless sufficient to contribute substantially
to his demotion in the government in September 1969.

The CMLN also extensively used the method of African palaver. It held its meetings as a rule every Thursday. In the practice of the Malian junta, we also can observe an almost inevitable tendency to concentrate power in the hands of the chairman. In all these respects the actual practice of the Malian junta deviated from the secret written rules stated in a small booklet that every member possessed.

Probably the most important deviation from the stated rules was due to an inherent conflict between the hierarchical structure of the military establishment and the egalitarian tendencies of a brotherhood of plotters equally exposed to risks. The Ghanaian, Sierra Leonean, and Malian juntas set out to resolve or minimize these tensions in different fashions. In all three cases the junta chairman was exposed to often silent pressures not to show off at the expense of the ordinary members. General Ankrah recognized this and toed the line during the first year and one-half, mainly because he was an "invited" member. Later, after General Kotoka's death, he became more self-confident and self-indulgent and tried to convert his formal prominence into the position of a civilian president of the Republic. At this juncture he was effectively stopped by a coalition of civilian supporters of Afrifa and by J. W. K. Harlley, the power-broker in the junta and then the number-two man.

In Sierra Leone, Juxon-Smith, the invited chairman, consistently fought back the egalitarian pressures by referring to and exploiting his superior military rank and seniority. It is believed that he was once arrested by Major Blake, and a move to finally outvote him in the council, contemplated by the original nucleus, was overtaken by the counter-coup/mutiny on April 17, 1968. In Mali tensions of this kind were generated not between the CMLN and its chairman, Lieutenant Traoré, but between a majority in the junta and its first vice-chairman, Capttain Diakité, who was the most senior and oldest officer among the plotters.

Thus the mode of actual functioning in the structured and relatively stable juntas did not vary appreciably between the countries with a British and French bureaucratic heritage, except for the presence of police officers in the English-speaking juntas. More important factors seem to be variations in seniority, age, and professional profile among junta members (these variations were greatest in Ghana and smallest in Mali) and the circumstances of formation and expansion of the original nucleus (e.g., whether the junta's titular head had belonged to the original nucleus). In all observed juntas there was a discrepancy between the formal and informal power structure, but we shall dwell on this later. Among the stable juntas in the sample, we are not aware of clear cases of consistent internal alignments and cleavages along regional-ethnic lines. The Dahomeyan young cadres or Young Turks came closest to such a division, but not all the way. And, finally, in terms of norms structures all observed juntas were relatively homogeneous and/or capable of concealing such differences behind a facade of corporate solidarity. The near breakup of the Ghanaian NLC and Sierra Leonean NRC could have occurred more on personal and tactical political grounds than on the basis of deep norms incongruence.

LEADERSHIP

In our discussion of composition and internal organization we unavoidably touched on the problem of leadership. The juntas resulting from the seven successful coups clearly were led by the leaders of the nucleus at the moment of the coup only in three cases (General Soglo, Brigadier Lansana, and Lieutenant Moussa Traoré). In one case the leader of the nucleus formally ceded his predominant position four days after the takeover to his immediate superior, who at the last moment refused to join the plotters. The result was a kind of condominium (Lieutenant-Colonel A. Alley and Major M. Kouandété of Dahomey). In three cases the subsequent juntas in fact were headed by invited military officers, always senior to those in the nucleus (General J. A. Ankrah, Lieutenant-Colonel A. Juxon-Smith, and Colonel J. Bangura--in the last two cases after brief periods of interregnum ranging from one to five days). It seems plausible to conclude that the most important factors influencing the outcome are the

level of military hierarchy from which the coup is
launched and the difference between the British and
French heritage. When the coup leader is the commanding and highest ranking active officer in the
army, he remains the head of the subsequent junta,
at least until the next coup (General Soglo and
Brigadier Lansana). When this is not the case--i.e.,
when the coup is directed from an intermediary or
low level in the military hierarchy against the civilian regime and/or against the top brass--the
nuclei in the countries of British tradition tend to
invite the most agreeable senior officer to take
over the chairmanship. In the French-speaking half
of our sample this happened in Dahomey in December
1967, but only formally and under duress (in order
to make the French less irritated with the coup).
The Malian nucleus was not very much concerned with
the inevitable conflict between the ranks and the
real power position that resulted from their failure
to have at least a "swing man" figurehead brought in.
It seems that British-trained officers have a higher
respect for rank hierarchy and bureaucratic propriety
than French-trained officers.

When the chairmen are invited in, although here
the sample is clearly too small to make valid generalizations, the predominant criterion of selection
is corporate unity and cohesion based on established
impersonal norms of bureaucratic organization. The
nucleus of the second Sierra Leone junta, headed by
Major Blake, manipulated and rigged these procedures
for a while, but not too much. The motives behind
the manipulation were personal, regional-ethnic, and
perhaps in a small part also related to probable
political alignments and sympathies.

The noninvited chairman's position results from
his prominence in the plotting phase. In the cases
of General Soglo and Brigadier Lansana these positions were ascriptive, while the Malian nucleus
elected Lieutenant M. Traoré to this position very
shortly before the coup in preference to the previous
leader, Captain Diakité. The motives for this
switch were Lieutenant Traoré's superior personal
courage and modesty, lack of intellectual ambitions,
greater closeness to the majority in the original
nucleus in terms of age, education, outlook, and rank,
as well as his personal congeniality.

177

The stability of the juntas' leadership is directly related to the susceptibility of the military establishment to internal mutinies. Every junta leader tries to make his own coup the last one, but not all succeed in this effort. We discussed earlier the problem of contagion and now will state only that sharp cleavages in the military establishment at large, between the junta and the rest of the officer corps, or between the junta and NCOs and enlisted men, as well as those within the junta, are the primary causes of instability of junta leadership and the junta itself. In the present sample one leader (General Soglo) was ousted as a result of a conflict between his junta and the intermediary and junior officers left out of power; two leaders (Brigadier Lansana and General Ankrah) lost their positions due to political and personal disagreements within the respective juntas; and one leader (Brigadier Juxon-Smith) was arrested by mutinous NCOs and soldiers. It appears that the critical intervening factors are the ability of the junta leaders to inspire confidence and trust, to maintain dialogue and channels of communication within the ruling junta and between the junta and the potential contending groups in the military, to cultivate the junta's public image, and to display diplomatic skills. A theoretical alternative, to keep the army under tight control and suppress potential internal opposition, did not seem to work in the four cases in our sample if not combined with "positive" measures. The consequences of the two unsuccessful conspiracies and coups in our sample (Ghana in 1967 and Mali in 1969) seem to have been overcome by a combination of force, increased caution, and somewhat better public relations within the army.

THE INSTITUTIONAL FRAMEWORK AND
INFORMAL ORGANIZATION OF
DECISION-MAKING ON THE
NATIONAL LEVEL

A comparison of the five juntas that operated in the four countries for more than several days-- two in Dahomey and one each in Ghana, Sierra Leone,

178

and Mali, with the variance in duration between
eight months and three and one-half years--shows
substantial variation in formal organizational structure (see Figures 1-5 in earlier chapters). Both
Dahomeyan juntas were ill-defined: the first, General Soglo's, was informal and fluid; that of the
young cadres was variable and vague in composition
and structurally policentric. In the other three
countries the juntas were closed or almost closed,
precisely defined (in terms of composition and internal rules), and structured institutions. The
size of these bodies varied over time: 7, 8, 7, 8,
7, 6 members in Ghana; 7, 8 in Sierra Leone; 14, 13
in Mali. All had secretariats charged with prepar-
ing the sessions, supervising channels of communication with other governmental agencies, and exercising a measure of supervision over the implementation
of junta decisions. In two of three cases, the chairman of the junta was placed in charge of the junta's
secretariat (office).

The Military Committee of National Liberation
(CMLN) in Mali differed from the other two. Due to
a significant extent to its larger size, the CMLN
created a bureau consisting of five officers (chairman, first and second vice-chairmen, permanent
secretary, and commissioner for settling conflicts).
This elected inner body carried out some of the functions exercised by the chairmen in Ghana and Sierra
Leone, such as fixing the agenda for the meeting
and deciding on preliminary procedural questions
(distribution of materials, communications with
other governmental agencies related to future meetings, and the like). Lieutenant Filifing Cissoko,
the permanent secretary, in fact was directing the
activities and administering the secretariat of the
CMLN, thus relieving the overworked and overburdened
chairman, Lieutant Traoré, of some administrative
chores. This became a source of considerable informal power for Cissoko.

The Ghanaian and Sierra Leonean juntas, had
only three types of members: chairman, deputy chairman, and ordinary members. The deputy chairman, often head of the police in the English-speaking countries, replaced the chairman during his absence but
otherwise wielded formal power only slightly greater

179

than that of the ordinary members. In both cases (Ghana and Sierra Leone) the deputy chairmen headed, in addition to their duties in the junta and in the police, the ministry for foreign affairs, probably in recognition of their wider previous political experience in general and in dealing with foreigners in particular.

We already have discussed the internal organization of the juntas and should add that one of them (the NRC in Sierra Leone) introduced the institution of a rotating member (out of the total of eight). This member, junior in rank, served for three months, usually helping the chairman in the NRC secretariat and/or discharging some of his numerous duties (for instance as the head of the ministerial department for interior). Although the origin of this institution was accidental, it seems to have helped the junta to remove pressure from the officer ranks to effectively share power with them. The Soglo junta in Dahomey, the NLC in Ghana, and the CMLN in Mali had to contend with pressures of this kind and the internal insurrections against all three from junior ranks were closely related to this problem. The junta of the young cadres carried out one thorough reshuffle of the Council of Ministers, which in fact had the effect of one tour of rotation of junior officers in ministerial positions. Thanks to its fluidity and instability, the young cadres junta overcame this problem in an arbitrary and irregular fashion.

Following an almost successful insurrection led by a young lieutenant in April 1967 the Ghanaian NLC gave thought to possible ways of associating a larger section of the officer corps, other than the already participating senior officers, with the regime. Lieutenant General Kotoka, while the general officer commanding, used to visit the garrisons around the country regularly to talk to the troops and meet the officers in the mess after parades. Due to a much larger size and dispersion of the army units at great distances from Accra (unlike the situation in Sierra Leone), the top brass decided against the institutionalized widening of the army's involvement in politics for practical, security, and corporate cohesion reasons.

All juntas, whether structurally stable or not, shared a number of features. They were in fact, if not always in law, the highest decision-making and supervising bodies on the national level. The juntas were legally responsible to no one, including the armed forces they claimed to represent. An institutional assembly of (senior) officers functioned only in Ghana, and irregular meetings of a similar kind were held on several occasions in Dahomey (more often under the government of young cadres than under General Soglo) and Mali. But these were clearly consultative bodies, not military parliaments. In all cases there were functioning or attempted civilian consultative bodies. In time all juntas developed informal power structures different from the formal ones. None of them commanded sufficient manpower among the military officers in terms of numbers, quality, and relevant skills and expertise to enable the junta not to rely heavily on the civilian bureaucracy and civilian advisers. All of them in fact represented military-civilian coalitions in which the relative weight of the four basic ingredients (junta, military officers involved in running the state, civilian bureaucrats, and influential advisers) varied.

Taking each of these common features separately, we shall now analyze the differences between the five stable juntas. In Dahomey no junta was legally proclaimed to be the highest institution of the Republic. The de facto preeminence of the two Dahomeyan juntas was assured by the fact that their heads simultaneously occupied the post of president of the Republic (General Soglo in 1965-67; Major M. Kouandété in 1967; Lieutenant-Colonel A. Alley in 1967-68) and chairman of the Council of Ministers (General Soglo in 1965-67; Major Kouandété in 1967-68). Since the constitution was suspended and the National Assembly, municipal councils, and other elective bodies disbanded, the junta heads commanded full legislative and executive powers. Whatever was decided in a small circle of real power-holders usually was approved without much difficulty in the Council of Ministers, dominated by the junta, and enacted by either a presidential decree or an executive order. When, in the spring of 1968 after a new constitution was adopted by referendum, the Supreme Court declared one of these executive acts (an election law) unconstitutional the junta simply suspended temporarily both the new constitution and the Supreme Court.

The juntas in Ghana, Sierra Leone, and Mali suspended the respective constitutions, dissolved the parliaments or what was left of them, dissolved other elective bodies on regional and local levels, dismissed the civilian governments and their ministers, disbanded political parties and other organizations, and formally prohibited all political activity. Unlike their Dahomeyan colleagues the NLC, NRC, and CMLN took care to enact quasi-legal provisional charters that vested them with supreme power of rule by decree. The juntas were placed above all existing or newly created, recreated, or reappointed bodies (such as the provisional government in Mali and, from 1967, the Executive Council in Ghana).

As far as the relationship between the junta as the highest decision-making and legislative body and the government proper is concerned, our sample contains two clear and distinct types or models of organization. The Sierra Leonean National Reformation Council combined in itself the functions of the previous institutions of the governor-general, House of Representatives, prime minister, and cabinet. The junta members divided among themselves all ministerial portfolios while civilians occupied only advisory and nominally nonpolitical administrative posts such as secretaries-general to the NRC and secretaries of the ministerial departments.

Another extreme evolved under the Military Committee of National Liberation (CMLN) in Mali. There the junta assumed the prerogatives of the president and the National Assembly but set up a Council of Ministers as a separate institution. Only two members of the junta plus one more senior military officer were vested with direct ministerial responsibilities, the rest of the 15 portfolios being distributed among civilian allies of the CMLN. In September 1969, 10 months after the coup, this scheme was modified by having the CMLN chairman combine with this position the post of the chairman of the Council of Ministers. Previously the latter post was occupied by the first vice-chairman of the CMLN. The number

of junta members in the Council of Ministers increased
at the expense of the civilians.

The Ghanaian NLC started with a scheme that formally was almost identical with the setup later
adopted in Sierra Leone (the Sierra Leoneans may have
emulated the Ghanaians), but in July 1967 the Ghanaians shifted toward the system applied in Mali a
year later.

The Dahomeyan system under General Soglo, chron-
ologically the earliest of the five, was very similar to the original Malian type, the basic difference
being a formally structured junta. The two top members of the informally existing junta held three
portfolios in the Council of Ministers (General Soglo
as chairman and Colonel P. Aho as minister of defense,
and interior and security). The junta had supreme
decision-making and legislative powers (by presidential decree) and contained in its midst the head of
state.

From the institutional point of view the Dahomey
coup in December 1967 only slightly changed this
setup. General Soglo and Colonel Aho were sacked
and replaced by Lieutenant-Colonel Alley and Major
Kouandété, who divided among themselves the posts of
head of state and chief executive. Most of the
civilian ministers were replaced by junior officers.
Formally, two new institutions appeared on the surface, the Military Revolutionary Committee and the
Military Tribunal, but in fact not all of the influential officers were among their members. The informal junta consisted de facto of the president of
the Republic, chairman of the Council of Ministers,
two or three influential ministers, two or three influential members of the Military Revolutionary Committee, and the chairman of the Military Tribunal.
This informal junta, as under General Soglo, over-
lapped with the Council of Ministers.

We shall discuss the informal structure of
decision-making shortly but we deem it pertinent to
note that the formal organizational setups on the
national level do not seem to have resulted from any
predetermined or thoroughly copied blueprint. They
rather reflected the immediate needs and circumstances of the juntas' operation. The plotters always
replaced the top civilian decision-makers irrespective

of their formal position (president-cum-chief executive, prime minister), while relations with the Council of Ministers and its members depended on the tenor of their attitude toward the new rulers. Consciously or unconsciously, the new juntas assimilated or reacted to the organizational schemes of the ousted civilian government.

For instance, the Malian model of military rule strongly resembled the governmental scheme that evolved under Modibo Keita between August 1967 and the coup. The junta simply replaced the National Committee for the Defense of Revolution, another extra-constitutional highest decision-making and supervising body placed above all other institutions in the country. The Dahomeyan juntas did not formally deviate from the previously existing institutional framework. The Ghanaian (1966-67) and Sierra Leonen setups resulted from the replacement of the four existing institutions (head of state, parliament, chief executive, cabinet) by one body. Apart from the institutional precedent, the organizational framework on the national level also mirrored the relations with civilian politicians, civil service or state administration, as well as the intentions of the military rulers as to the sharing of power with civilians and evolution toward constitutional rule.

During the rule of all five of the stable juntas there existed several kinds of consultative bodies. Purely military consultative organs were present in all cases except under the NRC in Sierra Leone. They varied in regularity and rank of members. The army members of the Ghanaian NLC regularly attended conferences of about 50 senior officers from the rank of major up, held every two months. They aired the pending issues of governance and kept in touch with sentiments among the upper layer of the military establishment. These conferences were held in Burma Camp and often lasted an entire day. The assembly had its subcommittees. Toward the close of each conference senior police officers would be invited to join, but the army top brass never went to similar gatherings in the central police headquarters. Military assemblies were held seldom and/or irregularly under the two juntas in Dahomey and Mali. In Mali

and under General Soglo in Dahomey these were restricted to the officer corps. Under the government
of the young cadres, military assemblies also included the most politicized and active NCOs. The
divided Dahomeyan military also created several kinds
of military committees charged with supervising the
ruling juntas. With no executive powers these committees turned out to be another variation on military consultative bodies and were rather ineffective
too.

    Mixed military-civilian or civilian-military
consultative bodies were known to all stable juntas.
Under General Soglo in Dahomey, the NLC in Ghana,
and the NRC in Sierra Leone there existed permanent
organs of this kind, while in Mali and under the
young cadres in Dahomey they were ad hoc bodies such
as several subcommissions of the Military Revolutionary Committee in Dahomey and the National Conference
of Cadres and "expanded meetings" of the junta under
the Malian CMLN. In the spring of 1969 the Malian
junta announced the formation of an 80-member National
Consultative Council to consist of civilians and 16
army officers, but so far (April 1971) this decision
has not been implemented.

    The purely or predominantly civilian varieties
of consultative bodies on the national level operated in Dahomey (December 1967-June 1967), Ghana
(March 1966-August 1969), Sierra Leone (April 1967-
April 1968), and Mali. In the first three cases
there existed permanent civilian consultative councils to the junta, while the Malian CMLN only appointed civilian commissions from time to time to
advise on specific and restricted matters (e.g., administrative reform, a new economic plan). In Ghana
and Sierra Leone the juntas formally created two
subvarieties of permanent civilian consultative bodies.
The first subvariety consisted of the Economic Advisory Committee (later called Economic Committee)
of the NLC and the Economic Advisory Committee to
the NRC. Both bodies were compact in size (around
six-seven members) and typically consisted of senior
civil servants running the economic ministries by
proxy and/or civilian confidants of the military
rulers. Both bodies were given full access to relevant information and to the most influential junta

members and were for prolonged periods of time housed next to the junta office. This subvariety in fact developed into advisory-executive institutions or into economic subcabinets. In Ghana the NLC created several other advisory-executive, advisory-investigative, and advisory-adjudicative committees and commissions (such as the Committee of Administration and the Expediting Committee).

The second and politically less influential subvariety was represented by the numerically much larger Political Advisory Committee (later renamed the National Advisory Committee) in Ghana and the National Reformation Advisory Council in Sierra Leone. These two were basically auxiliary public relations institutions that contained prominent figures, representatives of corporate bodies, and some former politicians. They were useful to the juntas as legitimizing symbols in the absence of the disbanded parliaments. The political advisory bodies tried to compete with the economic subvariety and lost miserably. The difference in organization and access to administration and executive power, the top priority given to economic recovery by the military, the presumably apolitical and highly technical nature of the economic committees' work, their close personal contact with the military rulers, the rulers' distrust of politicians, and a far greater self-confidence in dealing with political matters all worked positively for the economic subvariety.

In Dahomey under General Soglo these two subtypes were combined within the Committee of National Renovation. It included a commission dealing with economic and financial matters, but unlike their colleagues in Ghana and Sierra Leone its members did not enjoy close relations with the military rulers or speedy access to all relevant information (although they formally had a right to it) and to the state administration. The commission remained a strictly consultative subvariety.

It is difficult to disentangle all the factors that seem to have shaped the complicated and checkered development of the consultative bodies. This development reflected the need of the military rulers for qualified advice on technically complex matters; the perceived desirability of a better public image at home and abroad, of strengthened internal legitimacy, and of a manifest association with various politicized segments of population without surrendering power; and finally, this development reflected military-civilian relations in general and the intentions of the military rulers. Modern French and British bureaucratic traditions also left an imprint on the organization of these bodies. For instance, the Committee of National Renovation in Dahomey shared many features with the French Social and Economic Council.

All stable juntas in our sample developed informal power structures that included both officials and individuals who held no formal position. Even around the fluid and ill-structured juntas of Dahomey, which by definition are supposed to coincide with an informal power structure, there were influentials, predominantly civilians, who did not or could not appear at even informal meetings of office-holders who considered themselves "insiders." Yet in the more or less narrow areas of their competence and/or interest, they exerted a greater influence on, for instance, General Soglo than the high officers of the army. The informal influence of Mme. Soglo was particularly evident. General Soglo often listened privately to the advice of E.-D. Zinsou, his foreign minister, on external affairs and of his nephew, N. Soglo, finance minister, on economic problems. Next, the consensus on important matters was reached among the top officers--Colonel Aho, Lieutenant-Colonel Alley, Major Sinzogan, and Major Adandéjan--and subsequently a final decision was taken in the Council of Ministers.

The stable and formally structured Ghanaian junta had in the orbit around General Ankrah, its chairman, and Deputy Chairman J. W. K. Harlley, the head of the Economic Advisory Committee, E. N. Omaboe, a relative of General Ankrah. Omaboe enjoyed privileged access to both officers and not infrequently was invited to junta meetings. Between March 1966 and July 1967 his influence in economic matters was greater than that of many titular members of the NLC. A similar position vis-à-vis the NRC in Sierra Leone was occupied by two foreign economic advisers--G. Conrad and B. Quinn, the resident representative of the International Monetary Fund.

The informal structure of confidants, relatives, and friends tends to grow as time passes. After an initial period of uncertainty and disorientation, interest groups find their way to the new rulers, according to their assignments and in particular according to the most influential members of the junta and the power-brokers. The trend toward concentration of power in the hands of the "inner" group and the chairman, observed almost universally, creates two or more partly overlapping power circles of which only one is the formal junta.

The existence of these informal structures, interacting in varying fashions in different situations and areas of decision-making, has its underpinning in part in the inevitable division of labor, in the complexity of modern government even in small and poor polities, and in differentiation within every junta along the lines of such norms as life style, age, professional and political background, and rank. Nevertheless the hiatus between the normative and real share of power also signals a breakdown in internal communication and mutual trust and predates the creation of the lines of fracture and conflict. For instance, the predominant position within the CMLN in Mali of four to five officers around Lieutenant Traoré is closely related to the most serious source of the junta's internal instability, the rivalry between Traoré and Captain Diakité. An informal power structure, when it is known and includes controversial or for some reason unpopular figures, undermines the junta's relations with the officer corps and could tarnish the junta's public image (for example, it has been asserted that Mme. Soglo had offended many Dahomeyan officers under the general and greatly contributed to his downfall).

We already have stated some of the reasons why the military rulers, even if they do not particularly trust the civilians, are obliged to rely heavily on civilian advisers, top officials, civil servants, and prestigious and prominent leaders and citizens. The juntas must comply for reasons of legitimation, in order to assure a sufficient measure of public support and in order to govern effectively. There is some overlap between these three objectives, with a corresponding overlap in the categories of civilians approached by or attracted to the juntas.

The first set of considerations brings into the junta's orbit civilians who possess various symbols of social prestige, e.g., popular traditional leaders, chiefs, priests, judges. Since the military in the four countries in our sample refused to use the previously existing political organizations for their own purposes as the Algerian junta did, the second set of considerations leads the juntas to approach local power-brokers and leaders of professional organizations, corporate bodies (universities, trade unions, chambers of commerce, denominational organizations), newspapermen, and public relations men (there was a special public relations committee under the NRC in Sierra Leone).

The juntas do not possess and/or effectively control sufficient sources of qualified manpower to meet the exigencies of governance, and they lack the relevant expertise and experience. The military junta, often disdaining and underestimating professional civilian politicians, believes that its members and other amateurs in uniform can do the jobs of skilled civilians in many high positions. At the same time it recognizes that there are also areas of government that require special training and experience. In addition, certain circumstances might prompt a junta not to commit all available manpower from among the officer corps to the running or supervising of the civilian administration. Moreover, if there is a perceived high congruence of norms and goals between the junta and the top civilian bureaucrats and groups of civilian politicians, the junta is likely to opt for government by proxy, retaining only the monopoly of making basic decisions and the veto in less important areas.

The pattern of the functional division of labor in decision-making under the five stable juntas in our sample shows several regularities. In all cases the military junta completely monopolized decision-making in defense and security matters. Institutionally, this invariably was achieved by having military officers as ministers of defense, and interior and security, and as directors of internal security agencies in French-speaking countries. This was an irreducible military position in the cabinet and Council of Ministers under military rule. The post of minister of defense usually was held either by the junta's leader himself (General Soglo, Major Kouandété, Brigadier Juxon-Smith, General Ankrah), by his deputy or a strongman (Colonel Aho, Lieutenant-General Kotoka), or by an influential member of the junta (Captain Cissoko in Mali). If the transition to civilian rule was gradual and orderly, the ministry of defense was the last to be released. Functionally, monopolization in the areas of defense and security was maintained by withholding these matters from meaningful discussions with civilians. In Ghana, principal secretaries in the ministries of defense and interior sat on the Defense Council, but both were subordinated to their military ministers.

The juntas invariably took great interest in foreign policy. Institutionally, their role was expressed through holding the portfolio of external affairs and through availing themselves of foreign travel in state delegations and socializing with diplomats. But holding the external affairs portfolio was not a uniform practice. General J. A. Ankrah and Inspector J. W. K. Harlley were charged with running the Ghanaian ministry for external affairs but not throughout the entire period; Police Commissioner W. L. Leigh held appointment in the department while the NRC was in power; Major B. Sinzogan had this role under the young cadres in Dahomey but he was posted only after E.-D. Zinsou, civilian foreign minister of the previous Soglo government, turned down the offer. The Malian junta felt too inexperienced, lacked confidence, and wanted to utilize fully the external connections and skills of J. M. Koné and S. Coulibaly, the first two foreign ministers. General Soglo of Dahomey used Zinsou for the same purposes, while Major Kouandété needed him in order to gain the goodwill of Paris.

Whatever the institutional arrangements, and however strong the actual influence of civilian ministers, senior civil servants in the ministries for external affairs, and other civilian influentials, the final say on all important matters in this area was held by the military junta. For instance, the anti-Chinese moves in Dahomey under Soglo and Ghana under the NLC were taken despite and over the contrary advice and resistance of civilian officials. In less vital foreign policy matters, the civilian ministers (Zinsou and to a greater extent S. Coulibaly) and civil servants enjoyed very considerable autonomy to the point that the military minister became a figurehead. But the civilians could always be over-ruled.

We discussed earlier the importance of the economic consultative bodies under the juntas in the English-speaking countries of our sample. In all four countries the juntas were greatly concerned with and gave top priority to economic, budgetary, and financial recovery. In the two French-speaking countries of the sample the military never took over, even nominally, the ministries of finance and of economic development, letting civilian technocrats and experienced ministers run the show under their supervision.* In Ghana and Sierra Leone the junta members nominally controlled these ministries, in the former for a part of the total period of rule and in the latter throughout the period. But regardless of the formal arrangement the juntas accepted almost all recommendations of civilian ministers, civil servants, and other civilian experts. The military had no independent means of gathering and evaluating relevant information or of generating its own competent opinion and monitoring the performance of the economy. Instead it relied on common sense and trust. But the civilians still needed the junta's formal approval on all important measures.

In all other areas of decision-making the juntas retained ultimate veto power, but their interest and impact varied greatly--from great concern for labor unrest during numerous strikes and attention to chieftancy affairs in Ghana, to some interest in agriculture and communications in Dahomey, to virtual indifference in some areas of welfare, education, and health.

THE ORGANIZATION OF PUBLIC
POWER OUTSIDE THE CAPITAL

The total number of military holders of political and civilian administrative offices and the re-

---

*The Malian CMLN departed from this practice in September 1970 after my research was terminated.

191

placing of civilian office-holders by the military gives the main dimensions of the spread of military rule over the four polities. In this respect Mali and Sierra Leone represent two extremes.

The CMLN in Mali dismissed the governors of all six regions and appointed the commanders of the corresponding military zones in their stead soon after the coup. Later these two functions became separated in most of the regions, with the highest ranking officer discharging the function of military governor and an officer of lower grade and/or seniority acting as the military commander. In addition, the latter often held additional civilian jobs such as the mayor of the main town of the region. The military governors, like French préfets, represented the junta (the president) and reported to the minister of interior, Captain C. S. Cissoko. The military commanders were under the chief of staff and through him under the minister of defense, the same Captain C. S. Cissoko. Since most civilian mayors and commandants de cercle also were dismissed, being too closely connected with the former regime, their posts were formally filled by military officers stationed nearby. In fact, all these were double and triple job arrangements while actual business was carried out by civilian administrators who either remained in the posts they held under the Keita government or else were simply transferred to a corresponding job elsewhere. This system can be called extensive military tutelage.

At the other extreme, the National Reformation Council in Sierra Leone limited the regularized political involvement of the small officer corps, chiefly concentrated in Freetown, to only about 10 officers at a time. The NRC debated a proposal to appoint military governors of the four administrative units (three provinces and one area) but retained senior civil servants as provincial commissioners (governors). Except for inspection tours by one or two junta members, nothing had changed in the organization of state administration outside Freetown. This system of military control of the apex of the political system only can be called limited military tutelage.

The Dahomeyan system was close to that of Sierra Leone as no military officers were appointed to civilian offices outside the capital. However, the Dahomeyan army is substantially larger and its units are more dispersed in the country. These factors facilitated informal political influence and occasional interference with civilian préfets and sous-préfets by local military commanders. High military officers who were stationed elsewhere (chiefly in the capital) also interfered in the localities of their origin and/or where they had relatives and interests. As in Sierra Leone the system of government outside the capital in Dahomey underwent practically no change.

The Ghanaian system under the NLC was half-way between the Malian and Sierra Leonean extremes. The NLC replaced the highly politicized civilian regional commissioners, who under Nkrumah were party-government bosses, by regional committees of administration. These bodies included the highest military and police officers posted in a given part of the country. The military officers, mostly commanders of battalions stationed in a region, lieutenant-colonels and colonels in rank, headed most of the six regional committees. They were rotated several times during the entire period of military rule, with two distinct principles of selection applied in the 1966-67 and 1967-69 periods (see Chapter 3).

Following the British tradition in the Gold Coast, the regional chairmen acted as representatives of the head of state—the NLC and its chairman—and directed, at least in theory, the work of the regional administration and of regional representatives of national ministries. They were assisted by a top civil servant in Accra, close in rank to a principal secretary, who in fact ran regional administration by proxy. Unlike the Malian practice the Ghanaian junta placed at the helm of the disbanded elective municipal (except in Great Accra) and local councils not military officers but civilian town and district committees of administration, and management committees. These bodies had to report to the highest local police officer and to the NLC member responsible for local government, but this did not appreciably affect the mode of their operation. The system was in fact very close to that during the terminal period of British rule.[8]

It follows that the organization of public power under the five stable juntas varied in form, but in fact it was the same or very similar to the system that existed either immediately before the coup or under the regime that preceded the ousted government.

Apart from administrative traditions the juntas were influenced in this area by the degree of politization of subnational and local administration under the ousted regime; its association with former unpopular practices; the military's community of norms with the civilian bureaucracy; the junta's objectives and its willingness, or the lack thereof, to commit the officer corps to active involvement in administration; the size of the officer corps; and the dispersion of army units outside the capital. It seems that the amount of leisure time among the officer corps also was a factor.*

THE RELATIONSHIP BETWEEN THE JUNTA AND THE MILITARY AND POLICE ESTABLISHMENTS

All juntas usually declare that they represent the army and (in English-speaking countries) the police or, when the coup is directed against the top brass, that they represent the real spirit of the army. They accuse their military adversaries of betraying the norms of professionalism and the trust of the army. All stable juntas in our sample had to contend with serious problems in their relations with the corporate bodies they claimed to represent.

We already have dwelt on the divisive influences on the military establishment from the external (to the polity) and internal social environment, on

---

*It appears that the complexity of corporate social life, within the same system of norms and traditions, is related to the size of the military establishment. Thus the self-preoccupation of an organization counterbalances a larger supply of potential administrators in bigger armies. This is a corollary of similar propositions in the theory of organization.

various inroads of politics and politicians that
tend to promote existing cleavages in the army and
to create new ones (see Chapters 6 and 7). Military
intervention in politics as such often divides the
army, and in addition there is a phenomenon of external contagion and/or internally induced proclivity
to internal coups. All stable juntas in this sample
invariably tried to cover up and heal the wounds of
division and to preserve the outward appearance of
corporate unity. They also all tried to assure that
no one in the army would stage a coup against them.

The data indicates that the lower the level in
the military establishment from which the coup is
launched the more difficult it is to restore corporate unity, short of total reorganization of the
armed forces. The Sierra Leone Force experienced the
greatest obstacles of this kind after a junta of army
NCOs and enlisted men arrested, mistreated, and
jailed the entire officer corps of the army and police. The damage produced by this event on the
army's morale, effectiveness, discipline, and mutual
trust cannot be overemphasized. The Malian coup
staged at the level of captains and lieutenants, and
the 1967 coup in Dahomey at the level of major and
captain, also negatively affected the armed forces
but less severely than in Sierra Leone. The problems
of the Soglo junta in Dahomey, the NLC in Ghana,
and the NRC in Sierra Leone (the levels of general,
colonel, and major respectively) were not related to
the coups but to their subsequent policies and behavior vis-à-vis the rest of the officer corps.

In this study the post-coup problems of the juntas with the rest of the army, and mainly with the
officer corps and NCOs, were as follows: (1) of a
corporate-hierarchical nature, (2) of a material
nature, (3) related to the sharing of state power,
and (4) related to political disagreements and norm
and goal conflicts in the army. These four basic
ingredients or some of them were present in varying
combinations in internal military politics under the
five stable juntas.

The Soglo junta was exposed to varieties 3 and
4 as intermediate and junior officers were clamoring
for participation in the inner councils and closer
association with the prerogatives of power; they had

different perceptions of the army's most desirable role as well as of political problems. These factors remained operative under the succeeding junta of young cadres but spilled onto lower levels of the military hierarchy. In addition, the second Dahomeyan junta had to contend with the problem of a conflict between the military hierarchy and the informal power structure in the army. The same problem affected the Malian CMLN, and to a lesser extent the NLC in Ghana. In all three cases the hiatus was eliminated or reduced through prematurely retiring or "kicking upstairs" those senior officers who did not participate in the coup, were not considered reliable, and could not claim a position in the informal structure of power commensurate with their high rank. Thus the second Dahomeyan junta retired senior officers who were members of the previous junta (General Soglo, Colonel Aho, and Major Adandéjan); the Malian CMLN retired two colonels (Colonel S. Traoré, chief of staff under Modibo Keita, and Colonel P. Drabo, his successor after the coup), four lieutenant-colonels, and five majors[9]; while the NLC in Ghana sent abroad to diplomatic posts several generals and brigadiers, discharged one colonel, and retired three or four senior officers.

The problem of conditions of service became most acute under the NRC in Sierra Leone and served as the single most important immediate motivation of the mutineers who ousted the junta. The NRC initially pledged not to increase the material standards of the military because it lacked legitimacy and popular support. In order to gain these two objectives the junta imprudently neglected the interests of its own "electorate." A higher load of extra work and the impact of inflation were felt most painfully in the lower ranks while the junta and the army officers foolishly disregarded the need for better relations with the troops. The Ghanaian NLC and the Malian CMLN took care of the material interests of the military (and in Ghana also of the police) establishments, and soon after the coups rewarded these groups with improved material and other conditions of service.

The combination of factors 3, 1, 4, and 2 (in this order) was operative in Mali and in Ghana under

the NLC. The two abortive plots against the NLC and
the CMLN were prompted by the desires of their architects to displace or to replace the ruling juntas,
to implement a different political platform (in Mali),
to promote themselves (particularly in Ghana), and
to gain certain material benefits from the change
(this was true of the three executors of the Ghanaian
coup in April 1967 and of the lower ranks participating in the Malian plotting associated with the
name of Captain D. X. Diarra). The Malian junta--
less secure, differently motivated, and affected by
puritanism--tried to minimize cleavages on these
grounds. The CMLN members did not promote themselves
in rank and did not increase their income dramatically. The Ghanaian NLC disregarded both--partic-
ularly in respect to rapid self-promotion--and almost
paid a high price as a result. Other methods to reduce pressures for sharing power were internal consultative bodies, informal procedures with the same
effect, and bringing other military officers into
positions of authority.

Each of the five stable juntas in our study
applied a different mix of these instruments. The
Dahomeyan juntas relied on informal procedures and
irregular consultative bodies under General Soglo
and on the same mechanisms plus a greater involvement
of the officer corps in administering the country
under the young cadres. The Ghanaian NLC used all
three methods but had a more regular consultative
mechanism. The NRC in Sierra Leone utilized informal procedures and, unlike all the other juntas,
introduced the institution of a rotating junior member of the ruling body. The Malian junta used irregular internal consultative assemblies and more regular informal consultative procedures and brought the
bulk of the officer corps into the business of administering and supervising the state.

The success of the five juntas in managing their
relations with the rest of the army varied substantially. Four of the five experienced real, attempted,
or alleged internal military insurrections (against
General Soglo in Dahomey, against the NLC in Ghana,
against the NRC in Sierra Leone, and against the
CMLN in Mali). Two of these four actually were ousted
by force from within the military establishment

(General Soglo and the NRC), while a third (the NLC) narrowly escaped.

The data indicates that military intervention and subsequent military rule invariably negatively affects the internal cohesion of the army. On the other hand in most cases it promotes or preserves the privileged material position of the military establishment and its "legal" claim to a large share of available economic resources and also contributes to making the military better equipped and armed. In order to assess the outcome of military intervention: the price of politization and of active exposure to general social cleavages, the duration of disequilibrating and imbalancing effects on the military establishment, and the net corporate gains for the military should be compared in each individual case with the net impact of each intervention in terms of its social gains (if any) and costs (always present), as well as with the country's real defense requirements. And then there remains a problem of observer perceptions, norms, and preferences.

THE RELATIONSHIP BETWEEN THE JUNTAS AND CORPORATE BODIES, PARA-POLITICAL AND INTEREST GROUPS

We argued earlier that whatever form military rule took in these four countries it in fact represented one or another variety of military-civilian coalition. These coalitions showed various combinations of four basic components--the junta, the other military, the civil administration, and other civilian influentials. Variations in relative weight and juxtaposition of these components have been observed cross-polity, cross-time, at different levels of government (national, subnational, local), and in different areas of decision-making. Now we shall attempt to deal more extensively with the two civilian components of the coalitions and with those politicized and politically relevant groups and organizations that either were left out of the ruling coalitions or remained on their periphery.

When a military coup occurs, the victorious African military, for whatever stated or concealed reasons, triumphantly "bans" politics. In the present study the manifest explanations for these moves were as follows: a threat to the internal security and integrity of the country (Dahomey and Sierra Leone); tyranny, corruption, mismanagement, and other real or alleged sins of civilian politicians (Ghana, Mali). The military presented itself as the antithesis of these wrongdoings--as supra-regional, supra-partisan, uncorrupt, common sense patriots and the only hope of the nation. The common denominator of these manifest platforms of the military juntas could be stated as follows: "That was bad politics, we had to set the country straight, and since it cannot be done overnight we shall close the shop for a while and clean up the mess--until 'normal' conditions are restored."

To satisfy the cynics we will say that at least in four or perhaps in five cases out of the sample of nine military coups these assertions were either outright or partial lies, in order to conceal very real personal, group, and corporate interests that had preciously little to do with the welfare of the nation (the 1967 coups in Dahomey and Ghana and two in Sierra Leone). Actually not a single coup in the sample occurred without an appreciable dose of narrow group and corporate interests. On the other hand it should be stated that the perceptions of at least some coup leaders were different. Many of them sincerely stood by their own rhetoric and went as far as to believe that their quick self-promotion to brigadiers and generals, as well as pay raises, to take only the most visible manifestations of self-seeking, were either in the national interest or only a modest compensation for the dangerous labor of the nation's saviors.

These perceptions, combined with the traits of their professional training in the systems of British and French norms, shaped to a significant extent the juntas' relations with politically relevant organizations and groups of civilians. In varying degrees all military members of the juntas had assimilated an apolitical or anti-political ethos--distrust, underestimation of or outright disdain for civilian politicians, ideology, and too much talk. Instead they tended to apply a straightforward and plain amateur approach to problems, assuming that the language and style of government should be as clear and precise as military commands. It turned out to be a naive expectation. One should note that the police members of the Ghana and Sierra Leone juntas were less addicted to this fallacy because of their extensive previous training in politics.

Second, the military rulers were to different degrees but invariably affected by the limitations of the technocratic mind and tended to view social problems in terms of efficiency, rationality, clarity of administrative procedures, cleanliness (the absence of explicitly illicit, but not of all forms of corruption and semilegal self-enrichment), and sound logistics. Hence initially all the coups were announced as cleansing operations with a limited goal of bringing all these qualities back into the civilian administration andcivilian life in general, with the army serving as a model and as the repository of everything good.

Third, the military rulers, at least at the beginning, did not grasp the complexity of arriving at a consensus outside the barracks. They thought that the physical removal of the "bad guys," appeals to patriotism, and reinforced discipline in administration and in the economy, supported by occasional threats of punishment and naked force, would do the job. Hence there was no need for the politician's double-talk, ideology, and patient persuasion, or the organization of the population (the "masses") for political action.

Fourth, although they grabbed state power illegally and unconstitutionally, strangely enough the military rulers were influenced by Western liberal ideas. Some of them sincerely and idealistically believed in such ideas.[10] The others were reacting to the curtailing of liberal norms of political democracy under the previous regime and wanted to be different--for the sake of being different and in order to bolster legitimacy and foreign aid from the West. Although they had become authoritarian rulers some still were convinced of the virtues of having the military stay clear of politics. Whatever the source or rationale, these ideas in the military rulers' minds became an objective element of political reality. The result was a peculiar combination of

military authoritarianism, brazen threats directed
to unspecified political opponents, and actually restrained and rather lenient dealing with the remnants of the previous regime. The juntas also were
reluctant, in some but not all cases, to press the
point and to exploit to the fullest the advantages
of state power and the possibilities of patronage.
The military rulers in Ghana and Mali, for example,
were restrained by what they considered a negative
example of indiscriminate meddling into the internal
affairs of nonpartisan and para-political corporate
bodies and organizations. The professional ethics
largely inherited from the colonial army seem to
have been related to the distrust of politicians,
and hence to the limited influence of consultative
bodies. On the other hand the military ethics tended
to reduce the direct administrative and para-political
involvement of the officer corps in running the state.

Fifth, the military rulers had no traditions of
political involvement to profit from and only General
Soglo had some experience from his short "supra-
partisan" intervention in 1963. A rather low level
of education, particularly political education, and
of general culture, often ineptness in handling the
language of politics, on the whole very modest intellectual qualities, and in at least two cases men-
tal instability (Brigadier Juxon-Smith, General Afrifa) created serious additional problems for the
military rulers.

Sixth, the actual resources of skilled manpower
with relevant experience that the military rulers
possessed were limited indeed--in numbers and even
more in quality. On the other hand this deficiency
was in some but not all cases counterbalanced by a
corresponding paucity of skills among the civilians
and by political fragmentation and atomization in
the polity. The latter, under conditions of threatened
suppression of opposition, produced situations remi-
niscent of a political vacuum (Mali, Sierra Leone
during at least a part of NRC rule, and Dahomey).

All five stable juntas disbanded the existing
political parties and often prohibited political activities under threat of severe punishment. It took
them some time to discover that one cannot legislate
politics away. In fact, these bans boiled down to

officially proclaimed and only partly followed moratoria on some forms of manifest political activity and organization, and to the substitution of other forms and methods.

Several factors undermined the effectiveness of the bans. The junta and the military in general could not rule in a vacuum. For a variety of reasons stated earlier, they needed civilian allies, influential leaders of public opinion, and advisers. To legitimize their rule and/or to maintain public support, the military itself had to engage in detested political activities and official propaganda, and to start learning by trial and error all those "devious" skills of talking without really meaning it--hinting without promising and promising without necessarily delivering.* Second, a substantial number of junta members very soon after the coup somehow came to like the idea of running the state. This new perspective made them accept more readily the need for persuasion, for accepting the remaining political and para-political groups, for forging public opinion, and maneuvering. Third, after an initial period of shock and disarray the para-political and interest groups, former and aspiring politicians and influentials, adjusted themselves to the new situation and set out to make contacts with the holders of supreme power. Fourth, with limited resources at their disposal and only imperfect control of the country, the military rulers could not eliminate all forms of politically relevant action even if they had badly wanted to.

All five juntas retained the trade unions. In Ghana and Mali their leaderships were purged because of close association with the ousted regimes. All five regimes tried to bring trade unions closer to the new government, included trade union representatives in the political (and less influential) consultative bodies, and posed as a third impartial party

---

*Compare the initial promises of the NRC in Sierra Leone and those of the young cadres in Dahomey with their performance. Actually all five juntas at one point or another broke promises solemnly given to the nation.

between the trade unions and management. Both Dahomeyan juntas came to power thanks to trade union
opposition to the previous regimes, and both, particularly the regime of the young cadres, went far in
acquainting the trade union leadership with confidential information related to the real financial state
of the nation. The Malian junta for some time entertained the thought of using the trade unions as a
transmission belt to the population and a substitute
for a political party.

The austerity policies of the juntas, the fact
that the state employees form a majority of wage earners in the four countries and that the trade unions
represent primarily the interests of state employees,
the ineptness and the lack of patience on the part
of several juntas, brought them at one stage or another into open conflict with the trade unions. These
open clashes hastened the downfall of General Soglo,
were in the offing in Sierra Leone at the time of
the counter-coup, led to harsh government retaliation
and brutality in Ghana, brought troops into the
streets of Cotonou under the young cadres in Dahomey,
and prompted the Malian CMLN to disband the national
trade unions' provisional leadership. However, the
general weaknesses of the labor movement in Tropical
Africa and the limited objectives, political ambitions, and reformist policies of many trade union
leaders allowed four of the five juntas in this sample to survive such conflicts.

We earlier touched on the relations of the
juntas with the civilian administration and bureaucracy. The impact of military rule on these institutions was not appreciable or lasting. During the
first several months it improved discipline (mainly
reporting to the job, reducing absenteeism during
the day, and so forth), but often without commensurate gains in efficiency. The change of masters produced some confusion and uncertainty, and temporarily
even had a paralyzing effect. Regardless of the formal organization of power the real impact of military
rule on state administration seems to have been an
increase in its autonomy. The military removed or
minimized party and "political" pressures on the
bureaucrats, without bringing in their own system of
effective control. Even if the juntas were to employ

203

all the military officers and NCOs in the country
on a full-time basis, they could not really super-
vise the civilian administration. Besides, the juntas espoused Western notions of the administration's
corporate autonomy and apolitical nature. The Ghanaian junta in particular restored the autonomy and
raised the pay scales of the civil service during the
first year and a half of the NLC rule. The NLC relied heavily on information, advice, execution, and
supervision provided by top civil servants, even in
areas where the junta members retained a monopoly on
ultimate decisions. This cordial entente of the
military and civilian bureaucrats was somewhat spoiled
by civilian politicians who were allies of the NLC,
and the new "golden age" came to an end with the
termination of military rule.

The relations between the junta and the civilian
administration were less cordial in Dahomey, Sierra
Leone, and Mali due to a lower congruity of norms
and goals, smaller initial political capital of the
juntas, more strained military-civilian relations in
general, and several other factors. In the long run
no junta changed anything of substance in the organization and functioning of the civil administration.
Some, but very few, corrupt civil servants were sacked,
and if anything the experience taught civilian bureaucrats about the dangers and unpredictability of associating themselves with political parties. It is
doubtful that the efficiency and the responsiveness
of the civil bureaucracy improved, while corruption
only took different and less conspicuous forms.

Much of what was said about the civilian bureaucracy and the general style of the military rulers
in dealing with corporate bodies also applies to
the universities in Ghana and Sierra Leone and to
the institutions of higher learning in Mali. In all
three cases the juntas espoused the general Western
notions of the autonomy and apolitical nature of
these institutions. The actual situations in these
three countries differed substantially. In Ghana
both the largest universities (Legon and Kumasi) by
and large had been covert strongholds of silent opposition to Nkrumah's regime. Therefore they welcomed
the advent of military rule, shared many but not all
the goals of the military-civilian coalition that

ran the country, and became at best an ally and collaborator, at worst a constructive and rather well-intended critic of certain aspects of the military rule (the journal Legon Observer presents this position well). The junta helped the universities financially and thus assured cooperation with them on the basis of conservative British-inspired norms of liberalism.

On the other hand the University College at Fourah Bay in Sierra Leone and the biggest and most important schools of higher learning in Bamako (e.g., the Teachers' College and National School of Administration) before the coup had been rather strongly influenced by the two ousted and disbanded political parties--the APC in Sierra Leone and the US-RDA in Mali. The general negative reception to the coups in Sierra Leone, and the heavy residues of the US-RDA ideology and of vested interests in the ousted regime among the students and faculty in Mali, made these establishments important centers of more or less silent, if not necessarily passive, opposition to the two military regimes. The juntas lacked the political instruments, skills, and allies to deal with these problems; several times they tried to or did in fact apply administrative measures (cutting the budgetary allocation in Sierra Leone; arrests, a trial, and jail sentences in Mali) but did not resolve the problem.[11]

THE TRANSFER OF POWER

In only two of the five stable juntas was there a quasi-legal and orderly transfer of power by the military to civilian authorities. In our sample, and so far in all of Africa, the only really clear case of voluntary, well-prepared and -executed, and orderly handing-over of power to constitutionally elected civilian politicians occurred in Ghana.

In Dahomey the military rulers were very dangerously split and had been exposed to strong financial pressure exerted by France and internal political pressures from most civilian groups. Besides, before finally arriving at the handing-over ceremonies the junta blatantly violated the freshly adopted

205

constitution and imposed on the country a civilian
politician of its own liking--one who was expected
to be a puppet. Zinsou's appointment was only at
his insistence and ex post facto confirmed by the
electorate, which did not have much choice. Civilian
discontent with military rule in Sierra Leone was
so universal and strong by the spring of 1968 that
when two senior officers of the Sierra Leone Force
handed power over to the civilian government legally
elected in 1967 it was hardly an expression of voluntary abdication.

Even this brief review casts grave doubt on the
proposition that the military acts as a selfless
cushion between feuding civilian elites--as a stabil-
izer, a neutral caretaker--or is a functional substitute for the deficient system of assuring competitive alternation in office of competing groups of
civilian politicians. Let us examine in this light
the only example in Africa of a voluntary and orderly
transfer of power by the military to a constitutionally
elected civilian political leadership.

When the Ghanaian military-police junta shot
its way through to Flagstaff House in Accra on February 24, 1966, it declared an end to tyranny and
abuse of power and set as its manifest goal a restoration of a true, as opposed to a rigged, democracy.

The junta disbanded the presumably undemocratic
CPP, instead of ordering it purged of tyrannical and
corrupt leaders and letting the population judge the
relevance of the party's program and appeal without
the distorting influence of possession of state
power. The NLC imprisoned and kept in detention for
long periods of time about a thousand persons closely
connected with the previous regime. In most cases
no specific charges were lodged and the courts were
not asked to rule on whether the detained had violated positive laws. By several police and administrative methods, the junta forcibly removed from
public life two to three thousand functionaires, organizers, and other activists of the former party.[12]
Although a minority of detainees possibly needed
police protection and the treatment in Ghanaian jails
probably was more liberal than under the previous
regime, the junta only substituted the notorious institution of preventive detention with "protective

206

custody"--old wine in new bottles. The NLC enacted
numerous decrees and regulations designed to intimidate the CPP sympathizers,[13] including those who
disliked and silently opposed Nkrumah's practices
but were in agreement with the substance of the party's platform.

In addition to administrative and police measures the junta and its civilian allies from among
the former chiefly bourgeois opposition to the CPP
and from among the civil service launched a successful political campaign aimed at discrediting the
CPP and Nkrumah. To this purpose they used the
courts, numerous commissions of inquiry, and the state-
owned mass media (newspapers, radio, and television).
Not only were the leaders of the former defeated opposition welcome in Ghana but also the junta gave
them important jobs in the state administration,
such as that of attorney-general, and appointed them
to various consultative panels, committees, commissions, and other para-governmental bodies. Although
a ban on overt political activities was formally
maintained, the standards of its application were
quite different and more lenient for the former opposition than for those known to have had a CPP affiliation and/or affinity. These double standards were
particularly obvious in the case of Busia, former
leader of the opposition United Party. After having
served and given an initial exposure as the head of
the Political Advisory Committee to the junta, he
was made director of a semi-official Center for Civic
Education. Using the symbols of association with
state power and taxpayer money, he was the only known
politician to be allowed to travel freely about the
country holding meetings and spreading what was essentially the rhetoric and the platform of his future
Progress Party. He skillfully capitalized on his
initial, and by Western standards unfair, advantage
over other potential competitors.

The NLC used the power of administrative appointments to place former opponents of the CPP and Nkrumah
in positions of power and patronage--from special
commissioners in the national Executive Council to
members of appointed municipal and local committees
of management. Busia confirmed in April 1967 that
the former opposition shared "some ideas and ideals

. . . with those who organized the coup."[14] At the same time the junta carefully watched that only reformed former CPP members and turncoats could have a seat even on consultative bodies that were supposed to represent the public opinion of the entire population. The same was true of the Constitutional and Electoral commissions that were to lay the ground rules for a return to civilian rule.

When it came to the formation of a Constituent Assembly the junta substituted for the previously announced method of popular elections a system of delegating representatives from the local and municipal bodies it had appointed previously, plus direct designation from the top. The NLC knew that despite the officially administered police quarantine the CPP still had a substantial following in the country and, if allowed, had a chance of winning a democratically held election. Yet it packed the Constituent Assembly with the party's opponents. The possibility that despite all manipulations the right wing of the former CPP, headed by K. Gbedemah, could still win prompted the NLC to openly pressure and blackmail the Constituent Assembly into adopting a temporary (up to three years) institution of a military-police collective head of state. In fact, it tried to extend further the period of military tutelage in order to bar an unfavorable (to the NLC) determination of the voters. General Afrifa conspicuously appeared on numerous ceremonial occasions with the late Asantehene (traditional ruler of the Ashantis). In July-August 1969, using his official helicopter as head of state, he came very close to what was considered campaigning for Busia and his party. Afrifa's threat to stage another coup if the election results were not to his liking was an open secret. Local power-brokers in most parts of the country got the message, and given the fact that a bloc pattern of voting predominates in Ghana, the application of the described catalog of measures gave a desired result. In a technically clean election the former opposition gained an absolute majority in the parliament, and on October 1, 1969, the junta presented it with executive power.

The present study suggests that, at least as far as West Africa is concerned, nothing seem further

208

from reality than the assertion that military intervention is a functional substitute for the orderly
alternation of political parties in office. The
military juntas were not politically neutral just as
their civilian counterparts in the state administration were not. The period of the junta's incumbency
invariably changed the political climate in differing
degrees, and the relative strength of competing political parties and groups caused, or significantly
contributed to, rearrangements of political alliances
and of politically relevant webs of patron-client
relationships.

CONCLUSION

We have examined a number of what seem to us
salient characteristics of military rule in four
relatively small and young independent polities in
West Africa. The difficulties of conducting research
on such a sensitive topic, while the military still
controls the country or soon afterward, limit the
reliability of the data collected and severely limit
the possibilities of replicating the study. At the
same time the smallness of the sample, dictated
primarily by limited resources, time included, negatively affected the generalizability of our findings
on the whole of Tropical Africa. Therefore our conclusions ought to be taken as tentative.

This study indicated that the military establishments in the four countries--Dahomey, Ghana,
Sierra Leone, and Mali--at the time of their active
intervention in politics in 1965-68 were, and to this
day still are, to a large extent alien institutions
in the new independent polities. From their inception they have developed under the strong influence
of the former colonial metropoles. However, the underlying causes of military intervention are predominantly inherent in the domestic sociopolitical
environment of these countries, despite heavy economic,
cultural, and to a lesser extent political dependence
of the formally independent states on Britain and
France, and on the West in general. Furthermore the
subsequent development under military rule also has
been governed predominantly by domestic factors and

209

evolved under the impulses of original African and
of assimilated political practices.

Although the military intervene in politics for
a variety of manifest and concealed reasons, the
single strongest motivation for intervention, at
least in this sample, has been the protection of narrow corporate and personal security interests and of
the "legal" claim on a share of scarce national resources so far unjustified by the countries' defense
requirements. Therefore, it seems erroneous to view
the military in West Africa as selfless patriots
and modernizers. Military intervention helped the
armies of the four countries to achieve the objectives of improved corporate security and welfare,
but invariably at the expense of internal cohesion.

No military regime can really "outlaw" the omnipresent politics. It can only create a different
ruling military-civilian coalition that runs the
country under the conditions of, or similar to,
martial law and modifies the forms and overt methods
of political expression. Nor can military rulers
purge themselves of politics internally. In fact,
the longer they stay the more fragmented and vulnerable to divisive influences of the wider sociopolitical environment they become. Military rule is subject to the same or very similar regularities that
are observed in most known civilian political systems, such as the duality and hiatus between the
manifest framework and the informal power structures.

The predominance of domestic impulses of developments prior to and after the military coups allows
us to view the wave of military intervention in West
Africa in the 1960s as a delayed echo of decolonization and as a step either toward "nationalizing" the
formerly alien institution into the fabric of African
political life or, possibly, to its rejection.
Through this incursion, the officer corps, most often
unconsciously and while defending its own interests
and imperfectly mirroring the strains in the society,
breaks in one direction a wall that separated it from
the previous ruling group of the civilian elite.
When in power, the military is not a neutral cushion
between antagonistic civilian groups and parties.
It displaces and harms some of them, promotes others,
and becomes itself an active and influential interest

group that causes rearrangements of political alliances and patron-client para-political relations.

The selflessness and neutrality of the military
is a myth. Nevertheless, one of the possible results
of the military's meddling in politics is a better
mutual understanding among the military and some
civilian elites, and willy-nilly the acceptance by
the the civilians of the officer corps as a recognized and important member of the establishment. It
is in this specific sense that one can view the "in-
tegrative" impact of military intervention, despite
its having wrecked the institutions of the preceding
civilian order.

One can question the social costs of military
intervention, as compared to some positive gains.
Those who have and/or had sympathies for the ousted
"radical" regimes in Ghana and Mali can lament the
fact that Nkrumah and Keita were incapable of self-
adjustment in time, wasted chances, and allowed the
conservatives and (in Ghana particularly) reaction-
aries to capitalize on necessary and long-overdue
corrections in government policies.

Have the military interventions moved these two
societies forward at all, or have they marked a re-
gression? It seems that military intervention in itself does not solve fundamental social problems and
even retards their solution. The West African armies
are too small in terms of highly skilled manpower,
experienced and talented leaders, administrators and
managers. The African military as the ruling power
is hindered by the limitations of the technocratic
mind, by its anti-political ethos, and by its selective adherence to Western liberal ideals. The military lacks the political instruments to shoulder the
task at which the civilian leaders with political
parties at their disposal flatly failed. Hence the
military juntas cannot achieve more than a somewhat
more disciplined and clean civilian administration
can--unsupported by political organizations and un-
hindered by partisan politics. It is unrealistic to
expect anything more from the juntas at their very
best.

We see the most significant dimension of political development resulting from institutional breakdowns and from a rather conservative retrenchment

211

and reconstruction under the military in the following developments: the advanced experience of the
social elites; a better understanding of objective
limitations and of the complexity of political and
social processes; a better "feel" for the interests
and real weight of other competing political and para-
political groups; and an enhanced, albeit conservative, rationality. In short, the realistic dimensions
of social change introduced by military intervention
appear most clearly when we view political development as basically a learning process, which in Tropical Africa is still predominantly that of the elites.

CHAPTER 2
    1. "Projet de Constitution de la République
du Dahomey," supplement, <u>Aun</u>, No. 157 (December 3,
1963); S. M. Apithy, <u>Telle est la Vérité</u> (Paris,
1968); M. Glélé, <u>Naissance d'un état noir</u> (Paris:
Librairie Général de Droit et de Jurisprudence,
1969), Chapter 21.
    2. <u>WA</u>, May 24, 1969, p. 594; <u>BAN</u>, No. 539
(February 2, 1969), p. 10876; <u>ARB-EFTS</u>, IV, 9
(October 1967), 845, 846; S. Decalo, "The Politics
of Instability in Dahomey," <u>GA</u>, No. 2 (1968); W.
Skurnik, "The Military and Politics: Dahomey and
Upper Volta," in C. Welch, Jr., ed., <u>Soldier and
State in Africa</u> (Evanston, Ill.: Northwestern Uni-
versity Press, 1970), pp. 80-81.
    3. <u>AFP</u>, No. 5719 (July 3, 1965).
    4. <u>JORD</u>, No. 1 (January 1, 1966), p. 2; <u>Décret</u>,
No. 121.
    5. See Ahomadegbé's letter in <u>M</u>, December 29,
1967.
    6. D. Wood, "The Armed Forces of African
States," Adelphi Papers, No. 27 (London: Institute
for Strategic Studies, 1966), p. 8.
    7. <u>Ibid.</u>; U.S. Arms Control and Disarmament
Agency, <u>World Military Expenditures</u> (Washington,
D.C.: The Agency, 1969), p. 13.
    8. <u>Budget National de Functionnement de la
République du Dahomey</u> (Porto-Novo: Imprimerie Nationale, 1968), pp. 79-85.
    9. Wood, "The Armed Forces of African States,"
p. 9.
    10. Glélé, <u>Naissance d'un état noir</u>, pp. 316-
17; L. Hamon, ed., <u>Le rôle extramilitaire de L'Armée
dans le Tiers Monde</u> (Paris: Presses Universitaires
de France, 1966), pp. 70-80.
    11. <u>AN</u>, January 1966, pp. 13-19.
    12. <u>AuN</u>, December 24, 1965, p. 1.
    13. Ordonnance No. 3, PR/CRN; <u>JORD</u>, No. 4
(February 15, 1966), p. 2.

14. A. Gnonlonfoun, "Un an du régime Soglo au Dahomey," AN, February 9-15, 1967, p. 7.

15. A. Gnonlonfoun, "Le Régime provisiore face aux problèmes," AN, No. 965 (March-September 1966).

16. AuN, November 13, 1966, p. 6.

17. AuN, April 24, 1966, pp. 1, 3.

18. G. Agboton, "Quelques moyens de réalisation de l'unité nationale," AuN, October 9, 1966, p. 6.

19. AuN, September 8, 1966, pp. 1, 3.

20. Gnonlonfoun, "Un an du régime Soglo au Dahomey," p. 11; Année Politique Africaine (Dakar: Societe Africaine, 1966), pp. 111-29.

21. "La Pente se dresse à nouveau," AN, September 15-21, 1966.

22. AFP, No. 6071 (August 30, 1966); "L'Heure des Grandes Decisions," AN, September 15-21, 1966.

23. R. Lemarchand, "Dahomey: Coup Within a Coup," AR, XIII, 6 (1968), p. 51; Décret, Nos. 106 PR and 147 PR, JORD, 1967, pp. 360-61.

24. Ordonnance No. 8, JORD, June 1, 1967, pp. 359-60.

25. "Une epreuve de force syndicats-gouvernement," MTM, December 16, 1967.

26. AFP, No. 6462 (December 12, 1967); FM, December 13, 1967; Dov Ronen, Dynamics of Political Transition in Dahomey (forthcoming.), Chapter 7.

27. AFP, No. 6467 (December 17-18, 1967).

28. H. Fagla, "Dahomey: d'un conflit de générations à un coup d'état," FEA, January 1968, p. 11.

29. AFP, No. 6475 (December 28, 1970).

30. AuN, December 24, 1967, p. 1.

31. AFP, No. 6471 (December 22, 1967).

32. O, December 17-23, 1967, p. 2.

33. Ibid.

34. Lemarchand, "Dahomey: Coup Within a Coup," p. 53.

35. MD, June 8, 1968.

36. DI, February 20 and 22, 1968.

37. Decret No. 441, December 22, 1967; Ordonnance No. 17 and Decret No. 19 bis PR/SGG, JORD, 1968.

38. AFP, No. 6505 (February 2, 1968); Constitution du Dahomey du 31 mars, 1968 (Paris: Documentation Française, 1969), Art. 103-106, p. 14.

39. <u>Constitution du Dahomey du 31 mars, 1968,</u> Art. 39.

40. <u>AN</u>, May 15-21, 1968, pp. 5, 14.

41. <u>AuN</u>, May 19, 1968, p. 1.

42. <u>M</u>, June 10, 1968, p. 1; A. Gnonlonfoun, "Union Nationale?", <u>JA</u>, July 1-7, 1968.

43. <u>AFP</u>, No. 6612 (June 13, 1968); "The Proclamation of the 22" (mineo.; Cotonou, June 1968).

44. Author's interviews; S. Olatundji, "Pourquoi le Président Zinsou a écarté Alley de l'Etat Major," <u>AN</u>, No. 1102 (September 19-25, 1968).

45. <u>MA</u>, No. 353 (July 4, 1968); <u>AN</u>, No. 1091 (July 4-10, 1968).

46. <u>TP</u>, July 29, 1968; <u>AFP</u>, No. 6651 (July 29, 1968); <u>AuN</u>, August 1, 1968.

47. <u>WA</u>, April 30, 1970, p. 597.

CHAPTER 3

1. There are numerous books on the modern political history of the Gold Coast (Ghana). See, for example, D. Austin, <u>Politics in Ghana 1946-1960</u> (London: Oxford University Press, 1964); David Apter, <u>Ghana in Transition</u> (New York, 1963); H. Bretton, <u>The Rise and Fall of Kwame Nkrumah: A Study of Personal Rule in Africa</u> (London: Pall Mall, 1966); W. B. Harvey, <u>Law and Social Change in Ghana</u> (Princeton, N.J.: Princeton University Press, 1966). Robert Pinkney's <u>Ghana Under Military Rule</u> (Methuen, 1972) came out after the completion of this study.

2. See A. Zolberg, <u>Creating Political Order: The Party-States in West Africa</u> (Chicago: Rand McNally, 1966), esp. pp. 22-25, 95-98.

3. See K. A. Busia, <u>The Courage and Foresight of Busia, Great Historic and Prophetic Statements Issued by Professor K. A. Busia While in Exile</u> (Accra: George Boakie, 1969).

4. Kwame Nkrumah, <u>Speech Delivered by the Life Chairman on the Occasion of the Tenth Anniversary 12th June 1959 of the Convention People's Party</u> (Accra, 1959); Kwame Nkrumah, <u>I Speak of Freedom</u> (New York, 1961), p. 209.

5. This seems to me an accurate statement by Nkrumah's friend and sympathizer, Thomas Hodgkin of Oxford University. "Ghana's Turn," letter in <u>T</u> (March 5, 1966).

6. Zolberg, _Creating Political Order_, p. 87.

7. _Ibid._, pp. 96-97.

8. On this point, see an interesting account by Samuel Ikoku, _Le Ghana de Nkrumah_ (Paris, 1971). This book, written by a high Nigerian associate of Nkrumah, gives a critique of the regime he served and also Ikoku's self-defense. The weakest, the least accurate, and least documented part of the book is on the coup and subsequent military rule.

9. The base year in this computation was 1934 (100), with the highest level achieved in July 1960 (119). See computations by Birmingham in W. B. Birmingham, J. Neustadt, and E. N. Omaboe, eds., _A Study of Contemporary Ghana, Vol. 1, The Economy of Ghana_ (London: Allen and Unwin, 1966), reproduced by D. Austin and R. Rathbone, "Ghana Labour Unions and Political Organizations," in _Trade Unions and Politics_, No. 3 (London: Institute of Commonwealth Studies, 1967), pp. 100-101 (collected seminar papers).

10. On Nkrumah's foreign posture, see W. S. Thompson, _Ghana's Foreign Policy, 1957-1966: Diplomacy, Ideology and the Nkrumah Period_ (Princeton, N.J.: Princeton University Press, 1969).

11. A Western leftist critic of Nkrumah's socialism is presented in B. Fitch and M. Oppenheimer, "Ghana: End of an Illusion," special issue of _MR_, Vol. XVIII, No. 3 (July-August 1966).

12. See J. M. Lee, _African Armies and Civil Order_ (New York: Praeger Publishers, 1969), esp. pp. 26-28; H. Kitchen, ed., _A Handbook of African Affairs_ (New York: Praeger Publishers, 1964), p. 201; W. Gutteridge, _Armed Forces in New States_ (London: Oxford University Press, 1962), _Military Institutions and Power in the New States_ (New York, 1965), and _The Military in African Politics_ (London, 1969).

13. Valerie Bennett, "The Effect of British Colonial Policy on Civil-Military Relations in Gold Coast-Ghana (1921-1966)," (unpublished Ph.D. thesis, African Studies Program, Boston University, 1971), pp. 186-88. Bennett gives an account of the Ghanaian army's history up to 1966.

14. See General Alexander's memoirs: H. T. Alexander, _African Tightrope: My Two Years as_

216

Nkrumah's Chief of Staff (New York: Frederick A. Praeger, 1966).

15. K. Gbedemah's statement, *National Assembly Debates*, 4.12.1957, C. 304-10.

16. In December 1958 two opposition MPs were detained after Major Awhaitey stated that the two approached him to stage a coup. See Austin, *Politics in Ghana*, pp. 381-84 and Appendix B.

17. A. A. Afrifa, "The Future of Politics in Ghana," *LO*, supplement, October 27, 1967.

18. Thompson, *Ghana's Foreign Policy, 1957-1966*, Book III, p. 9.

19. These security officers on loan rendered the most determined armed resistance to the coup and a dozen of them allegedly were killed in Flagstaff House on February 24, 1966. See D. H. Louchheim, "Soviet Lost Lives in Army's Ghana Coup," *WAP*, March 1, 1966, pp. A-10.

20. Inspector-General Harlley's statement in *Ghana Reborn* (New York: Ghana Information Services, December 1966), p. 12.

21. Jon Kraus, "The Men in Charge," *AR*, April 1966, p. 20.

22. Ernest Lefever, *Spear and Scepter* (Washington, D.C.: The Brookings Institute, 1970), p. 55.

23. See memoirs of two participants in the 1966 coup, A. A. Afrifa, *The Ghana Coup: 24th February 1966* (New York: Humanities Press, 1966); A. K. Ocran, *A Myth Is Broken* (London: Longmans, 1964).

24. Lefever, *Spear and Scepter*, p. 55.

25. Stockholm International Peace Research Institute, *Yearbook of World Armaments and Disarmament 1968-69* (New York: Humanities Press, 1969), pp. 210-11.

26. Lee, *African Armies and Civil Order*, p. 44; Lefever, *Spear and Scepter*, pp. 74-77.

27. "Steps by Ghana to Avert Crisis," *G*, February 23, 1966.

28. The account of the coup is based on personal interviews and the following somewhat conflicting sources: Kodwo Ewudzie, *The Challenge of Our Time* (Accra: Foxborow Research Publications, September 1967); Peter Barker, *Operation Cold Chop: The Coup that Toppled Nkrumah* (Accra: Ghana Pub-

lishing Corporation, 1969); Ruth First, Power in Africa (New York: Pantheon, 1970), esp. pp. 363-76; Afrifa, The Ghana Coup; Ocran, A Myth Is Broken; Lefever, Spear and Scepter.

29. Ocran, A Myth Is Broken, pp. 60-62.

30. Ibid., p. 59.

31. Barker, Operation Cold Chop, pp. 161-63.

32. LO, special supplement, February 17, 1967, p. iv.

33. GT, May 11 and 23, 1967, p. 1.

34. Commissioner Harlley contributed significantly to an upward revision of his and the police role in the coup both through official Ghanaian publications and through interviews, e.g., Barker (Operation Cold Chop) and Lefever (Spear and Scepter).

35. Ocran, A Myth Is Broken, p. 81.

36. The list included Lieutenant-General J. A. Ankrah, chairman, Ga, 50 years old; Police Commissioner J. W. K. Harlley, deputy chairman, Ewe, 46; Major-General E. K. Kotoka, Ewe, 39; Colonel A. A. Afrifa, Ashanti, 29; Brigadier A. K. Ocran, Fanti, 36; Assistant Commissioner of Police, J. E. O. Nunoo, Ga, 49; Deputy Commissioner of Police A. K. Deku, Ewe, 43; and Deputy Commissioner of Police B. A. Yakubu, Northerner, 40, with new ranks that were self-conferred on the day of the coup. GT, February 26, 1966, p. 1; Ewudzie, The Challenge of Our Time, pp. 9-14; Lefever, Spear and Scepter, p. 61.

37. LO, special supplement, February 17, 1967, p. iv.

38. T. Hodgkin called it a "counter-revolution"--see T. Hodgkin, "Counter-Revolution in Ghana," LM, No. 4 (April 1966). I have difficulty calling the Nkrumah-CPP regime a revolution. On this score I am in agreement with R. Rathbone in "Education and Politics in Ghana," Africana Collecta (Gütersloh: Bertelsmann Universitatsverlag, 1968) and in "Politics and Factionalism in Ghana," CH, Vol. LX, No. 355 (March 1971), and with Austin's analysis of the CPP regime in Politics in Ghana.

39. "The Proclamation for the Constitution of a National Liberation Council for the Administration of Ghana and for Other Matters Connected

Therewith," GT, February 26, 1966, p. 1; Lieutenant-General J. A. Ankrah's broadcast in GT, February 28, 1966, p. 1; both documents are reprinted in Ewudzie, The Challenge of Our Time, pp. 9-24.

40. See M. Owusu, "The 1969 General Election and the Culture of Politics in Swedru-Ghana 1966-1969," in D. Austin, ed. (forthcoming).

41. Ocran, A Myth Is Broken, p. 94.

42. Owusu, "The 1969 General Election," p. 35.

43. See Lieutenant-General Ankrah's broadcast in GT, February 28, 1966.

44. On the Ghanaian foreign policy under the NLC, see W. S. Thompson, "Ghana's Foreign Policy Under Military Rule," AR, XV, 5-6 (May-June 1969), 8-12.

45. The most famous and often cited example concerned the sale of the pharmaceutical factory at Kwabenya to Abbot Laboratories of Illinois. Under strong public pressure, mainly from the University of Ghana, the American firm rescinded the agreement. The heated public debate could be followed in the issues of Legon Observer, November 1967-January 1968. The government position is best expressed in R. S. Amegashie, "Commissioner for Industries Replies to the Critics" (mimeo., Accra, 1968). The text of the amended agreement was published in GT, November 13, 1967, p. 7.

46. J. M. Due, "Agricultural Development in the Ivory Coast and Ghana," JMAS, XII, 4 (December 1969), 659.

47. Ghana, The Budget 1966-67 (Accra, 1968), Part II, Table V: Ghana, The Financial Statement 1967-68 (Accra, 1969), Tables I and V; Ghana, The Financial Statement 1968-69 (Accra, 1970), Tables I and V. This material also is presented in R. Price, "Theoretical Approach to Military Rule in New States: Reference Group Theory and the Ghanaian Case," WP, Vol. XXIII (April 1971).

48. The figures in this paragraph are compiled from E. N. Omaboe, "The State of the Economy Today," LO, December 22, 1968, p. 3.

49. Ghana, Economic Survey 1969 (Accra: Central Bureau of Statistics, 1970), p. 15. For a more thorough analysis of NLC economic policies, see G. K. Agama, "Monetary Aspects of Stabilization

Policy in Ghana 1966-1969" (mimeo., Princeton University, 1971).

50. See Agama, "Monetary Aspects."

51. A. A. Afrifa, "Dawn of a New Era," GTO, October 1, 1969.

52. WA, July 26, 1969, p. 856; LO, December 22, 1969, p. 4.

53. See a brief description and discussion of the NLC rule in D. Austin and R. Rathbone, "The Politics of Demilitarization: The Ghana Case" (mimeo., Institute of Commonwealth Studies, London, May 1966).

54. Lieutenant-General E. K. Kotoka and two other officers were killed during an almost successful attempt to replace the NLC with another junta consisting of a lieutenant-colonel and two majors. This counter-coup was staged by Lieutenant S. Arthur, who was temporarily left in command of a 120-man reconnaissance squadron stationed in Ho, 120 miles east of Accra. The disgruntled lieutenant was motivated by the desire for self-promotion and by adventurism. A military tribunal sentenced Lieutenant Arthur, 27, and Lieutenant M. Yeboah, 26, who killed General Kotoka, to death by a firing squad, and Second Lieutenant Osei Poku, 23, to 30 years of imprisonment. The first two were executed on May 9 in the presence of a large crowd. The entire unit was investigated, and 9 NCOs were sentenced to a total of 142 years of imprisonment. LO, special edition, Vol. II, No. 8/1 (April 22, 1967); GT, May 3-May 10, 1967; GT, August 2, 1967, p. 1.

55. See the NLC statement in "Ghana Leader Loses Post over 'Gifts,'" T, April 3, 1969.

56. These posts bore slightly different titles under Kotoka, Ankrah, Ocran, and Otu.

57. Ghana Armed Forces Act 1962 (Amendment), Decree, 1968.

58. K. A. Busia, a former leader of the opposition United Party and the second chairman of the Political Advisory Committee, answered public criticisms in March 1967: "The Political Committee is not a United Party committee. . . . The former members of the United Party serving on the Political Committee constitute exactly one-third of its mem-

bership. They are there not as a group, but as individuals. They observe the law banning their
party, and have made no attempt to act in concert
to fulfill any agreed policy." K. A. Busia, "One
Year After the Coup," LO, supplement, April 14,
1967, p. ii.

59. See a speech by a PAC member, G. D. G.
Folson, in LO, No. 25 (December 8-21, 1967), pp.
9-10.

60. GT, July 1, 1967, p. 1.

61. GT, July 18, 1967, p. 6.

62. M. Owusu, "The 1969 General Election,"
pp. 15, 55, 57.

63. GT, June 24, 1967, p. 1; and author's interviews. According to its prominent member, Joe
Appiah, the Political Advisory Committee had in
fact decided to disband itself. Its successor,
the National Advisory Committee, was dissolved in
November 1968.

64. GT, June 8, 1967, p. 1; and author's interviews. See a description of the CCE in W. Boye-
Anowomah, "Center for Civic Education," GT, September 19, 1967, p. 7.

65. See Ankrah's denials in GT, August 7, 1968,
p. 1.

66. GT, January 30, 1968, p. 1. The decree,
No. 223, was officially entitled the Elections and
Public Offices' Disqualification Decree. See also
GTO, XII, 3 (1968), 2-3.

67. GT, November 15, 1968, p. 1.

68. GT, November 13, 1967, p. 13.

69. Ibid.

70. See a review of the CPP regime and, less
thoroughly, of the NLC rule in Jon Kraus, "Arms
and Politics in Ghana," C. Welch, Jr., ed., Soldier
and State in Africa (Evanston, Ill.: Northwestern
University Press, 1970), pp. 154-221.

71. Apart from the already mentioned abortive
coup of April 17, 1967, an almost mutiny in March
1969, and the rumors of a possible Ewe coup in
April 1969, such apprehensions were raised by the
trial of Air Marshal M. A. Otu, who was arrested
on November 21, 1968, and accused on television by
J. W. K. Harlley of plotting with prominent Nkrumahists to overthrow the NLC--see GT, December 18,

1968, p. 1.   This strange affair strained army-police relations.   The charges were never substantiated and Otu was reinstated under the civilian government as chief of defense staff.   Apart from this, the NLC was quite aware of the fate of the sister National Reformation Council regime in Sierra Leone in April 1968.

72.   The first substantial outline of a return to civilian rule was presented by General J. A. Ankrah in his New Year's Eve message on December 31, 1967, but he dragged his feet subsequently. GT, January 1, 1968, p. 1.

73.   GT, January 27, 1968, p. 1; E. Akufo-Addo, "Synopsis of the Draft Constitution," GTO, XII, 3 (1968), 6-7; also published in AR, XIII, 4 (April 1968), 9-12.

74.   General Ankrah's statement in WA, No. 2684 (1968), p. 1330.

75.   See the NLC decree in GT, November 11, 1968, p. 1.

76.   GT, April 8, 1969, p. 1.

77.   Ghana, Constitution of the Republic of Ghana (Accra: Ghana Publishing Corporation, 1969), First Schedule, Transitional Provisions, Part I, Art. I, p. 139.

78.   Ibid., Art. 71:2:b: ii, p. 58.

79.   Ibid., pp. 147-48.

80.   Ibid., p. 148.

81.   Ibid., chapters XIII and XV, pp. 109-10, 113-14.

82.   The campaign and electoral results are extensively presented in M. Danquah, ed., The Birth of the Second Republic (Accra: Editorial and Publishing Services, 1970).

83.   Afrifa, "Dawn of a New Era."

84.   NYT, September 1, 1970, p. 2.

85.   WA, No. 2850 (1972), p. 108.

86.   Ghana, Public Relations Department, The Fall of the Second Republic (Accra, 1972), p. 12.

CHAPTER 4

1.   This process and the fundamental characteristics of Sierra Leone politics are described in the best books to date on Sierra Leone: Martin Kilson, Political Change in a West African State:

A Study of Modernization Process (Cambridge, Mass.: Harvard University Press, 1966); J. R. Cartwright, Politics in Sierra Leone 1947-67 (Toronto, 1970).

2. On general sources, see R. G. Saylor, The Economic System of Sierra Leone (Durham: Duke University Press, 1967).

3. See J. Peterson, "The Sierra Leone Creole: A Reappraisal," in C. Fyfe and E. Jones, eds., Freetown: A Symposium (Freetown: Sierra Leone University Press, 1968), pp. 101-24.

4. See Sierra Leone, Report of the Forster Commission of Inquiry on Assets of Ex-Ministers and Ex-Deputy Ministers (Freetown: Government Printer, 1968), section on Sir Albert Margai, pp. 59-67.

5. See V. Minikin, "The Development of Political Opposition in Sierra Leone 1961-1967" (unpublished M.A. thesis, West African Studies Center, University of Birmingham, October 1968).

6. S. Dixon-Fyle, "The Economy Needs Stronger Official Involvement," FT, Sierra Leone Survey Supplement, November 6, 1969.

7. See C. Allen, "Sierra Leone Politics Since Independence," AAF, Vol. LXVII, No. 268 (October 1968).

8. DM, January 26, 1967, p. 1.

9. HO, December 7, 1967, pp. 1, 3, 4.

10. DM, February 11, 1967, p. 1; T, February 9, 1967.

11. AFP, February 5-6, 1967; "Echec de L'impérialisme en Sierra Leone," HO, February 14, 1967, pp. 1-2.

12. Allen, "Sierra Leone Politics," pp. 36, 37; also the table in Minikin, "Development of Political Opposition."

13. See Sierra Leone, The Report of the Dove-Edwin Commission of Inquiry into the Conduct of the 1967 General Election in Sierra Leone and the Government Statement Thereon (Freetown: Government Printer, 1967).

14. See a description of these events by an eyewitness, H. Fisher, "Elections and Coups in Sierra Leone 1967," JMAS, VII, 4 (April 1969), 611-36. I also extensively used my notes taken in the courtroom in 1970 during the Lansana treason trial in Freetown.

15. Estimates vary between 40 and 14, while The New York Times gives the lowest figure of at least 4 (NYT, March 22, 1967). Cartwright quotes Siaka Stevens' statement of 9 killed and 54 wounded. See Cartwright, Politics in Sierra Leone 1947-67, p. 252.

16. WA, November 15, 1969; T, March 28, 1967; and my notes.

17. See a transcript of the speech in Fisher, "Elections and Coups," p. 631.

18. Ibid., p. 636.

19. Ibid., p. 632; DM, March 24, 1967, p. 1.

20. "UN Envoy to Lead Junta in Sierra Leone," G, March 25, 1967.

21. FM, March 29, 1967.

22. See J. M. Lee, African Armies and Civil Order (New York: Praeger Publishers, 1969), p. 27.

23. The pay scales are given in ibid., pp. 94-95. Compare them with the per capita national income in 1967 of Le 92.3 per annum in Bank of Sierra Leone, Sierra Leone in Figures (Freetown, 1969).

24. Sierra Leone, Report of the Dove-Edwin Commission, paragraphs 129, 134.

25. "The NRC Royal Sierra Leone Military Forces Decree," No. 13 (May 19, 1967).

26. DM, July 20, 1967, p. 1.

27. "The NRC Anti-Corruption Squad Decree 1967," SLG, Vol. XCVII, No. 109.

28. See DM, January 20, 1968, p. 1.

29. See NRC Decree No. 28, issued on June 8, 1967, in SLG, Vol. XCVII.

30. See Attorney-General B. Macauley's statement in T, March 28, 1967.

31. See the accounts of this statement in SLTJ, VII, 1 (1967), 2; "No Dictatorship, Says Sierra Leone Leader," T, March 30, 1967; Fisher, "Elections and Coups," pp. 634, 635.

32. AFP, No. 6248 (March 26-28, 1967); DM, March 28, 1967, p. 1.

33. DM, March 3, 1967, p. 1.

34. Ibid.

35. AFP, No. 6274 (April 27, 1967); SLTJ, No. 2 (1967), pp. 44-45.

36. Sierra Leone, Annual Report and Statement
of Accounts (Freetown: Bank of Sierra Leone, 1968),
pp. 9-10.

37. See Captain S. M'boma's statement on the
SLMB in SLTJ, No. 3 (1967), pp. 80-82; "La Sierra
Leone modifie ses structures," MTM, October 10,
1967, pp. 2949-50.

38. See Sierra Leone, Annual Report (1968),
p. 15, and Annual Report and Statement of Accounts
(Freetown: Bank of Sierra Leone, 1969), p. 49.

39. The trade surplus in 1968 was Le 4.4 million compared to the deficits of Le 12.6 million
in 1966 and Le 14.7 million in 1967. See Sierra
Leone, Sierra Leone in Figures (Freetown: Bank of
Sierra Leone, 1969).

40. Sierra Leone NRC (Newspaper) Law No. 4,
1967 (Freetown: Government Printing Office, 1967).

41. See the NRC rebuttal in SLN, HCL/INF/oo6,
November 30, 1967.

42. See "Juxon-Smith and Fourah Bay" and Davidson Nicol's statement in WA, November 8, 1969, pp.
1331, 1338-39.

43. DM, October 17, 1967, p. 1; MTM, October
28, 1967, pp. 2849-50.

44. A. T. Juxon-Smith, Address Delivered by
the Chairman, NRC, Brigadier A. T. Juxon-Smith,
on the Occasion of the Opening Session of the Civilian Rule Committee on Wednesday, 21 February
1968 (Freetown: Government Printing Office, 1968),
p. 10.

45. See the NRC decree in DM, January 17,
1968. The original list of 62 selected members
was published in DM, January 30, 1968, p. 1. It
differs slightly from the mineographed roll-call
list of the first working session (Freetown, February 27, 1968).

46. Joint Statement by APC and SLPP Representatives to the Civilian Rule Committee (mimeo.,
Freetown, February 22, 1968), 3 pp.; Civilian Rule
Committee Memoranda Submitted Jointly by the Representatives of the APC and the SLPP (mimeo., Freetown, February 1968), 3 pp.

47. HT, April 22, 1968; R. Howe, "Sierra
Leone Struggles Back to Democracy," CSM, April 22,
1968.

48. *AFP*, No. 6571 (April 20, 1968).
49. *AFP*, No. 6570 (April 19, 1968).

CHAPTER 5
1. See the only book to date in English on the Malian political system, F. G. Snyder, *One-Party Government in Mali* (New Haven: Yale University Press, 1965); also see S. M. Sy, *Recherches sur l'exercise du pouvoir politique en Afrique Noire* (Paris: Pédone, 1965). For a comparison of Mali, Ghana, and Guinea, see S. Amin, *Trois Expériences Africaines de Développement* (Paris: Presses Universitaires de France, 1965). The origin of the Union Soudanaise is described in R. Schachter-Morgenthau, *Political Parties in French-Speaking West Africa* (Oxford: Clarendon Press, 1964), and its functioning in the early 1960s in A. Mahiou, *L'Avenement du Parti Unique en Afrique Noire* (Paris: Librairie Générale de Droit de Jurisprudence, 1969).
2. See an optimistic description and analysis of government and party institutions in N. S. Hopkins, "Government in Kita: Social Institutions and Processes in a Malian Town" (unpublished Ph.D. thesis, Department of Anthropology, University of Chicago, 1967).
3. See the professional background of the delegates to the Sixth Congress in September 1962 in Mahiou, *L'Avènement du Parti Unique*, p. 32.
4. The US-RDA options are presented by the radical S. Badian-Kouyaté, *Les Dirigeants Africains Face à Leur Peuple* (Paris: François Maspers, 1964). See an analysis of US-RDA economic policies in W. I. Jones, "Planning and Economic Policy in Mali" (unpublished Ph.D. thesis in political science, University of Geneva, 1971).
5. See N. S. Hopkins, "Socialism and Social Change in Rural Mali," *JMAS*, VII, 3 (1969), 465-67.
6. On the relationship between Malian merchants and the state bureaucracy, see C. Meillassoux, "A Class Analysis of the Bureaucratic Process in Mali," *JDS*, VI, 2 (1970), 97-110.
7. See Modibo Keita's last Independence Day speech in which he proudly pointed out the increase in the length of asphalt roads from 350 km. in 1961 to 1,230 km. in 1968. Ban, No. 524 (1968), p. 10559.

8. See G. Compte, "Comment Modibo Keita a été renversé," JA, No. 464 (1969), p. 32.

9. BAN, No. 559 (June 25, 1969), p. 11260. The expenses of national sovereignty (the presidency, National Assembly, foreign affairs), general administration expenses, and outlays for education, health, other social and welfare services, and public debt showed the greatest increase. On the other hand the budgetary expenditure on defense was reduced by 11 percent, due to the closing of French military bases and despite the creation of a national army. Expenditures on the police and judiciary of a national army. Expenditures on the police and judiciary increased only slightly. See Amin, Trois Expériences Africaines, pp. 77, 108.

10. See R. Schachter-Morgenthau, "Mali and Tanzania: Some Observations About Socialism in Tropical Africa" (mimeo., Boston, 1971).

11. MTM, July 29, 1967.

12. AFP, No. 6369 (August 23, 1967); the letter of A. Moumouni, "La Situation Politique au Mali," M, September 19, 1967.

13. Lieutenant-Colonel Muguet, Les Armées Nationales des Etats Voisins: Nigérie, Ghana, Guinée, Mali, No. 712/A (Paris: Centre Militaire d'Information et de Spécialisation pour l'Outre-Mer, 1964), p. 31; N. S. Hopkins, "Social Control in a Malian Town" (mimeo., paper for the African Studies Association meeting, New York, 1967); Hopkins, "Government in Kita."

14. NM, No. 1 (1968), pp. 102.

15. About 175 public officers, including ministers, ambassadors, and financial inspectors, were denounced publicly and were dismissed or resigned; at least one, the deputy mayor of Bamako, committed suicide. MTM, December 2, 1967.

16. AFP, No. 1450 (1968), p. 22; AN, No. 1106 (1968), p. 22; AN, No. 1090 (1968), p. 4; AFP, No. 1486 (1968), p. 6; WA, No. 2678 (1968), p. 1151.

17. NM, No. 4 (September 1968).

18. See a more detailed description of the coup in Anton Bebler, "The Making of a Coup," WA, No. 2782 (October 3, 1970), pp. 1151-52.

19. See short official biographies of both in "Mali," supplement to JA, No. 438 (1969).

20. Colonel Sékou Traoré, army chief of staff, enumerated these activities on the occasion of the third anniversary of the army: spreading literacy, popularizing the party line, ideological education, administrative duties, running kindergartens, running social and medical centers in the bases, participation in harvesting and public works. ES, February 22, 1966, pp. 1-3. In addition, the army helped to organize cooperatives and train the People's Militia.

21. Muguet, Les Armées Nationales, p. 31. D. Wood gives lower figures: army, 3,500; Gendarmerie, 1,000; civil police, 600. See D. Wood, "The Armed Forces of African States," Adelphi Papers, No. 27 (London: Institute for Strategic Studies, 1966), p. 10.

22. Wood, "The Armed Forces of African States," p. 10.

23. In addition to Colonel Sékou Traoré, Major Diallo, commanding officer of the People's Militia, and Major Cisse, the military commander in the Fifth Region, also tried to resist. Eight senior officers refused to support the coup and were temporarily detained. AFP, No. 6746 (February 20, 1968).

24. See this formulation in Captain Diakité's statement in ES, March 24, 1969, p. 1.

25. AFP, No. 6747 (November 21, 1968).

26. See Lieutenant Moussa Traoré's declaration in ES, November 23, 1968, pp. 1, 4.

27. See Captain Diakité's declarations in ES, November 26, 1968, p. 1, and December 12, 1968, p. 4.

28. See P. Biarnes, "La Junte Militaire de Bamako s'engage à organiser des élections avant la fin de 1969," M, November 7, 1968.

29. See the junta's catalog of accusations in two statements by Captain Diakité, ES, December 12, 1968, p. 1, and March 24, 1969, p. 1.

30. ES, December 26, 1968, p. 1.

31. AFP, No. 6755 (November 30, 1969); ES, December 9, 1968, p. 3.

32. AFP, No. 6764 (December 11, 1968).

33. J. Suret-Canale, expert of the French Communist Party, put the figure at 44 in H, September 29, 1969.

34. AFP, No. 6793 (January 16, 1969).
35. For example, Mohamed Mahmoud Duld Cheik, cadi of Toumbouctou, was again allowed to move outside the town. ES, January 14, 1969, pp. 1, 4.
36. ES, November 30, 1968, p. 1.
37. See Captain Diakité's initial declaration, ES, December 19, 1968, pp. 1-4.
38. ES, December 9, 1968, pp. 1-3.
39. CPA, No. 1 (1969), p. 39.
40. See Captain Diakité's statement in ES, March 24, 1969, p. 1.
41. ES, June 3, 1969, pp. 1-2.
42. ES, June 24, 1969, p. 1; ES, July 29, 1969, p. 1; ES, July 30, 1961, pp. 1-4; ESH, August 4, 1969, p. 1, 5.
43. ES, September 14, 19, 1969, p. 1.
44. ESH, September 29, 1969, p. 2.
45. There were several mass strikes in Bamako schools in protest against poor cafeteria services and a planned reform of higher education. See CPA, No. 1 (1969), p. 33; CPA No. 2 (1969), p. 28. A. Touré, director of the Teachers' College, one faculty member, and three administration members, as well as two students, were arrested and tried in March 1970 on charges of anti-state conspiracy in view of establishing an illegal political party. Touré was sentenced to two years in jail.
46. About 10,000 employees were laid off out of 30,000 in the 27 state enterprises. See "Choix Difficile pour les Militaires," RFEPA, No. 40 (April 1969), p. 13.
47. The budget deficit was reduced from FM 4.4 billion in 1968 to FM 1.7 billion in 1969, the total expenditure from FM 23.5 billion to FM 23.3 billion, but defense and security outlays increased from FM 2.98 billion to FM 3.19 billion. See BAN, No. 559 (June 25, 1969), pp. 11261-62.
48. The crisis was averted by massive imports on credit from the United States, France, and West Germany. See ESH, September 29, 1969, p. 3.
49. AFP, No. 6971 (August 19, 1969). Altogether 33 officers, NCOs, and soldiers were tried. Three main defendants—Captain D. S. Diarra, Captain A. Diarra, and Sergeant B. Traoré—were sentenced to life terms of hard labor; eight were acquitted. See AA, December 8-21, 1969, pp. 7-8.

50. <u>ES</u>, May 19, 1969, pp. 1, 3, 4.
51. "Résolution Générale du 2me Congrès du Syndicat National de l'Education et de la Culture" (mimeo., Bamako, April 1970), 5 pp.

CHAPTER 6
1. See the table in M. Glélé, <u>Naissance d'un état noir</u> (Paris: Librairie Générale de Droit et de Jurisprudence, 1969), pp. 299-301.
2. It seems that the actual payoffs by Nkrumah to the Ghanaian businessmen were very modest. John Esseks shows a complex interplay between Nkrumah's nationalism and his socialist-statist ideology in "Government and Indigenous Private Enterprise in Ghana," <u>JMAS</u>, IX, 1 (1971), 11-29.
3. The military intervention in Dahomey in October 1963 clearly contradicts the generalization of Ruth First that the "first Army coups [in Africa] were pay strikes." See Ruth First, <u>Power in Africa</u> (New York: Pantheon, 1970), p. 21.
The October 1963 intervention also makes dubious another sweeping statement that army corporate reasons are invariably present during military interventions. (<u>Ibid.</u>, p. 19.)
4. There could be, particularly in Mali, some connection between the pre-colonial centralizing traditions and the post-independence civilian orders. A. Zolberg makes this point in <u>Creating Political Order: The Party-States in West Africa</u> (Chicago: Rand McNally, 1966), p. 130.
5. See the memoirs of Generals A. A. Afrifa and A. Ocran: Afrifa, <u>The Ghana Coup: 24th February 1966</u> (New York: Humanities Press, 1966); A. K. Ocran, <u>A Myth Is Broken</u> (London: Longmans, 1968).
6. "Dahomey: Le prix de la banqueroute," <u>RFEPA</u>, No. 1 (1968), pp. 29-31; Dov Ronen, "The Military Intervention," in <u>Dynamics of Political Transition in Dahomey</u> (forthcoming).
7. See <u>BAN</u>, February 5, 1969, p. 10876; <u>ARB-EFTS</u>, October 1967, pp. 845-46; S. Decalo, "The Politics of Instability in Dahomey," <u>GA</u>, No. 2 (1968), p. 9.
8. See John C. De Wilde, <u>Expériences de Développement Agricole en Afrique Noire</u> (Paris: Maisonneuve et Larose, 1968), Chapters 1, 2.

9. In 1967 officially recorded Malian exports of cattle stood at 42,970 head, whereas custom statistics of the neighboring states showed imports from Mali of over 120,000 head. P. Decraene, "Le Mali fait face à une situation financière très difficile," M, November 28-29, 1969).

10. See R. Schachter-Morgenthau, "Mali and Tanzania: Some Observations About Socialism in Tropical Africa" (mimeo., Boston, 1971).

11. Former Ugandan President Milton Obote, head of the only legal political party, the Uganda People's Congress (UPC), did not use his powers in time to assure loyalty of the commander of the army and the air force. Although he had had apprehensions about Major-General Idi Amin, Obote had not fired him. This fact and the cooperation of General Amin with Police Inspector-General E. W. Oryema made the coup, in the absence of the president from the country, extremely easy, did not visibly divide the army, and as far as we know assured the new junta a wide popular support, at least in the capital and among the Baganda. The divisive techniques used by Obote, mainly the promotion of army and police officers from his own ethnic group, the Langi, and the creation of a large presidential guard and the expansion of security services under his relative, A. Adoko, did not give the desired results in time and may well have provoked the coup. (See NYT, January 26, 1971, p. 1, and January 27, 1971, p. 3.)

The former Yugoslav ambassador to Uganda, L. Reljic, assumed but did not show that Obote's downfall was a result of "neocolonialist conspiracy" promoted by Obote's active foreign policy of non-alignment, his criticism of British relations with South Africa, and his internal policies that "harmed . . . the interests . . . of foreign powers." Reljic failed to analyze the internal causes of the coup, did not demonstrate how in the particular case of Uganda "domestic capital" in collusion with British interests "provided the main material support" for the coup, and passed in silence over the wide support the January coup received among numerous social groups, including the membership of the UPC. See L. Reljic, "The Background of Coups d'Etat in Africa," RIA, Vol. XXII (March 20, 1971), pp. 21-22, and compare with the analysis and prediction of the Uganda coup in H. Bienen, "Military and Society in East Africa: Thinking Again Praetorianism" (mimeo., Princeton University, Center of International Studies, 1971).

12. Such views are found mainly on the Western political left, in the political East, in the African radical press, and in the Arab press. Ideological and political hardliners took these allegations for granted and found in them another confirmation of their world view even before Nkrumah declared t that the Ghanaian plotters were offered $13 million in advance by the U.S. ambassador. He did not disclose any supporting evidence, however. See Kwame Nkrumah, Dark Days in Ghana (London: Lawrence and Wishart, 1968), p. 49.

13. See Waldemar Nielsen, The Great Powers and Africa (New York: Praeger Publishers, 1969); Anton Bebler, "The Strategies of the Great Powers in Africa," Teorija in Praksa, Nos. 8-9 (Ljubljana, Yugoslavia, 1971).

14. Glélé makes these points in Naissance 'd'un état noir, p. 317.

15. See J. Colas, "Social and Career Correlates of Military Intervention in Nigeria: A Background Study of the January 15th Coup," Annual Meeting of the Inter-University Seminar on Armed Forces and Society, Chicago, October 1969, p. XVII.

16. H. Fisher, "Elections and Coups in Sierra Leone 1967," JMAS, XII, 4 (April 1969), 636. The NLC members, particularly Major Jumu, had close personal ties with Ghanaian and Nigerian officers dating back to days at Sandhurst.

CHAPTER 7

1. H. Bienen, "Military and Society in East Africa: Thinking Again Praetorianism" (mimeo., Princeton University, Center of International Studies, 1971), pp. xvii, 39-40, 179.

2. See J. M. Lee, African Armies and Civil Order (New York: Praeger Publishers, 1969), pp. 25-51.

3. See M. Janowitz, The Military in the Political Development of New Nations (Chicago: University of Chicago Press, 1964), p. 12.

4. See relative figures in ibid., pp. 20-21, and in the SIPRI Yearbook of World Armament and Disarmament 1968/1969 (New York: Humanities Press, 1969).

5. D. Wood, "The Armed Forces of African States," Adelphi Papers, No. 27 (London: Institute for Strategic Studies, 1966), p. 17; R. May, "Sierra Leone as a Reconciliation System, 1951-68" (unpublished M.S. thesis, University of Birmingham, 1968), p. 23.

6. Major Blake, the chief architect of the second Sierra Leone coup on March 23, 1967, is said to have been aggrieved by his slow promotion. The complaint that there were in 1967 too many full colonels (12) in the Ghanaian army had been a frequent topic of discussion among the junior officers, and the mechanism of rigorous selection on promotion examinations of lieutenants largely motivated Lieutenant S. Arthur, author of the almost successful counter-coup on April 17, 1967. Lieutenant Arthur failed on such an examination on April 4 and started entertaining the idea of a coup on April 10, 1967. See the statements of Lieutenant Arthur and Lieutenant Yeboah in GT, May 3, 1967, and Attorney-General V. Owusu's statement in GT, May 4, 1967, p. 7.

7. See Lee, African Armies and Civil Order, pp. 50-51.

8. See R. Clignet, "Ethnicity, Social Differentiation and Secondary Schooling in West Africa," CEA, Summer 1967, p. 375.

9. See A. K. Ocran, A Myth Is Broken (London: Longmans, 1968), p. XVI, contrary to what Ernest Lefever says in Spear and Scepter (Washington, D.C.: The Brookings Institute, 1970), p. 39.

10. May, "Sierra Leone," p. 24; and AC, No. 6 (March 17, 1967).

11. See the design on Table 1 in Lee, African Armies and Civil Order, p. 4.

12. The RWAFF had after World War II four battalions in Nigeria, two battalions in Ghana, and one battalion in Sierra Leone; the rough population ratio of the three countries was 25:3.4:1. Ibid., p. 27.

13. R. Price has not been careful on this point; General J. A. Ankrah, for example, is a good example of the curious Afro-British symbiosis of norms. He has combined in social life such British hobbies as

horce racing with a polygamous family and 22 children. R. Price, "Theoretical Approach to Military Rule in New States: Reference Group Theory and the Ghanaian Case," WP, Vol. XXIII (April 1971).

14. See the memoirs of the Ghanaian generals, A. A. Afrifa and A. K. Ocran: Afrifa, The Ghana Coup: 24th February 1966 (New York: Humanities Press, 1966); Ocran, A Myth Is Broken.

15. Lee, African Armies and Civil Order, Chapter 2.

16. See a handy description of these institutions and their relevance to military intervention in politics in E. Luttwak, Coup d'Etat: A Practical Handbook (London: Penguin, 1969), pp. 90-103.

17. General C. Soglo of Dahomey is a good example of the transition from the colonial army to the national army. Born in 1909, he volunteered for service in the French army in 1930 and later married a French woman. He fought in France in 1939-40 and in 1944-45, later served in Morocco, the Ivory Coast, Indochina, and Senegal. His advancement accelerated after the French adopted policies aimed at granting autonomy to African territories. He returned to independent Dahomey as a French military adviser to the government of his own country. See W. A. E. Skurnik, "The Military and Politics: Dahomey and Upper Volta," in C. E. Welch, Jr., ed., Soldier and State in Africa (Evanston, Ill.: Northwestern University Press, 1970), footnote on p. 106.

18. SIPRI Yearbook, Table 1A.16.

19. See Wood, "The Armed Forces of African States," p. 10.

20. Dahomey budget allocations rose slowly from $0.5 million in 1960 to $1.1 million in 1963 (the military seized power for the first time in October 1963) and then jumped to $4 million in 1964, remaining stationary until 1968. SIPRI Yearbook, Table 1A.16.

21. This is true of all innovations in the Dahomeyan army since independence: the Civic Service (with Israeli aid), expansion of the engineers company to be used for civic work (with French aid), an elite paratroop company (with French equipment and money, Israeli advice). See

interview with Major A. Alley in AuN, June 5, 1966, p. 3.

22. The agreement with Great Britain was concluded in January 1968. In October, 170 infantry men and 130 paratroopers were flown for exercises to Stanford base, used by NATO. See GT, January 10, 1968, p. 1, and October 7, 1968, p. 7.

23. This question is raised, inter alia, in H. Bienen, The Military Intervenes: Case Studies in Political Development (New York: Russell Sage Foundation, 1968), p. xvi.

24. J. A. Ankrah, former chairman of the NLC, for example, was active in real estate under Nkrumah and is now a retired general and a well-to-do owner of several rented villas. The same is true of General Soglo of Dahomey, who rented two of his houses to the U.S. embassy, and, allegedly, of General A. A. Afrifa; J. W. K. Harlley, former inspector-general of Ghanaian police; and Colonel P. Aho of the Dahomeyan army. It was reported that four senior inspectors of the Ghanaian police used the police headquarters in Accra for meetings of executive officers of a private company of which they were the principal owners. (GT, May 11, 1967, p. 12.) This list could be expanded.

25. M. Glélé, Naissance d'un état noir (Paris: Librairie Générale de Droit et de Jurisprudence, 1969), pp. 315-17.

CHAPTER 8
1. One of the most recent ones is by Ernest Lefever in Spear and Scepter (Washington, D.C.: The Brookings Institute, 1970), p. 27: (1) a security coup replaces a civilian regime incapable of providing order and external and internal security--subtype is the custodial coup; (2) a reform coup aims at reversal of internal and/or external policies of the civilian regime, including the intention of a fundamental change in the sociopolitical order; (3) a new elite coup replaces only the government and the political elite by a new group, without significantly changing the order and policies; and (4) a punitive coup is promoted basically by corporate grievances and aspirations of the military establishment.

2. P. Biarnes, "La Junte Militaire de Bamako s'engage à organiser des élections avant la fin de 1969," M, November 27, 1968.

3. See Kwame Nkrumah, Voice from Conakry: Broadcasts to the People of Ghana Made in Conakry Between March and December, 1966, on Radio Guinea's "Voice of the Revolution" (London: Panafrican Publications, 1967).

4. See N. S. Hopkins, "Socialism and Social Change in Rural Mali," JMAS, Vol. VII, No. 3 (1969), and "Government in Kita: Social Institutions and Processes in a Malian Town" (unpublished Ph.D. thesis, Department of Anthropology, University of Chicago, 1967).

5. See Modibo Keita's speech at the Catholic Lycée de Filles Notre-Dame du Niger in AN, February 23, 1966, p. 5.

6. ESH, April 17, 1966, p. 1.

7. On this point, see R. Price, "Military Officers and Political Leadership: The Ghanaian Case," CP, III, 3 (April 1971), 367-68. However, in my opinion the author grossly overstates the case when he argues that the alliance with the police "severely constrained . . . the latitude of action of the Army officers in taking steps toward desired reforms." No one on the council contributed more to trying to implement reforms than J. W. Harlley. R. Price seriously exaggerates the army members' ability to envision and formulate a coherent program of government action and their difference from the police members in terms of self-enrichment and aggrandizement.

8. See M. Owusu, "The 1969 General Election and the Culture of Politics in Swedru-Ghana 1966-1969," in D. Austin, ed. (forthcoming), p. 69.

9. JORM, No. 292 (1969), p. 6, and No. 294 (1969), p. 74. Major B. Poudiougou replaced Colonel Drabo in March 1969; see JORM, No. 296 (1969), p. 101; ESH, March 4, 1969, pp. 1, 6.

10. This seems to be the case with Generals Afrifa and Ocran; see A. A. Afrifa, The Ghana Coup: 24th February 1966 (New York: Humanities Press, 1966); A. K. Ocran, A Myth Is Broken (London: Longmans, 1968).

11. See Davidson Nicol, "Civic Responsibility and Academic Freedom in Africa: Introduction to

236

the College Annual Report of the Principal, Fourah
Bay College, University of Sierra Leone (September
1966-August 1967)," MN, VII, 1-2 (1968-69), 73-81.

12. There were basically two waves of arrests
--in February-March 1966 and in April 1967. The
last group of 70 detainees--including the former
ministers of defense, interior, and state protocol
(J. K. Baako, K. Addison, and K. Edusei) and 33
military men--was released in April 1968. (GT,
April 25, 1968, p. 1.) It should be added that
these persons were not detained throughout the entire period 1966-68.

13. These regulations prohibited all communications with Nkrumah ("State Security Decree") and
required all persons released from protective custody to report to the nearest police station forth-
rightly (NLC Decree No. 144). The NLC created
"military tribunals to try exceptionally certain
categories of offenses committed by non-military
personnel for any of which will carry a maximum
sentence of death by a firing squad." See Owusu,
"The 1969 General Election," pp. 2, 3; "Ghana Government Press Release No. 25/67," reproduced in
Kodwo Ewudzie, The Challenge of Our Time (Accra:
Foxborow Research Publications, 1967), pp. 27-28.

14. Owusu, "The 1969 General Election," p. 43.

SELECTED BIBLIOGRAPHY

LIST OF BIBLIOGRAPHIC
ABBREVIATIONS

A	Africa
AA	AfricAsia
AAc	Afrique Actuelle
AAF	African Affairs
AC	Africa Confidential
AFP	Agnece France Presse
AN	Afrique Nouvelle
AR	Africa Report
ARB	Africa Research Bulletin (political series)
ARB-EFTS	Africa Research Bulletin (economic, financial, and technical series)
AuN	L'Aube Nouvelle (Cotonou)
B	Bingo (Paris)
BAN	Bulletin de L'Afrique Noire (Paris)
BCEAO	Banque Centrale des Etats de l'Afrique de l'Ouest, Bulletin
CA	Courrier d'Afrique
CEA	Cahiers d'Etudes Africaines
CH	Current History
CP	Comparative Politics
CPA	Chronologie Politique Africaine (Paris)
CSM	Christian Science Monitor
DA	Documentation Africaine
DI	Dahomey Information
DG	Daily Graphic (Accra)
DM	Daily Mail (Freetown)
DT	Daily Telegraph (London)
EC	Etudes Congolaises
ES	Essor (Bamako)
ESH	Essor Hebdomadaire
F	Le Figaro
FEA	France-EurAfrique (Paris)
FM	Fraternité-Matin
FT	Financial Times
G	Guardian
GA	Génève-Afrique
GT	Ghanaian Times

GTO	Ghana Today
H	L'Humanité
HO	Horoya (Conakry)
HT	International Herald Tribune (Paris)
JA	Jeune Afrique
JDS	Journal of Development Studies
JMAS	Jounral of Modern African Studies
JORD	Journal Officiel de la République du Dahomey
JORM	Journal Officiel de la République du Mali
LM	Labour Monthly
LO	Legion Observer
M	Le Monde
MA	Le Moniteur Africain
MD	Le Monde Diplomatique
MN	Minerva
MR	Monthly Review
MTM	Marchés Tropicaux et Méditerranéens
NM	Nouvelles du Mali (newsletter of Malian Embassy in Belgrade)
NYT	New York Times
O	Opinion du Pays (Cotonou)
RA	Revue Africaine
RFEPA	Revue Française d'Etudes Politiques Africaines
RIA	Review of International Affairs (Belgrade)
SLG	Sierra Leone Gazette
SLN	Sierra Leone Newsletter (SL High Commission, London)
SLTJ	Sierra Leone Trade Journal (Freetown)
SQ	Sociological Quarterly
T	Times (London)
TP	Togo Press
WA	West Africa
WAP	Washington Post
WP	World Politics
WT	World Today (London)

PUBLIC DOCUMENTS

Dahomey. Budget National de Fonctionnement de la République du Dahomey. Porto-Novo: Imprimerie Nationale, 1968.

_____. Constitution du Dahomey du 31 Mars, 1968. Paris: Documentation Francaise, 1969.

Ghana. Constitution of the Republic of Ghana. Accra: Ghana Publishing Corporation, 1969.

_____. Economic Survey 1969. Accra: Central Bureau of Statistics, 1970.

_____. Speeches by Colonel I. K. Acheampong. Accra, July 1972.

_____. The Budget 1966-67. Accra, 1968.

_____. The Finalcial Statement 1967-68. Accra, 1969.

_____. The Financial Statement 1968-69. Accra, 1970.

International Bank of Reconstruction and Development, International Development Association. Economic Development in Mali, Evolution, Problems and Prospects. Vol. I, Main Report. Washington, D.C.: IDA, May 1970.

Juxon-Smith, A. T. Address Delivered by the Chair-man, NRC, Brigadier A. T. Juxon-Smith, on the Occasion of the Opening Session of the Civilian Rule Committee on Wednesday, 21 February 1968. Freetown: Government Printing Office, 1968.

Sierra Leone. Annual Report and Statement of Ac-counts. Freetown: Bank of Sierra Leone, 1968.

_____. Annual Report and Statement of Accounts. Freetown: Bank of Sierra Leone, 1969.

_____. Report of the Forster Commission of In-quiry on Assets of Ex-Ministers and Ex-Deputy Ministers. Freetown: Government Printer, 1968.

_____. The Report of the Dove-Edwin Commission of Inquiry into the Conduct of the 1967 General Election in Sierra Leone and the Government

Statement Thereon. Freetown: Government Printer, 1967.

UN Economic Commission for Africa. Demographic Handbook. New York: ECA, 1968.

_____. "Economic Indicators for Africa," JA, No.
474 (February 3, 1970).

United Nations. United Nations Statistical Yearbook.
New York, 1969.

U.S. Arms Control and Disarmament Agency. World
Military Expenditures. Washington, D.C.: The
Agency, 1969.

BOOKS

Afrifa, A. A. The Ghana Coup: 24th February 1966.
New York: Humanities Press, 1966.

Alexander, H. T. African Tightrope: My Two Years
as Nkrumah's Chief of Staff. New York: Frederick A. Praeger, 1966.

Amin, S. Trois Expériences Africaines de Développement. Paris: Presses Universitaires de
France, 1965.

Apithy, S. M. Telle est la Vérité. Paris, 1968.

Apter, David. Ghana in Transition. New York, 1963.

Austin, D. Politics in Ghana 1946-1960. London:
Oxford University Press, 1964.

Badian-Kouyaté, S. Les Dirigeants Africains Face à
Leur Peuple. Paris: François Maspers, 1964.

Barker, Peter. Operation Cold Chop: The Coup That
Toppled Nkrumah. Accra: Ghana Publishing Corporation, 1969.

Bienen, H. The Military Intervenes: Case Studies in Political Development. New York: Russell Sage Foundation, 1968.

Bing, Geoffrey. Reap the Whirlwind. London: Mc-Gibbon and Kee, 1968.

Birmingham, W. B., J. Neustadt, and E. N. Omaboe, eds. A Study of Contemporary Ghana. Vol. 1, The Economy of Ghana. London: Allen and Unwin, 1966.

Bretton, H. The Rise and Fall of Kwame Nkrumah: A Study of Personal Rule in Africa. London: Pall Mall, 1966.

Cartwright, J. R. Politics in Sierra Leone 1947-67. Toronto, 1970.

Danquah, M., ed. The Birth of the Second Republic. Accra: Editorial and Publishing Services, 1970.

De Wilde, John C. Expériences de Développement Agricole en Afrique Noire. Paris: Maisonneuve et Larose, 1968.

Diagne, P. Pouvoir politique traditionnel en Afrique Occidentale. Paris: Présence Africaine, 1967.

Diakité, Y. Une main amie. Paris, 1969.

Ewudzie, Kodwo. The Challenge of Our Time. Accra: Foxborow Research Publications, 1967.

Finer, S. The Man on Horseback. London: Pall Mall Press, 1962.

First, Ruth. Power in Africa. New York: Pantheon, 1970.

Forde, D., and P. M. Kaberry, eds. West African Kingdoms in the Nineteenth Century. London: Oxford University Press, 1967.

Glélé, M. <u>Naissance d'un état noir</u>. Paris: Librairie Générale de Droit et de Jurisprudence, 1969.

Gutteridge, W. <u>Armed Forces in New States</u>. London: Oxford University Press, 1962.

Hamon, L., ed. <u>Le rôle extramilitaire de L'Armée dans le Tiers Monde</u>. Paris: Presses Universitaires de France, 1966.

Harvey, W. B. <u>Law and Social Change in Ghana</u>. Princeton, N.J.: Princeton University Press, 1966.

Huntington, S. <u>Political Order in Changing Societies</u>. New Haven: Yale University Press, 1968.

_____, ed. <u>Changing Patterns of Military Politics</u>. New York: The Free Press, 1962.

_____. <u>The Soldier and the State: The Theory and Politics of Civil-Military Relations</u>. New York, 1964.

Ikoku, Samuel. <u>Le Ghana de Nkrumah</u>. Paris, 1971.

Janowitz, M. <u>The Military in the Political Development of New Nations</u>. Chicago: University of Chicago Press, 1964.

Johnson, J., ed. <u>The Role of the Military in Underdeveloped Countries</u>. Princeton, N.J.: Princeton University Press, 1962.

Kilson, Martin. <u>Political Change in a West African State: A Study of Modernization Process</u>. Cambridge, Mass.: Harvard University Press, 1966.

Kitchen, H., ed. <u>A Handbook of African Affairs</u>. New York: Praeger Publishers, 1964.

Lee, J. M. <u>African Armies and Civil Order</u>. New York: Praeger Publishers, 1969.

Lefever, Ernest. Spear and Scepter. Washington, D.C.: The Brookings Institute, 1970.

Lombard, J. Structures de type "féodal" in Afrique Noire. Paris: Mouton, 1965.

Luttwak, E. Coup d'Etat: A Practical Handbook. London: Penguin, 1969.

Mahiou, A. L'Avènement du Parti Unique en Afrique Noire. Paris: Librairie Générale de Droit et de Jurisprudence, 1969.

Merritt, R., and S. Rokkan, eds. Comparing Nations: The Use of Quantitative Data in Cross-National Research. New Haven: Yale University Press, 1966.

Nielsen, Waldemar. The Great Powers and Africa. New York: Praeger Publishers, 1969.

Nkrumah, Kwame. Dark Days in Ghana. London: Lawrence and Wishart, 1968.

_____. I Speak of Freedom. New York, 1961.

_____. Voice from Conakry: Broadcasts to the People of Ghana Made in Conakry Between March and December, 1966, on Radio Guinea's "Voice of the Revolution." London: Panafrican Publications, 1967.

Ocran, A. K. A Myth Is Broken. London: Longmans, 1968.

Omari, T. Peter. Kwame Nkrumah: The Anatomy of an African Dictatorship. Accra, 1970.

Saylor, R. G. The Economic System of Sierra Leone. Durham: Duke University Press, 1967.

Schachter-Morgenthau, R. Political Parties in French-Speaking West Africa. Oxford: Clarendon Press, 1964.

Selltiz, C., et al. Research Methods in Social Re-
    lations. New York: Holt, Rinehart and Winston,
    1961.

Snyder, F. G. One-Party Government in Mali. New
    Haven: Yale University Press, 1965.

Stockholm International Peace Research Institute.
    Yearbook of World Armaments and Disarmament
    1968-69. New York: Humanities Press, 1969.

Sy, S. M. Recherches sur l'exercice du pouvoir poli-
    tique en Afrique Noire. Paris: Pédone, 1965.

Thompson, W. D. Ghana's Foreign Policy, 1957-1966:
    Diplomacy, Ideology and the Nkrumah Period.
    Princeton, N.J.: Princeton University Press,
    1969.

Van Doorn, J., ed. The Military Profession and Mili-
    tary Regimes. The Hague, 1968.

Welch, C., ed. Soldier and State in Africa. Evanston,
    Ill.: Northwestern University Press, 1970.

Zolberg, A. Creating Political Order: The Party-
    States in West Africa. Chicago: Rand McNally,
    1966.

ARTICLES AND PERIODICALS

Afrifa, A. A. "Dawn of a New Era," GTO, October 1,
    1969.

Agama, G. K. "Monetary Aspects of Stabilization
    Policy in Ghana 1966-1969." Princeton Univer-
    sity, 1971. (Mimeo.)

Agboton, G. "Quleques moyens de réalisation de
    l'unité nationale," AuN, October 9, 1966, p. 6.

Akufo-Addo, E. "Synopsis of the Draft Constitution,"
    GTO, XII, 3 (1968), 6-8. Also published in AR,
    XIII, 4 (April 1968), pp. 9-12.

Allen, C. "Sierra Leone Politics Since Independence," AAF, Vol. LXVII, No. 268 (October 1968).

Austin, D., and R. Rathbone. "Ghana Labour Unions and Political Organizations," in Trade Unions and Politics, No. 3. London: Institute of Commonwealth Studies, 1967. (Collected seminar papers.)

Bebler, Anton. "The Making of a Coup," WA, No. 2782 (October 3, 1970), 1151-52.

_____. "The Strategies of the Great Powers in Africa." Teorija in praksa, Nos. 8-9 (Ljubljana, Yugoslavia, 1971).

Biarnes, P. "La Junte Militaire de Bamako s'engage à organiser des elections avant la fin de 1969," M, November 7, 1968.

"Choix Difficile pour les Militaires," RFEPA, No. 40 (April 1969).

Clignet, R. "Ethnicity, Social Differentiation and Secondary Schooling in West Africa," CEA, Summer 1967, p. 375.

Compte, G. "Comment Modibo Keita a été renversé," JA, No. 64 (1969).

"Dahomey: Le prix de la banqueroute," RFEPA, No. 1 (1968).

Decalo, S. "The Politics of Instability in Dahomey," GA, No. 2 (1968).

Decraene, P. "Le Mali fait face à une situation financière très difficile," M, November 28-29, 1969.

Dixon-Fyle, S. "The Economy Needs Stronger Official Involvement," FT, Sierra Leone Survey Supplement, November 6, 1969.

Due, J. M.   "Agricultural Development in the Ivory Coast and Ghana," JMAS, Vol. VII, No. 4 (December 1969).

Fagla, H.   "Dahomey: d'un conflit de générations à un coup d'état," FEA, January 1968.

Feldberg, R.   "Political Systems and the Role of the Military," SQ, Vol. II (Spring 1970).

Fisher, H.   "Elections and Coups in Sierra Leone 1967," JMAS, VII, 4 (April 1969), 611-36.

Fitch, B., and M. Oppenheimer.   "Ghana: End of an Illusion," special issue of MR, Vol. XVIII, No. 3 (July-August 1966).

Gnonlonfoun, A.   "Un an du régime Soglo au Dahomey," AN, February 9-15, 1967.

Hodgkin, T.   "Counter-Revolution in Ghana," LM, No. 4 (April 1966).

Hopkins, N. S.   "Socialism and Social Change in Rural Mali," JMAS, Vol. VII, No. 3 (1969).

Howe, R.   "Sierra Leone Struggles Back to Democracy," CSM, April 22, 1968.

Kamarck, A.   "African Economic Problems and Prospects," AR, January 1969.

Kraus, Jon.   "Arms and Politics in Ghana," in C. Welch, Jr., ed., Soldier and State in Africa. Evanston, Ill.: Northwestern University Press, 1970.

_____.   "The Men in Charge," AR, April 1966.

Lavroff, D. G.   "Les coups d'état militaires en Afrique Noire," in Année Politique Africaine 1968. Dakar: Société Africaine d'Edition, 1969.

Lemarchand, R.   "Dahomey: Coup Within a Coup," AR, Vol. XIII, No. 6 (1968).

Meillassoux, C. "A Class Analysis of the Bureaucratic
    Process in Mali," JDS, Vol. VI, No. 2 (1970).

Nicol, Davidson. "Civic Responsibility and Academic
    Freedom in Africa: Introduction to the College
    Annual Report of the Principal, Fourah Bay Col-
    lege, University of Sierra Leone (September
    1966-August 1967)," MN, Vol. VII, Nos. 1-2
    (1968-69).

Nordlinger, E. "Soldiers in Mufti: The Impact of
    Military Rule upon Economic and Social Change
    in the Non-Western States," American Political
    Science Review, Vol. LXIV, No. 4 (December 1970).

Olatundji, S. "Pourquoi le Président Zinsou a
    écarté Alley de l'Etat Major," AN, No. 1102
    (September 19-25, 1968).

Omaboe, E. N. "The State of the Economy To-day," LO,
    December 22, 1968.

Owusu, M. "The 1969 General Election and the Culture
    of Politics in Swedru-Ghana 1966-1969," in D.
    Austin, ed., forthcoming.

Perlmutter, Amos. "The Praetorian State and the
    Praetorian Army," CP, Vol. I, No. 3 (April
    1969).

Peterson, J. "The Sierra Leone Creole: A Reapprisal,"
    in C. Fyfe and E. Jones, eds., Freetown: A
    Symposium. Freetown: Sierra Leone University
    Press, 1968.

Price, R. "Military Officers and Political Leader-
    ship: The Ghanaian Case," CP, Vol. III, No. 3
    (April 1971).

_____. "Theoretical Approach to Military Rule in
    New States: Reference Group Theory and the
    Ghanaian Case," WP, Vol. XXIII (April 1971).

Putnam, R. "Toward Explaining Military Intervention
    in Latin American Politics," WP, Vol. XX
    (October 1967).

Rathbone, R. "Education and Politics in Ghana," in
    Africana Collecta. Gütersloh: Bertelsmann
    Universitätsverlag, 1968.

_____. "Ghana Labour Unions and Political Orga-
    nizations," in *Trade Unions and Politics*, No.
    3. London: Institute of Commonwealth Studies,
    1967. (Collected seminar papers.)

_____. "Politics and Factionalism in Ghana,"
    CH, Vol. LX, No. 355 (March 1971).

Reljic, L. "The Background of Coups d'Etat in Africa,"
    RIA, Vol. XXII (March 20, 1971).

Ronen, Dov. "The Military Intervention," in *Dynamics
    of Political Transition in Dahomey* (forthcoming).

Skurnik, W. A. E. "The Military and Politics: Da-
    homey and Upper Volta," in C. Welch, Jr., ed.,
    Soldier and State in Africa. Evanston, Ill.:
    Northwestern University Press, 1970.

Spiro, H. "Political Stability in the New African
    States," in *Africa in Motion: The Annals of
    the AAPSS*. Philadelphia: AAPSSA, July 1964.

Staniland, M. "The Rhetoric of Centre-Periphery
    Relations," *JMAS*, Vol. VIII, No. 4 (1970).

Thompson, W. S. "Ghana's Foreign Policy Under Mili-
    tary Rule," *AR*, Vol. XV, Nos. 5-6 (May-June
    1969).

Welch, C. "Roots and Implications of Military Inter-
    vention," in C. Welch, Jr., ed., *Soldier and
    State in Africa*. Evanston, Ill.: Northwestern
    University Press, 1970.

UNPUBLISHED MATERIAL

All People's Congress and Sierra Leone People's
    Party. "Civilian Rule Committee Memoranda Sub-
    mitted Jointly by the Representatives of the APC

and the SLPP." Freetown, February 1968. (Mimeo.)

_____. "Joint Rule Committee." Freetown, February 22, 1968. (Mimeo.)

Austin, D., and R. Rathbone. "The Politics of Demilitarization: The Ghana Case." Seminar Paper, Institute of Commonwealth Studies, London, 1966. (Mimeo.)

Bennett, Valerie. "The Effect of British Colonial Policy on Civil-Military Relations in Gold Coast-Ghana (1921-1966)." Ph.D. thesis, African Studies, Program, Boston University, 1971.

Bienen, H. "Military and Society in East Africa: Thinking Again Praetorianism." Princeton University, Center of International Studies, 1971. (Mimeo.)

Colas, John N. "Social and Career Correlates of Military Intervention in Nigeria: A Background Study of the January 15th Coup." Annual Meeting of the Inter-University Seminar on Armed Forces and Society, Chicago, October 1969.

Dacks, G. "A Statistical Exploration of Causal Factors of Independent Military Political Activity in the Independent States of Sub-Saharan Africa." Manuscript, Department of Politics, Princeton University, 1970. (Mimeo.)

Hopkins, N. S. "Government in Kita: Social Institutions and Processes in a Malian Town." Ph.D. thesis, Department of Anthropology, University of Chicago, 1967.

_____. "Social Control in a Malian Town." Paper for the African Studies Association meeting, New York, 1967. (Mimeo.)

Jones, W. I. "Planning and Economic Policy in Mali." Ph.D. thesis in political science, University of Geneva, 1971.

Leader, S. "Military Professionalism and Political Intervention." Ph.D. thesis in political science, SUNY at Buffalo, 1970.

Luckham, R. "Authority and Conflict in the Nigerian Army, 1966: A Case Study in the Transfer of Military Institutions." Paper presented to the 7th World Congress of Sociology, Varna, September 1970.

May, R. "Sierra Leone as a Reconciliation System, 1951-68." M.S. thesis, University of Birmingham, 1968.

Minikin, V. "The Development of Political Opposition in Sierra Leone 1961-1967." M.A. thesis, West African Studies Center, University of Birmingham, October 1968.

Rapoport, David. "Praetorianism: Government Without Consensus." Ph.D. thesis, University of California at Berkeley, 1960.

Schachter-Morgenthau, R. "Mali and Tanzania: Some Observations About Socialism in Tropical Africa. Boston, 1971. (Mimeo.)

Syndicat National de l'Education et de la Culture [du Mali]. "Resolution Générale du 2me Congres du Syndicat National de l'Education et de la Culture." Bamako, April 1970. (Mimeo.)

Welch, C. "Civil-Military Relations in Commonwealth West Africa." Buffalo, 1970. (Mimeo.)

PAMPHLETS

Busia, K. A. The Courage and Foresight of Busia, Great Historic and Prophetic Statements Issued by Professor K. A. Busia While in Exile. Accra: George Boakie, 1969.

Ghana, Public Relations Department. The Fall of the Second Republic. Accra, 1972.

<u>Ghana Reborn</u>. New York: Ghana Information Services,
     December 1966.

Gurr, Ted. <u>New Error-Compensated Measures of Compar-
     ing Nations: Some Correlates of Civil Violence</u>.
     Center of International Studies Research Mono-
     graph No. 25. Princeton, N.J.: Princeton Uni-
     versity, 1966.

Muguet, Lieutenant-Colonel. <u>Les Armées Nationales
     des Etats Voisins: Nigérie, Ghana, Guinée, Mali</u>.
     No. 712/A. Paris: Centre Militaire d'Informa-
     tion et de Spécialisation pour l'Outre-Mer,
     1964.

Wood, D. "The Armed Forces of African States."
     Adelphi Papers, No. 27. London: Institute for
     Strategic Studies, 1966.

Diarra, Captain D. S., 100, 150
Dove-Edwin Commission of Inquiry, 78
Drabo, Colonel P., 196

Entente, 133

foreign policy, 190; of Dahomey, 16, 19, 25; of Ghana, 31, 40-41, 154; of Mali, 81, 84-85, 86, 154; of Sierra Leone, 67
Fourah Bay College, 78
France, 13, 16, 18, 19, 25, 84, 85, 124, 125-126, 129, 134, 145, 147-150, 155, 156, 159, 209

Gbedemah, K., 51, 52, 53, 54, 208
Genda, A., 70, 79
Gendarmerie, 171-172
Germany, Democratic Republic of, 33, 163
Germany, Federal Republic of, 130
Great Britain, 30, 31, 32, 33, 35, 40, 41, 64, 109, 125, 129-131, 134-135, 139-140, 143, 144, 145, 147-150, 155, 159-162, 167, 209
Guinea, 40, 67, 78, 126, 163-164

Hachémé, Captain, 23
Harlley, J. W. K., 36, 37, 38, 44, 46, 48, 51, 52, 131, 169, 170, 172, 175, 187, 190, 218 n.34,36, 235 n.24
Hassan, Brigadier, 33

International Monetary Fund, 41, 187
Israel, 150

Johnson, Captain F., 23, 172
Jumu, Major S. B., 68, 69
Juxon-Smith, A. F., 70, 72, 73, 79, 136, 142, 172, 174, 175, 178, 201

Kai-Samba, Major B. I., 68, 69, 70, 72, 142
Kattah, Brigadier, A., 52

Keita, Modibo, 81, 84, 85, 86, 87, 88, 109, 129, 133, 155, 164, 166
Kérékou, M., 20
Koné, J.-M., 93, 97, 190
Koné, Major Bala, 171
Kotoka, E. K., 36, 37, 38, 43, 44, 46, 132, 169-170, 180, 218 n.36
Kouandété, M., 19, 21, 23, 25, 148, 159, 183, 190

Lansana, Brigadier, D., 64, 68, 69, 70, 80, 106, 142, 165, 177, 178
Leigh, W. L., 68, 172, 190
Levantines, 43

Maga, H., 10, 12, 18, 21, 106, 156
Margai, Sir Albert, 65, 66, 67, 68, 69, 72, 78, 116, 125, 126
Margai, Sir Milton, 64, 65
Mensah, M., 14
Military Committee of National Liberation (CMLN), 89-90, 91-93, 94-99, 100, 101, 168, 175, 178-179, 180, 182, 188, 190, 192, 196-197, 203
military coups
classification, 157-158, 160-161; contagion, 135-137; in Dahomey, October 28, 1963, 10, 13; December 22, 1967 12, 106, 107; December 17, 1967, 19-20, 21, 108; December 12, 1969, 148; in Ghana, February 24, 1966, 36, 37, 116; April 17, 1967, 44, 50, 70, 116; internal coups, 151-152; in the Kongo-Brazzaville, 136; in Mali, November 19, 1968, 87, 88; August 12, 1969, 100; in Nigeria, January 15, 1966, 136; in Sierra Leone, March 21, 1967, 68, 69; March 23, 1967, 69, 70, 106; April 17, 1968, 79, 117, 126; in Togo, 13, 135
military intervention
economic conditions as related to military intervention, 30, 31, 34, 36, 64, 65, 76-77, 82-84, 86, 109-111,

256

military intervention
economic conditions as related to military intervention (cont'd)
113-116; frequency, causal-
ity, 3, 4, 5, 103, 210;
sociopolitical setting of,
4, 5, 8, 29, 30, 157
military rule
consultative bodies, 14, 16,
17, 19, 24, 46, 50, 51, 70,
75, 79, 96, 97, 181, 185,
186, 187; decision-making,
15-17, 25, 44-47, 48-50, 74-
76, 95, 96, 97, 98, 178-192,
192-193; duration, 104; institutions, 17, 18-19, 20,
21, 23, 24, 25, 26, 43-51,
72-75, 93, 94-98, 181-187,
208; juntas (composition),
120-122, 169-176, 178; (internal divisions), 101,
177-178; (leadership), 176-
178; (relationship with the
armed forces and police),
194-198; (resources), 189-
190, 207; legitimacy, 93,
158; military-civilian coalitions, 14, 43, 198, 202,
211; pre-modern military
rule in Africa, 5; withdrawal, 24-25, 54-55, 80, 205-
209

National Committee for the
Defense of the Revolution
(CNDR), 86
National Liberation Council
(NLC), 38-39, 40, 41-43,
44, 45-46, 48-50, 51, 179,
182, 183, 193, 197, 198,
204, 206-207
National Reformation Council
(NRC), 53, 70, 73, 74, 180,
182, 192, 198
Nkrumah, Kwame, 28, 29-30, 31,
32, 33, 34, 35, 36, 37, 39,
41, 42, 43, 66, 67, 85, 105,
112, 130-132, 133, 139, 140,
162, 163-164, 166, 207, 211
Nunoo, J. E. O., 43, 52, 170,
218 n.36
Nzeogwu, Major C., 36

Ocran, A., 37, 170, 218 n.36
Olympio, Sylvanus, 13, 156
Omaboe, E. N., 46, 47, 48,
187
Otu, M. A., 37, 221 n.71
Otu, General S. J., 34
Owusu, V., 50, 52

Parker, M., 79
People's Militia (in Mali),
85, 87, 88, 110
police
in Dahomey, 146; in Ghana,
33, 35-36, 38, 54-55; 56-57,
171; in Mali, 89, 214; nu-
merical strength in the sample, 6; in Sierra Leone, 70,
71, 72, 79-80, 171
political development, 4-5,
211-212
political parties
in Dahomey: PDD, 10, 11;
in Ghana: CPP, 28-30, 35,
38, 40, 48, 52, 53, 82, 103-
104, 105, 109, 155, 156, 164
207; NAL, 54, 208, PP, 54,
207; in Mali: US-RDA, 81-
82, 85, 87, 88, 93-94, 97,
99, 103-104, 105-106, 109,
155, 156, 164, 205; in Sierra
Leone: APC, 66, 67, 104,
107; SLPP, 64-66, 67, 69,
104, 155
Poudiougon, Major B., 236 n.9
Presidential Guard (Ghana),
34, 37

Quinn, B., 187

Royal West Africa Frontier
Force (RWAFF), 140, 144

Sinzogan, B., 19, 21, 187
Soglo, General Christophe, 11,
14-20, 24, 116, 124, 125,
155, 165, 177, 178, 183, 187,
190, 196, 201, 203, 234 n.17
Soglo, Mme., 15, 187, 188
Soglo, Nicéphore, 14, 15, 187
Stevens, Siaka, 66, 67, 68, 69,
78, 79, 80, 126

Tejan-Sie, Banje, 79
Touré, Sékou, 66, 67, 73, 126
133, 163

257

ABOUT THE AUTHOR

ANTON A. BEBLER is Researcher and Lecturer at the Faculty for Sociology, Political Science, and Journalism, University of Ljubljana, Yugoslavia. Previously he held two appointments: Research Fellow, Institute for International Politics and Economy in Belgrade (1963-70); and Research Associate, Center of International Studies, Princeton University (1970-71).

Dr. Bebler has published about 70 articles and reviews on political matters, mostly in Yugoslav journals (<u>Medjunarodni problemi</u>, <u>Teorija in praksa</u>, <u>et al</u>.) and in other periodicals, made several programs for the Ljubljana TV Center, etc.

Dr. Bebler holds a B.A. and an M.A. from Belgrade University and a Ph.D. from University of Pennsylvania. He has also studied in Moscow, Ljubljana, Princeton, London, and Paris.

BOOKS WRITTEN UNDER THE AUSPICES OF
THE CENTER OF INTERNATIONAL STUDIES,
PRINCETON UNIVERSITY

Gabriel A. Almond. The Appeals of Communism. Princeton University Press, 1954.

William W. Kaufmann, ed. Military Policy and National Security. Princeton University Press, 1956.

Klaus Knorr. The War Potential of Nations. Princeton University Press, 1956.

Lucian W. Pye. Guerrilla Communism in Malaya. Princeton University Press, 1956.

Charles De Visscher. Theory and Reality in Public International Law. Trans. by P. E. Corbett. Princeton University Press, 1957; rev. ed. 1968.

Bernard C. Cohen. The Political Process and Foreign Policy: The Making of the Japanese Peace Settlement. Princeton University Press, 1957.

Myron Weiner. Party Politics in India: The Development of a Multi-Party System. Princeton University Press, 1957.

Percy E. Corbett. Law in Diplomacy. Princeton University Press, 1959.

Rolf Sannwald and Jacques Stohler. Economic Integration: Theoretical Assumptions and Consequences of European Unification. Trans. by Herman Karreman. Princeton University Press, 1959.

Klaus Knorr, ed. NATO and American Security. Princeton University Press, 1959.

Gabriel A. Almond and James S. Coleman, eds. The Politics of the Developing Areas. Princeton University Press, 1960.

Herman Kahn. On Thermonuclear War. Princeton University Press, 1960.

Sidney Verba. Small Groups and Political Behavior: A Study of Leadership. Princeton University Press, 1961.

Robert J. C. Butow. Tojo and the Coming of the War. Princeton University Press, 1961.

Glenn H. Synder. Deterrence and Defense: Toward a Theory of National Security. Princeton University Press, 1961.

Klaus Knorr and Sidney Verba, eds. The International System: Theoretical Essays. Princeton University Press, 1961.

Peter Paret and John W. Shy. Guerrillas in the 1960's. Frederick A. Praeger, 1962.

George Modelski. A Theory of Foreign Policy. Frederick A. Praeger, 1962.

Klaus Knorr and Thornton Read, eds. Limited Strategic War. Frederick A. Praeger, 1963.

Frederick S. Dunn. Peace-Making and the Settlement with Japan. Princeton University Press, 1963.

Arthur L. Burns and Nina Heathcote. Peace-Keeping by United Nations Forces. Frederick A. Praeger, 1963.

Richard A. Falk. Law, Morality, and War in the Contemporary World. Frederick A. Praeger, 1963.

James N. Rosenau. National Leadership and Foreign Policy: A Case Study in the Mobilization of Public Support. Princeton University Press, 1963.

Gabriel A. Almond and Sidney Verba. The Civic Cul-
    ture: Political Attitudes and Democracy in
    Five Nations. Princeton University Press, 1963.

Bernard C. Cohen. The Press and Foreign Policy.
    Princeton University Press, 1963.

Richard L. Sklar. Nigerian Political Parties: Power
    in an Emergent African Nation. Princeton Uni-
    versity Press, 1963.

Peter Paret. French Revolutionary Warfare from Indo-
    china to Algeria: The Analysis of a Political
    and Military Doctrine. Frederick A. Praeger,
    1964.

Harry Eckstein, ed. Internal War: Problems and Ap-
    proaches. Free Press, 1964.

Cyril E. Black and Thomas P. Thornton, eds. Commu-
    nism and Revolution: The Strategic Uses of Po-
    litical Violence. Princeton University Press,
    1964.

Miriam Camps. Britain and the European Community
    1955-1963. Princeton University Press, 1964.

Thomas P. Thornton, ed. The Third World in Soviet
    Perspective: Studies by Soviet Writers on the
    Developing Areas. Princeton University Press,
    1964.

James N. Rosenau, ed. International Aspects of Civil
    Strife. Princeton University Press, 1964.

Sidney I. Ploss. Conflict and Decision-Making in
    Soviet Russia: A Case Study of Agricultural
    Policy, 1953-1963. Princeton University Press,
    1965.

Richard A. Falk and Richard J. Barnet, eds. Security
    in Disarmament. Princeton University Press,
    1965.

Karl von Vorys. _Political Development in Pakistan._
Princeton University Press, 1965.

Harold and Margaret Sprout. _The Ecological Perspective on Human Affairs, With Special Reference
to International Politics._ Princeton University
Press, 1965.

Klaus Knorr. _On the Uses of Military Power in the
Nuclear Age._ Princeton University Press, 1966.

Harry Eckstein. _Division and Cohesion in Democracy:
A Study of Norway._ Princeton University Press,
1966.

Cyril E. Black. _The Dynamics of Modernization: A
Study in Comparative History._ Harper and Row,
1966.

Peter Kunstadter, ed. _Southeast Asian Tribes, Minorities, and Nations._ Princeton University Press,
1967.

E. Victor Wolfenstein. _The Revolutionary Personality:
Lenin, Trotsky, Gandhi._ Princeton University
Press, 1967.

Leon Gordenker. _The UN Secretary-General and the
Maintenance of Peace._ Columbia University
Press, 1967.

Oran R. Young. _The Intermediaries: Third Parties
in International Crises._ Princeton University
Press, 1967.

James N. Rosenau, ed. _Domestic Sources of Foreign
Policy._ Free Press, 1967.

Richard F. Hamilton. _Affluence and the French Worker
in the Fourth Republic._ Princeton University
Press, 1967.

Linda B. Miller. _World Order and Local Disorder:
The United Nations and Internal Conflicts._
Princeton University Press, 1967.

Wolfram F. Hanrieder. West German Foreign Policy, 1949-1963: International Pressures and Domestic Response. Stanford University Press, 1967.

Richard H. Ullman. Britain and the Russian Civil War: November 1918-February 1920. Princeton University Press, 1968.

Robert Gilpin. France in the Age of the Scientific State. Princeton University Press, 1968.

William B. Bader. The United States and the Spread of Nuclear Weapons. Pegasus, 1968.

Richard A. Falk. Legal Order in a Violent World. Princeton University Press, 1968.

Cyril E. Black, Richard A. Falk, Klaus Knorr, and Oran R. Young. Neutralization and World Politics. Princeton University Press, 1968.

Oran R. Young. The Politics of Force: Bargaining During International Crises. Princeton University Press, 1969.

Klaus Knorr and James N. Rosenau, eds. Contending Approaches to International Politics. Princeton University Press, 1969.

James N. Rosenau, ed. Linkage Politics: Essays on the Convergence of National and International Systems. Free Press, 1969.

John T. McAlister, Jr. Viet Nam: The Origins of Revolution. Alfred A. Knopf, 1969.

Jean Edward Smith. Germany Beyond the Wall: People, Politics and Prosperity. Little, Brown, 1969.

James Barros. Betrayal from Within: Joseph Avenol, Secretary-General of the League of Nations, 1933-1940. Yale University Press, 1969.

Charles Hermann. Crises in Foreign Policy: A Simulation Analysis. Bobbs-Merrill, 1969.

Robert C. Tucker. <u>The Marxian Revolutionary Idea:</u>
<u>Essays on Marxist Thought and Its Impact on Rad-</u>
<u>ical Movements</u>. W. W. Norton, 1969.

Harvey Waterman. <u>Political Change in Contemporary</u>
<u>France: The Politics of an Industrial Democracy</u>.
Charles E. Merrill, 1969.

Richard A. Falk and Cyril E. Black, eds. <u>The Future</u>
<u>of the International Legal Order</u>. Vol. I,
Trends and Patterns. Princeton University Press,
1969.

Ted Robert Gurr. <u>Why Men Rebel</u>. Princeton University Press, 1970.

C. S. Whitaker, Jr. <u>The Politics of Tradition: Con-</u>
<u>tinuity and Change in Northern Nigeria, 1946-</u>
<u>1966</u>. Princeton University Press, 1970.

Richard A. Falk. <u>The Status of Law in International</u>
<u>Society</u>. Princeton University Press, 1970.

Henry Bienen. <u>Tanzania: Party Transformation and</u>
<u>Economic Development</u>. Princeton University
Press, 1967; rev. ed. 1970.

Klaus Knorr. <u>Military Power and Potential</u>. D. C.
Heath, 1970.

Richard A. Falk and Cyril E. Black, eds. <u>The Future</u>
<u>of the International Legal Order</u>. Vol. II,
<u>Wealth and Resources</u>. Princeton University
Press, 1970.

Leon Gordenker, ed. <u>The United Nations in Interna-</u>
<u>tional Politics</u>. Princeton University Press,
1971.

Cyril E. Black and Richard A. Falk, eds. <u>The Future</u>
<u>of the International Legal Order</u>. Vol. III,
<u>Conflict Management</u>. Princeton University
Press, 1971.

Harold and Margaret Sprout. <u>Toward a Politics of the</u>
     <u>Planet Earth</u>. Van Nostrand Reinhold, 1971.

Francine R. Frankel. <u>India's Green Revolution: Eco-</u>
     <u>nomic Gains and Political Costs</u>. Princeton Uni-
     versity Press, 1971.

Cyril E. Black and Richard A. Falk, eds. <u>The Future</u>
     <u>of the International Legal Order</u>. Vol. IV, <u>The</u>
     <u>Structure of the International Environment</u>.
     Princeton University Press, 1972.